£45.00
Dudley 2

Defense, welfare, and growth

Defense, welfare, and growth

Edited by
Steve Chan and Alex Mintz

ROUTLEDGE

London and New York

First published 1992
by Routledge
11 New Fetter Lane, London EC4P 4EE

Simultaneously published in the USA and Canada
by Routledge
a division of Routledge, Chapman and Hall, Inc.
29 West 35th Street, New York, NY 10001

Typeset in 10 on 12pt Linotron Times by
Falcon Typographic Art Ltd, Fife, Scotland
Printed and bound in Great Britain by
Mackays of Chatham PLC, Chatham, Kent

British Library Cataloguing in Publication Data
A catalogue record for this title is available from the British Library.

Library of Congress Cataloging in Publication Data
Defense, welfare, and growth / edited by Steve Chan and Alex Mintz.
p. cm.
Includes bibliographical references and index.
1. Military readiness – Economic aspects. 2. Economic conversion. 3. Military readiness – Economic aspects – Case studies. 4. Economic conversion – Case studies.
I. Chan, Steve. II. Mintz, Alex, 1949–.
HC79.D4D45 1992
335.4′3355 – dc20 91–41858 CIP

ISBN 0–415–07599–8

Contents

Figures

Tables

Contributors

Olav Bjerkholt, Assistant Director-General, Central Bureau of Statistics of Norway and Adjunct Professor of Economics, University of Olso. His main areas of research are macroeconomic planning and energy economics. He is the coeditor with Jørgen Rosted of *Macro-Economic Medium-Term Models in the Nordic Countries. Contributions to Economic Analysis* no. 164, Amsterdam: North-Holland, 1987.

Davis B. Bobrow is Dean of the Graduate School of Public and International Affairs, University of Pittsburgh, where he is also Professor of Public and International Affairs and of Political Science. He has held visiting appointments in the Graduate School of Political Science at Saitama University and at the International Unversity of Japan, and written on various aspects of Japanese foreign and defense policy in *Comparative Strategy, Futures, International Studies Quarterly, The Japan Quarterly, Journal of Conflict Resolution, Leviathan*, and *World Politics*.

Ådne Cappelen is Research Director, Central Bureau of Statistics of Norway. His main areas of research are large-scale macroeconomic models. He has published extensively in the area of defense economics.

Steve Chan is Professor of Political Science at the University of Colorado (Boulder). His research interests are in the area of international political economy. His publications include *Flexibility, Foresight, and Fortuna in Taiwan: Navigating Between Scylla and Charybdis* (with Cal Clark), and *East Asian Dynamism: Growth, Order, and Security in the Pacific Region*.

Amalia Cochran is a doctoral student of political science at the University of Colorado (Boulder). Her research interests include energy and security issues in developing nations.

David R. Davis is Assistant Professor of Political Science at Emory University. Entitled *The Defense Ledger*, his Ph.D. dissertation focuses on the political and economic consequences of defense spending for the developing world in both the domestic and international arenas.

Richard C. Eichenberg is Associate Professor of Political Science at Tufts University, where he teaches international relations, foreign policy, and security and arms control. His most recent book is *Public Opinion and National Security in Western Europe* (Cornell University Press, 1989).

Nils Petter Gleditsch is Senior Research Fellow, International Peace Research Institute, Oslo, and Editor of its academic quarterly *Journal of Peace Research*. Chairman of the Board of the Centre for Peace and Conflict Research, Copenhagen University; and Visiting Professor of Peace Research, Uppsala University (Winter 1991). His recent books are *Norge i Verdensamfunnet: En Statistisk Håndbok* [Norway in the World Community: A Statistical Handbook; in Norwegian], Oslo: Pax, 1988; and *Arms Races: Technological and Political Dynamics* (coedited with Olav Njølstad), London: Sage, 1990.

Uk Heo is a graduate student at the Political Science Department of Texas A & M University. His main area of research is the political economy of defense.

Chi Huang is Associate Professor of Political Science at Texas A & M University. His research interests focus on political methodology, the political economy of development, and the guns–butter tradeoff. He is the author or coauthor of articles published in *Comparative Political Studies, Journal of Conflict Resolution, International Studies Notes, American Political Science Review, American Journal of Political Science*, and *Defence Economics*.

In-Taek Hyun is a senior research fellow at the Institute of Social Sciences, Seoul, South Korea. His current research interests include comparative defense policy, alliance and defense burden sharing, and the political economy of defense spending in Japan and South Korea.

Robert E. Looney is Professor of National Security Affairs at the Naval Postgraduate School. Prior to joining the Naval Postgraduate School, he was a development economist at the Stanford Research Institute, and has been an economic consultant to the governments of Iran, Saudi Arabia, and Mexico. His is the author of *The Political Economy of Latin American Defense Expenditures* with a foreword by Martin Needler (Lexington, Mass.: Lexington Books, 1986); *Third-World Military Expenditure and Arms Production* with a foreword by Robert West (London: Macmillan, 1988); and *The Economics of Third World Defense Expenditures* with a foreword by Charles Wolf (Greenwich, Conn.: JAI Press, 1991).

Alex Mintz is the Cullen/McFadden Professor of Political Science at Texas A & M University. He is the author or coauthor of 'Defense Expenditures, Economic Performance and the Peace Dividend'; 'Guns vs. Butter: A Disaggregated Analysis'; 'The Political Economy of Military Spending in Israel' (all in the *American Political Science Review*); and 'Guns vs. Butter: The Indirect Link' (*American Journal of Political Science*). His contribution to the preparation of this book was supported by a grant from the National Science Foundation (No. SES–8911030).

Chung-in Moon is Associate Professor of Political Science at the University of Kentucky. Over three dozen of his articles have appeared in edited volumes and in such scholarly journals as *World Politics, International Studies Quarterly, International Interactions, Middle East Journal, Millennium,* and *Pacific Focus.* His books include *Pacific Dynamics, The United States and the Defense of the Pacific, Dilemma of Third World Defense Industry*, and *Third World National Security*. His current research interests comprise of comparative industrial policy and state, society, and military in contemporary South Korea.

Mohan Penubarti is a doctoral student of Political Science at the University of Colorado (Boulder). His research interests focus on economic development and political stability of South Asian countries.

Sheen Rajmaira is a doctoral student in the Department of Political Science at the University of Colorado. Among her research interests are United States, Soviet Union, and Chinese relations, arms races, and international political economy.

Karen A. Rasler is Associate Professor of Political Science at the University of California, Riverside. She is the coauthor of *War and State Making* (1989) and the author of numerous articles on internal war, structural change in world politics, and relative decline.

Bruce Russett is Dean Acheson Professor of International Relations and Chair of the Political Science Department at Yale University, and Editor of the *Journal of Conflict Resolution*. He has been president of the International Studies Association and the Peace Science Society (International). His recent books include *Controlling the Sword: The Democratic Governance of National Security*, and *World Politics: The Menu for Choice* (with Harvey Starr; 3rd edition).

Ron P. Smith is Professor of Economics at Birkbeck College, University of London. His research has applied econometric analysis to the effects of defense spending on capital formation and economic growth in various developed and developing countries.

William R. Thompson is Professor of Political Science at Indiana University. He is the author of *On Global War* (1988) and the coauthor of *Seapower and Global Politics: Since 1494* (1988) and *War and State Making* (1989). His current research interests focus on rise-and-fall dynamics, long waves, warfare patterns, commercial challenges, and grand strategy.

Michael D. Ward is Professor of Political Science at the University of Colorado (Boulder), where he also holds a research appointment in the Program on Political and Economic Change at the Institute of Behavioral Science.

Erich Weede is Associate Professor of Sociology at the University of Cologne, Germany. He has done research on deterrence and causes of war, on domestic conflicts and violence, and on economic growth and income inequality. He has published five books (in German), the most recent of which is *Wirtschaft, Staat and Gesellschaft* (Tübingen: Mohr, 1990) as well as numerous articles in English and German. Since 1988 he has been the European editor of *International Interactions*.

1 Defense, welfare, and growth: introduction

Steve Chan
University of Colorado

INTRODUCTION

In the early 1990s, the last decade of the century, momentous changes are taking place in the world. The European Community is scheduled to further remove barriers to trade and travel among its member countries in short order, so that Western Europe is poised to become a more integrated political and economic unit rivaling the power of the two superpowers. At the same time, political and economic liberalization has been sweeping the East European countries. Authoritarian rulers have fallen from power in these countries, just as the physical and political barriers separating them from the West have been falling in rapid succession (with the Berlin Wall being the most prominent symbol of these barriers). The Soviet Union's policies of internal reform and external détente under Mikhail Gorbachev have clearly contributed to a significant relaxation of political and military tension between the East and West.

Turning to the Pacific Basin, the relations among China, Japan, and the United States are more cordial today than probably at any other time in this century. While the bloody suppression of the prodemocracy demonstrators at Tiananmen Square has stemmed the forces of political liberalization in China, that country is likely to continue its military retrenchment and foreign cooperation in order to create and sustain a policy environment conducive to rapid economic modernization. China's capitalist neighbors in East Asia have featured some of the most dynamic economies in the world. Led by Japan, these modern 'trading' nations (such as South Korea, Taiwan, Singapore, and Hong Kong) have eschewed traditional instruments of military assertion and force projection abroad in favor of commercial expansion and economic competitiveness. Trade protectionism rather than military aggression poses a more realistic danger to their national security.

With the prominent exception of the U.S. invasion of Panama and the Iraqi invasion of Kuwait, the direct resort to arms in settling international disputes has become less fashionable as the decade of the 1980s came to a close. Military détente – if not necessarily political reconciliation – has come to the Falklands/Malvinas, India and Pakistan, Israel and Egypt, Iran and Iraq, North and South Korea, and China and the Soviet Union. Concomitantly, Moscow has withdrawn its troops from Afghanistan, and Hanoi has done the same in Kampuchea. Thus, the spirit of Hobbes has abated, and has been replaced by collaboration among the world's major powers in the Iraq–Kuwait crisis leading to Iraq's military defeat and the restoration of Kuwaiti sovereignty.

Given these recent developments, it is important for us to reexamine the rationales for and outcomes of national defense, which may affect and be affected by international tension, civilian welfare, and domestic industrial productivity. This collection of essays seeks to improve our understanding of the empirical relationships between defense exertion on the one hand, and a variety of socioeconomic performances on the other hand. They are mostly concerned with the socioeconomic consequences of defense exertion. Despite their different analytic and substantive foci, they all engage in explicit formulation of theoretical expectations and systematic evaluation of the pertinent evidence across space or time. Consequently, they enable us to assess the generalizability and robustness of various hypotheses regarding the effects of defense exertion.

The remainder of this Introduction is organized in three sections. First, I review various perspectives regarding the consequences of governmental allocations of money and manpower to the defense sector. Second, a similar literature survey is undertaken to identify the prevailing expectations about the welfare consequences of defense allocation. Finally, I relate the analyses presented in this volume to the previous research, and summarize the theoretical and substantive highlights of these analyses.

DEFENSE EXERTION AND ECONOMIC PERFORMANCE

There is no shortage of perspectives intended to shed light on the question of what consequences defense spending is likely to produce. Many of these perspectives have been influenced by the conditions or experiences of Western countries, especially those of the advanced industrial powers featuring capitalism and pluralistic democracy. At the same time, with the notable exceptions of the USSR, India, Israel, South Korea, and Taiwan, systematic empirical verification or clarification of the expectations derived from these perspectives has been largely limited to these same countries.

In this book, we will focus on the nonmilitary consequences of defense exertion. To the extent that efforts to boost one's defense capabilities result in a process of mutual armament escalation, national security is more likely to be undermined than enhanced. International disputes accompanied by arms races are much more likely to lead to war than international disputes in the absence of these races (see Goertz and Diehl 1986; Morrow 1989; Wallace 1979, 1980, 1982; Weede 1980a). Therefore, hypermilitary vigilance may actually be counterproductive in enhancing national security. The consequent increase in international tension and conflict is likely to provide a poor environment for domestic economic growth.

Defense exertion can take the form of allocating either money or manpower to the military establishment. These two forms represent conceptually the capital-intensive and labor-intensive approaches to national security, and are apt to have different empirical effects on the economy and society. A number of perspectives try to account for the nonmilitary consequences of defense exertion (Chan 1985). They focus on one or more of the three key determinants of GNP growth in classical economics: namely, labor, capital, and technology.

There is, first, the *modernization model*, which has been most closely associated with the work of Benoit (1972a, 1972b, 1973, 1978). This work acknowledges that defense spending necessarily reduces domestic civilian production, and crowds out civilian investment. However, it argues that these unfavorable effects are apt to be offset by the other more positive effects in developing countries. Defense spending and military service are suggested to instill modern skills and attitudes, help to develop basic economic infrastructure, and produce mild inflation which in turn encourages fuller utilization of the existing production facilities. In support of Benoit's thesis, Babin (1989) and Kick and Dev Sharda (1986) have found, respectively, that military spending and personnel tended to contribute to faster economic growth in the relatively long term (that is, after a dozen years or so). Several other analysts (for example, Dixon and Moon 1986; Weede 1983) have also discovered evidence indicating that large armed forces (as distinct from large military budgets) seem to be conducive to the development and formation of human capital.

A much more prevalent analytic reaction to Benoit's studies has been to challenge his conclusion that 'heavy defense expenditure does not . . . appear to have been associated with *lower* growth rates' (1973, 4). This conclusion has met methodological as well as substantive objections, such as Benoit's failure to account for the total inflow of foreign resources, the degree to which a country's production capacities are characterized by slack, and the over-time variations in the data series (see Ball 1983b; Biswas and Ram 1986; Brzoska and Wulf 1979; Deger 1986; Deger and Smith 1983; Dorfman 1972; Frederiksen and Looney 1983; Faini *et al*. 1984; Grobar and Porter 1989; Hagan 1972; Huisken 1983; Kaldor 1976; Lebovic and Ishaq 1987; Lim 1983; Nabe 1983; Smith and Smith 1980; Terhal 1981). Overall, the studies inspired by Benoit either failed to find evidence supportive of his conclusion or actually produced evidence that contradicts it.

One of the more powerful criticisms directed against Benoit's conclusion is that he gave too much emphasis to the positive effects of defense spending in mobilizing the available national resources and in instilling modern skills and attitudes in the developing world, and that he did not give enough emphasis to the negative effects of defense spending on savings and investment. It is the latter contention that undergirds the second major perspective on the economic consequences of defense spending. The *capital formation model* stresses private investment as the key determinant of economic growth. Two proponents of this model thus argued that 'the negative effect of military expenditures on saving (and investment) outweighs the positive modernization and technological effect on the growth rate' (Deger and Smith 1983, 346). Smith's (1937, 1980) other studies led him to conclude that for the developed Western economies there tended to be a rough one-to-one tradeoff between a country's military expenditures and its total investment. The existence of such a tradeoff has been observed in both the developed and developing countries (Cappelen *et al*. 1984; Deger 1986).

One strand of this literature emphasizes the military expenditures and commitments associated with the burden of international leadership. A hegemonic power bears a disproportionate amount of the costs of providing for public goods such as global peace, monetary stability, and free and orderly trade (Gilpin 1975; Kindleberger 1973, 1981; Krasner 1976). Over time, whether due to the free-riding by others and/or the continuation of outmoded policy practices by the leading state, the international system undergoes a period of relative deconcentration of power (Modelski 1987a, 1987b). To the extent that defense spending dampens capital formation and thus slows economic growth, it is a major contributing cause of the *hegemon's decline* (Smith 1977). It may therefore facilitate international status mobility and power transition, which may in turn intensify international rivalry and precipitate war (Organski and Kugler 1980).

The longitudinal evidence for the above argument, however, is much more supportive in the case of the United States during 1946–78 than Britain during 1813–1913, a finding that has led to the conclusion that 'the defense-investment tradeoff is not a generic factor in the relative decline of system leaders and, derivatively, the world system's distribution of power' (Rasler and Thompson 1988, 82). Another recent review of the U.S. case also concluded that 'defense spending is not an important determinant of investment' (Gold 1990, 3). Thus, it seems that the hypothesized defense–investment substitution effect was more limited among the great powers than might have been suspected. Similarly, several other studies on developing countries such as India, Taiwan, and the Middle Eastern nations were unable to establish any statistically significant tradeoff between defense spending and civilian investment (Chan 1988; Faini *et al*. 1984; Lebovic and Ishaq 1987). Indeed, as Smith and Georgiou (1983, 13) acknowledged forthrightly, 'the effect of military expenditure on growth through investment and capital formation is likely to be a long run one and so not picked by the short lags used in time series analysis.' As another consideration, Deger (1986) pointed out that capital formation in the developing countries may be constrained not only or necessarily by a shortfall in savings due to high military spending; one must also take into account the reduced *absorptive capacity* to utilize the available savings as a result of the hypothesized unfavorable impact of military spending on public funding for human resources.

A third perspective on the impact of defense spending on economic performance can be called the *balance of payment model*, or the *export-led growth model*. This model argues that defense spending tends to deprive resources and talents to the most dynamic sectors of the economy, that these sectors tend to be most heavily involved in the export business, and that countries that are most adept in expanding export have tended to grow fastest economically (Rothschild 1973). The decline in a country's foreign trade competitiveness in turn leads to a weaker currency, structural unemployment, and chronic trade deficits. Although some of these tendencies have been suggested by others (for example, Deger 1986; Dumas 1977; Melman 1970, 1972, 1974), there has apparently been little systematic data analysis to follow up on Rothschild's original work. A review of the U.S. data has led at least one economist to conclude that defense spending has not been a primary cause of the decline in that country's international competitiveness, and that overall this spending 'has been a relatively neutral feature of the American economic landscape' (Gold 1990, 3). One time series study on Taiwan – which happens to be one of the most successful 'trading states' in the recent decades – failed to show any strong impact, positive or negative, of defense spending on export expansion or export composition (Chan 1988).

The fourth and final perspective may be labeled the *technological displacement model*. It basically argues that by drawing scientific and engineering talents from the civilian sector to military research and development (R & D), defense spending tends to hamper the innovation and therefore the growth of civilian economy (for example, Dumas 1977; Lindgren 1984b; Russett 1970). Systematic analyses of this hypothesized impact, however, have failed to yield strong and unambiguous evidence. Thus, for example, Gleditsch *et al*. (1988, 211) were unable to discover 'very clear evidence of a competitive relationship' between military R & D and civilian R & D. The proportionate size of civilian R & D was positively correlated with productivity gains in only five of the eight advanced Western countries analyzed in their study, and the proportionate size of military R & D was negatively related with productivity gains in six of these eight cases. This argument receives support from the review of U.S. data by Gold (1990, 3), who argued that 'there is no long-term trade-off between defense and civilian R & D.' In another study focusing on a developing country, Deger and Sen (1983) hypothesized that military spending should affect the technological advance of different civilian industries in India, which has one of the largest armament industries in the Third World. Their statistical results were generally insignificant, and were therefore unable to establish any major impact, positive or negative, of defense spending on the technological progress in civilian productivity. This conclusion was supported by Terhal (1981).

Although most of the research on the economic impact of defense exertion has focused on GNP growth, two other kinds of economic performance – namely inflation and unemployment – have received at least some attention. Defense spending has been hypothesized to increase inflationary pressure because it creates demand without expanding supply. To the extent that this spending emphasizes expensive procurement and is capital-intensive under situations of an already overheated economy, it is especially apt to result in production bottlenecks for civilian goods. At the same time, to the extent that this spending produces chronic deficit financing and monetary expansion by the government, it gives further impetus to inflationary pressure (Deger 1986).

Empirical analyses of the possible reciprocal influences between defense spending and inflation rate have, however, produced rather mixed results. On the one hand, according to case studies on India (Terhal 1981) v. South Korea (Chan and Davis 1991), and Morocco (Fontanel 1982), military expenditures have contributed significantly to price rises in these countries. On the other hand, Granger analyses of the U.S., British, and Taiwanese data series indicated that these two variables have been independent of each other – that is, defense spending has not affected the inflation rate in these countries, nor has the inflation rate affected defense spending (Chan and Davis 1991; Kinsella 1989; Starr *et al*. 1984). However, there is some evidence of reciprocal influences between these variables for France and West Germany in the recent decades. Thus, it seems that the relationship between defense spending and inflation is quite context dependent. The *seignorage* privilege enjoyed by the United States and Britain as underwriters of the premier currencies for international trade has perhaps enabled them to export the deleterious effects of their domestic fiscal irresponsibility to their trade partners through monetary inflation. Taiwan's successful export drives, its fiscal conservatism, and its high rates of savings relative to consumption may explain its ability thus far to contain inflation in spite of a comparatively heavy defense burden.

A heavy defense burden may also raise the level of long-term unemployment through its negative impact on economic growth and export competitiveness. Granger analysis of the data from South Korea and Taiwan again failed to verify a statistically significant short-term impact of defense manpower recruitment or spending on unemployment, or vice versa (Chan and Davis 1991). However, Kinsella (1989) found that the U.S. defense spending has tended to produce initially a small drop in unemployment, followed by a delayed effect of a slight rise. This finding seems to be congruent with the expectation that government fiscal stimulation (including defense spending) is likely to provide a temporary relief to a sagging economy, but in the long term it increases the dependence of private firms on government contracts and impairs their competitiveness in international trade. Thus, rising structural unemployment has been alleged as a long-term consequence of 'Pentagon capitalism' (Melman 1970, 1972, 1974).

Several 'lessons' or caveats emerge from the above summary of the literature. It seems that disaggregated data on defense spending are necessary for more informed analysis. For example, how much of the overall military budget is devoted to the development of industrial or transportation infrastructure, to the investment in human capital, to the pursuit of research and development, or to the salaries of personnel, has obvious implications for the modernization and technological displacement models. At the same time, such data may be very difficult and perhaps impossible to collect for some countries that treat them as national security secrets. Second, more contextual conditions need to be incorporated in our analysis. Whether a country has abundant natural resources and a skilled workforce, whether its economy is supply- or demand-constrained, whether its defense spending is financed through taxation or deficit spending, and whether its tax laws favor consumption or savings again have an obvious bearing on the arguments advanced by the capital formation and export-led growth models. Third, the need for valid time series analysis is again underscored, because the hypothesized causal relationships usually involve lagged, nonlinear, and multiple effects (such as Boulding 1974; Deger 1986). Finally, the collateral governmental policies (e.g., taxation, investment credit, unemployment benefits, collective labor bargaining, pension funding, and health and education assistance) may either offset or exacerbate the deleterious effects of military spending, and as such should be taken into account in evaluating the former's impact on socioeconomic performance (Eichenberg 1984).

DEFENSE VERSUS WELFARE TRADEOFF?

Quite apart from the possible influence of defense spending on the economic performance of a national aggregate, this spending can have a differential impact on various population segments. Beginning with Russett's (1970) pioneering work, there has been a long series of analyses on the general topic of the so-called *guns-versus-butter tradeoff* (for example, Caputo 1975; Dabelko and McCormick 1977, 1984; Domke *et al*. 1983; Hollenhorst and Ault 1971; Johnson and Wells 1986; Lyttkens and Vedovato 1984; Mintz 1989; Peroff and Podolak-Warren 1979; Pryor 1968; Russett 1971, 1982). This hypothesized tradeoff can have both a direct and an indirect income-shifting effect.

In the direct form, *assuming* a fixed amount of resources, increased defense spending can decrease other kinds of governmental expenditures such as on welfare, housing, and education. In the indirect form, higher defense spending can result in higher inflation and unemployment as well as the forgone opportunity of future growth. In both forms, the quality of life for the poorer or more disadvantaged segments of the population is apt to suffer more than that for the richer or more advantaged segments, especially if defense spending has the effect of bidding up the market value of capital or expertise (such as when this spending is financed by public borrowing or is heavily driven by capital and technology). The gap between the rich and the poor thus tends to widen.

Although there are substantial variations across studies about the existence or strength of the guns-versus-butter tradeoff for different countries and time periods, the more recent and valid inquiries into this subject (Domke *et al.* 1983; Russett 1982) tend to cast doubts on the zero-sum conception of governmental allocation of resources for different purposes. Similarly, attempts to disaggregate and trace the direct and indirect effects of various types of defense spending (such as procurement, personnel, R & D) on different kinds of social welfare programs have been unable to turn up evidence of strong or widespread tradeoff in the case of the U.S. (Mintz 1989; Mintz and Huang 1989). Similarly, longitudinal analysis of the Taiwanese defense and welfare data has also been unable to establish any negative linkage between the changes in these two time series (Davis and Chan 1990).

Thus, the aggregate evidence from these more recent studies seems to support the observation that defense and civilian expenditures have a tendency to rise concomitantly over time (Clayton 1976). This tendency for governments to try to have *both* guns and butter and their concomitant reluctance or inability to raise the necessary taxes for these expenditures may constitute a major and enduring source of economic mismanagement and welfare underperformance. In this context, the pertinent tradeoff is no longer that between different types of public expenditures; it rather becomes one between current government consumption in general and future economic growth. It should also be noted that, according to the capital formation perspective reviewed earlier (Smith 1980), the burden of defense spending in the developed democracies falls almost entirely on investment because it is assumed that there would be strong political pressure against trimming social welfare programs. This tendency would probably also apply to those Latin American countries (for example, Argentina, Mexico) where organized labor has been part of the ruling pact. In contrast, in capitalist East Asia (for example, Japan, South Korea, Taiwan, Singapore) the authoritarian and anti-labor regimes have traditionally managed to suppress social overhead. Yet, by practicing fiscal conservatism and eschewing the temptation of trying to get 'a quart out of a pint pot,' they have maintained rapid economic growth, tamed inflation, and achieved egalitarian income distribution despite their relatively heavy defense expenditures (except for Japan).

The *basic needs approach* has provided a second perspective on the investigation of the defense–welfare substitution effects (Davis and Chan 1990; Dixon and Moon 1986; Moon and Dixon 1985; Morris 1979). It focuses on the possible impact of defense spending or military service on the 'bottom line' of the people's physical quality of life. In a cross-sectional study of the less developed countries, Dixon and Moon (1986) have found that military manpower (measured by the so-called military participation ratio) is positively correlated with the people's physical well-being, and that defense spending is negatively correlated with this well-being after appropriate statistical controls have been introduced. This association seems to imply that a high level of sociopolitical mobilization and military recruitment may constitute a form of investment in human resources, which in turn results in higher physical quality of life. However, a recent time series study of Taiwan (admittedly an atypical developing country) has not been able to find any significant impact, direct or indirect, of military manpower or defense spending on the over-time improvement in that island's physical quality of life (Davis and Chan 1990).

According to Deger (1986), the level of human resources (as emphasized by the basic needs approach) is important, because it determines the *absorptive capacity* of a developing country in utilizing the available savings. Even though defense spending may not directly crowd out civilian investment, it may very well curtail the ability of the civilian sector to take advantage of the available funds due to the constraints imposed by shortfalls in trained personnel, skilled entrepreneurs, administrative capacity, and social infrastructure.

Yet a third line of inquiry has focused on the impact of defense burden on the *size distribution of income*; that is, on the question of whether defense burden tends to exacerbate social or economic inequality. There is some tentative cross-national evidence suggesting that military manpower (but not military spending) is positively correlated with income equality (such as Andreski 1968; Chan 1989; Garnier and Hazelrigg 1977; Weede 1980b, 1983b; Weede and Tiefenbach 1981). It has been hypothesized that this association is due to the tendency for an incumbent elite to be more willing to share the national wealth with the masses, when it is faced with severe internal or external threats. Consequently, defense exertion – at least in the form of a higher military participation ratio – may have a positive impact in bringing about a more egalitarian society.

SUBSTANTIVE SPECIFICATION AND ANALYTIC CHALLENGES

The above brief review of the literature suggests several areas for analytic attention and improvement. First, there is an increasing need for appropriate longitudinal case studies of different countries' historical experiences to complement and verify the patterns that have been previously derived from cross-national research. It is possible that the results of cross-sectional analyses cannot be supported by time series investigations of individual countries at different stages of economic development.

Second and relatedly, these latter studies should incorporate crucial factors that are specific to particular countries. Thus, the oil revenues of the Gulf states, the export surplus of the Asian 'trading nations,' the massive U.S. aid to Israel and Egypt, and the privileged position of the U.S. dollar as the premier international currency have all played an important role in mediating the socioeconomic impact of defense allocations in these countries.

Third, we need a more discriminating approach that would enable us to differentiate the impact of various kinds of defense spending (for example, on manpower, domestic procurement, foreign arms imports, R & D) on various kinds of socioeconomic performance (for example, inflation, unemployment, income equality, physical quality of life). The aggregate figures used to measure and monitor defense burden may obscure and hide important details about possible tradeoffs.

Finally, we need to be more sensitive to the possibility that the influence relationships between defense allocations and socioeconomic performances may be direct, indirect, or even reciprocal. These relationships are likely to operate through multiple channels with mixed effects. And, as implied before, these channels may also differ significantly for different countries (Chowdhury 1991), so that cross-national generalizations would have to be sensitive to specific contextual factors.

The essays included in this volume pursue both cross-sectional and time series methodologies. They analyze a variety of countries in order to study the conditions under which defense allocations would or would not have a tangible impact on economic growth or social welfare. Also, they tackle a number of substantive and analytic issues raised earlier in an attempt to provide further empirical validation and substantive clarification.

In Chapter 2, Mintz, Huang, and Heo disaggregate the overall military spending by the U.S. government, and examine how various subcategories of this spending can affect the inflation and unemployment rates. Whereas previous research using aggregated defense dollars has not uncovered any evidence of military expenditures being influenced by the unemployment level, these authors show that the defense procurement programs (but not the other categories of military expenditure) have been affected by the unemployment level. Therefore, their results imply that U.S. officials have used this type of military expenditure as a countercyclical tool for managing ongoing economic downturns (the causal impact of unemployment on weapons procurement tends to be immediate rather than delayed).

In Chapter 3, Rasler and Thompson look into the British case in order to examine its implications for alternative explanatory models of hegemonic decline. Significantly, contrary to the popular expectation of the deleterious effects of defense burden on capital formation, they found no evidence of military expenditure crowding out investment in the British time series. Instead, the evidence points in the other direction of investment rates and economic growth influencing both public and private consumption levels. That is to say, the causal flow goes from macroeconomic performance to defense burden rather than the other way around. Britain's military expenditure tended to be determined by rather than to determine capital formation and economic growth. The authors of this chapter argue that the competition between investment and consumption (especially public consumption for military purposes) was only a derivative phenomenon of the onging processes of British decline, and not a fundamental cause of its initial onset.

The focus shifts from a previous imperial power to a smaller European country in Chapter 4. In this chapter, Cappelen, Gleditsch, and Bjerkholt introduce us to Norway's defense burden and its implications for that country's political economy. They undertake an econometric simulation to assess the 'peace dividend' of alternative cutbacks in Norway's defense posture. Their analysis shows the kind of 'what if' questions that needs to be answered in order for scholarly treatments of the defense–growth–welfare tradeoffs to gain policy relevance. It also shows sensitivity to those political, economic, and social factors that set the context for any feasible attempt to undertake the conversion of military programs for civilian purposes. Among such factors in Norway are the rising demand for old-age care, the concern with environmental protection, the impact of conscription on labor supply, and that of military retrenchment on exacerbating regional economic and income disparities.

In Chapter 5, Bobrow analyzes the Japanese case, which has been characterized by a relatively light defense burden, heavy foreign commercial dependence, and a close security and political tie with the United States. Tokyo's policy conduct offers an illuminating case of how a major power can avoid the nasty tradeoffs between military security, national autonomy, economic vitality, and the maintenance of a conducive foreign political and commercial environment. However, Bobrow rightly cautions that 'like many other slogans, that of guns-versus-butter obscures more than it illuminates if taken as a descriptive rather than symbolic statement.' His analysis is particularly informative in two respects. First, he shows the importance of 'bringing politics and political culture back,' so that we are cognizant of the practical context in which officials and bureaucrats try to 'satisfice' among competing demands for limited resources. Much of the work on guns–growth–welfare tradeoffs has been overly economistic without attending to the motivations and customs that influence actual policy practice. Second, Bobrow reminds us that countries do not exist in splendid isolation – that is, the cross-national transfers of resources (tangible as well as intangible) can help to dampen or exacerbate domestic tradeoffs. Therefore, we need to exogenize the analysis of guns–growth–welfare tradeoffs in order to take account of the pertinent actions or inaction of foreigners (friends as well as foes).

Ron Smith offers an example of the exogenous variables that can influence defense burden in Chapter 6, where he develops a model of military spending and applies it to the British and French data. His results show a tendency to free-ride on the part of these NATO (North Atlantic Treaty Organization) allies of the United States and, at the same time, for their military expenditures to be adjusted according to the perceived threat emitting from the Soviet Union. Smith's chapter also demonstrates the value of rigorous modeling and applied econometrics to inform theory as well as policy.

The above case studies of major advanced powers are followed by several analyses of the smaller or less developed countries. In Chapter 7, Michael Ward and his coauthors apply a neoclassical model of economic growth to India. This country is interesting because it is a regional hegemon, possesses a comparatively large industrial sector and, at the same time, features a large impoverished population. Contrary to the popular belief of a negative impact of defense burden on economic growth, the econometric analysis of the Indian time series fails to demonstrate a dampening effect of the former on the latter (either directly, or indirectly through investment).

From India we move on to South Korea in Chapter 8. Arguably, South Korea presents one of the more successful economic stories in the Third World and has, at the same time, a relatively heavy defense burden as a result of the historical legacy of its war with North Korea. Chung-in Moon and In-Taek Hyun give a rich tapestry of the historical, political, and economic factors influencing defense allocations in Seoul. They point to the rivalry with the North, the maintenance of the U.S. tie, and the management of the domestic political economy as the principal sources of these allocations. Interestingly, they argue that defense spending tends to be a function of macroeconomic conditions and of the officials' attempt to manage these conditions rather than the other way around (thus, again reversing the customary causal direction in the literature on the defense–growth tradeoff). Moreover, their analysis implies that the ongoing democratization process may encourage more demands for 'butter' and less for 'guns.' Coupled with a maturing economy and protectionism abroad, these developments suggest more difficult political choices for making the necessary tradeoffs in the future (as compared to previous times when these tradeoffs could be dictated by an authoritarian state that overpowered the civil society).

In Chapter 9, attention turns to another East Asian newly industralizing country. As for South Korea, Taiwan has featured a comparatively heavy defense burden, rapid economic growth, and successful export expansion. Moreover, this island has one of the most equitable distributions of income in the capitalist world. Steve Chan undertakes a longitudinal analysis to study the relationship between military participation and income equality in Taiwan. He finds that the trends in these variables do not support the popular proposition (derived from cross-sectional studies) that a large military establishment facilitates greater income equality. During the 1980s especially, the number of armed forces personnel had declined while income distribution had become less equal. Moreover, contrary to the cross-national pattern of an inverted U-curve (that is, income inequality is relatively low among the poor countries, rises with the onset of modernization, but then declines after the achievement of mass affluence), Taiwan shows the opposite tendency. Its income distribution became more equal during the period of economic takeoff (the 1950s, 1960s, and 1970s), but has since become less equal as the country poised itself to join the ranks of the developed countries (during the 1980s).

We move from East Asia to the Middle East in the next two chapters. Going beyond the typical analysis of association between the opportunity costs of defense for growth and welfare, Mintz and Russett ask in Chapter 10 how policy-makers actually cope with such possible tradeoffs. Focusing on the case of Israel and its Arab neighbors, these authors in effect carry out Bobrow's injunctions to examine the political and exogenous context of these tradeoffs. Their analysis suggests that the use of limited military force by both Israeli and Arab leaders has been sensitive to Israel's economic conditions (especially the health of its core industrial groups) and electoral cycles. The behavior of both sides is suggestive of policy attempts to counteract or exploit economic weakness or political vulnerability through the use of military force. Interestingly, in this as well as in the chapter by Rasler and Thompson, the defense costs react to macroeconomic and political priorities, and not the other way around.

The case study of Israel and its Arab neighbors is followed by Robert Looney's investigation (in Chapter 11) of the relationship between defense burden and human capital formation among the Arab Gulf states. Contrary to the customary argument of guns–welfare tradeoff, he finds that 'increases in military expenditure per soldier and in the military participation appear to take place simultaneously with expanded allocations to human capital.' It seems that enhanced government revenues among the capital-surplus oil-exporting countries (during Looney's period of analysis, 1974–84) had enabled increased funding for both military and education programs. In that sense, a 'rising tide lifted all boats.' It is not clear, however, how these countries confronted the budgetary squeeze brought on by the subsequent 'leaner' years of falling oil prices and reduced sales.

In Chapter 12, we turn to a cross-national study of developing countries in general. Focusing on the size of armed forces, Erich Weede argues that the military participation ratio represents a form of investment in human capital in the Third World. He shows empirically that this ratio is generally associated with faster economic growth. However, the results are less positive for the hypothesis that a high military participation ratio induces greater income equality. Overall, Weede's analysis calls attention to the need to discriminate among alternative forms of defense allocation (such as between manpower- and capital-intensive military programs), and to differentiate the growth and welfare impact of defense allocations for countries at different levels of development.

Finally, in Chapter 13 Richard Eichenberg performs the herculean task of pulling together the analyses of the preceding chapters, and offers a masterful synthesis. He not only looks at the state of our current knowledge on tradeoffs among defense, growth, and welfare, but also provides suggestions for future directions of research. In particular, he argues that we need to pay more attention to theories of domestic power and coalitional politics, the processes of budgetary allocation, the State's fiscal structure and revenue options, and its pursuit of external security and influence. He contends that our research agenda on allocutional politics must address foreign policy grand strategy.

REFERENCES

Abolfathi, F. 1979. Arms expenditures and economic growth: is there a linkage? Presented at the annual meeting of the Peace Science Society (International), southern section, Columbia, S.C., April.

Aldrich, John, Robert Duvall, and James Weldes. no date. The costs of national security: spending for defense and spending for welfare in the United States, 1948–1983. University of Minnesota, Minneapolis, mimeograph.

Amsden, Alice H. 1977. Kaldor's 'The military in development' – a comment. *World Development* 5: 753–61.

Andreski, Stanislav. 1968. *Military Organization and Society*. Stanford, Calif.: Stanford University Press.

Askari, Hussein and Vittorio Corbo. 1974. Economic implications of military expenditures in the Middle East. *Journal of Peace Research* 11: 341–3.

Babin, Nehama. 1989. Military spending, economic growth, and the time factor. *Armed Forces and Society* 15: 249–62.

Ball, Nicole. 1981. *The Military in the Development Process*. Claremont, Calif.: Regina.

Ball, Nicole. 1983a. *Third-World Security Expenditure: A Statistical Compendium*. Stockholm: Swedish National Defence Research Institute.

Ball, Nicole. 1983b. Defence and development: a critique of the Benoit study. In Helena Tuomi and Raimo Vayrynen (eds.), *Militarization and Arms Production*, pp. 39–56. New York: St. Martin's.

Ball, Nicole. 1985. Security expenditure and economic growth in developing countries. Presented at the East–West conference on North–South Relations, Frankfurt, 20–2 March.

Ball, Nicole. 1986. Security expenditures: measurement and trends. Presented at the meeting on 'Defense, Resources and Development,' Birkbeck College, London, 20–1 March.

Benoit, Emile. 1972a. Growth effects of defense in developing countries. *International Development Review* 14: 2–10.

Benoit, Emile. 1972b. A rejoinder to Professor Dorfman's comment. *International Development Review* 14: 12–14.

Benoit, Emile. 1973. *Defense and Economic Growth in Developing Countries*. Lexington, Mass.: D. C. Heath.

Benoit, Emile. 1978. Growth and defense in developing countries. *Economic Development and Cultural Change* 26: 271–80.

Biswas, Basudeb and Rati Ram. 1986. Military expenditures and economic growth in less developed countries. *Economic Development and Cultural Change* 34: 361–72.

Boulding, Kenneth E. 1974. Defense spending: burden or boon? *War/Peace Report* 13: 19–24.

Boulding, Kenneth E. 1979. The war industry. In Clayton C. Walton (ed.), *Inflation and National Survival* (The Academy of Political Science, Proceedings, Vol. 33, No. 2), pp. 91–100. New York: Academy of Political Science.
Brzoska, Michael. 1981. The reporting of military expenditures. *Journal of Peace Research* 18: 261–75.
Brzoska, Michael and Herbert Wulf. 1978. Military spending in less developed countries: boost or burden for the economy? Study Group on Armament and Underdevelopment, University of Hamburg, mimeograph.
Brzoska, Michael and Herbert Wulf. 1979. Rejoinder to Benoit's 'Growth and defense in developing countries' – misleading results and questionable methods. Study Group on Armament and Underdevelopment, University of Hamburg, mimeograph.
Cappelen, Ådne, Nils P. Gleditsch, and Olav Bjerkholt. 1984. Military spending and economic growth in the OECD countries. *Journal of Peace Research* 21: 361–73.
Caputo, David A. 1975. New perspectives on the public policy implications of defense and welfare expenditures in four modern democracies: 1950–1970. *Policy Sciences* 6: 423–46.
Carnegie Endowment for International Peace. 1981. *Challenges for U.S. National Security: Defense Spending and the Economy*. New York.
Chan, Steve. 1985. The impact of defense spending on economic performance: a survey of evidence and problems. *ORBIS* 29: 403–34.
Chan, Steve. 1987. Military expenditures and economic performance. In *World Military Expenditures and Arms Transfers: 1986*, pp. 29–37. Washington, D.C.: U.S. Arms Control and Disarmament Agency.
Chan, Steve. 1988. Defense burden and economic growth: unravelling the Taiwanese enigma. *American Political Science Review* 82: 913–20.
Chan, Steve. 1989. Income inequality among LDCs: a comparative analysis of alternative perspectives. *International Studies Quarterly* 33: 45–65.
Chan, Steve and David R. Davis. 1991. Defense allocation, inflation, and unemployment in South Korea and Taiwan: a Granger analysis. *Korean Journal of Defense Analysis*: forthcoming.
Chester, Eric. 1978. Military spending and capitalist stability. *Cambridge Journal of Economics* 2: 293–8.
Chowdhury, Abdur R. 1991. A causal analysis of defense spending and economic growth. *Journal of Conflict Resolution* 35: 80–97.
Clayton, James L. 1976. The fiscal limits of the warfare–welfare state: defense and welfare spending in the United States since 1900. *Western Political Quarterly* 29: 364–83.
Dabelko, David and James M. McCormick. 1977. Opportunity costs of defense: some cross-national evidence. *Journal of Peace Research* 14: 145–54.
Dabelko, David and James M. McCormick. 1984. Response to Lyttkens and Vedovato. *Journal of Peace Research* 21: 395–7.
Davis, David R. and Steve Chan. 1990. The security–welfare relationship: longitudinal evidence from Taiwan. *Journal of Peace Research* 27: 87–100.
Deger, Saadet. 1986. *Military Expenditure in Third World Countries: The Economic Effects*. London: Routledge & Kegan Paul.
Deger, Saadet and Somnath Sen. 1983. Military expenditure, spin-off and economic development. *Journal of Development Economics* 13: 67–83.
Deger, Saadet and Ron Smith. 1983. Military expenditure and growth in less developed countries. *Journal of Conflict Resolution* 27: 335–53.
DeGrasse, Robert W. Jr. 1983. *Military Expansion and Economic Decline: The Impact of Military Spending on U.S. Economic Performance*. Armonk, N.Y.: Sharpe.

Dixon, William J. and Bruce E. Moon. 1986. The military burden and basic human needs. *Journal of Conflict Resolution* 30: 660–84.

Domke, William K., Richard C. Eichenberg, and Catherine M. Kelleher. 1983. The illusion of choice: defense and welfare in advanced industrial democracies, 1948–1978. *American Political Science Review* 77: 19–35.

Dorfman, Robert. 1972. A comment on Professor Benoit's 'Conundrum'. *International Development Review* 14: 10–12.

Dumas, Lloyd J. 1977. Economic conversion, productive efficiency and social welfare. *Peace Research Reviews* 7: 17–52.

Eichenberg, Richard C. 1984. The expenditure and revenue effects of defense spending in the Federal Republic of Germany. *Policy Sciences* 16: 391–411.

Faini, Ricardo, Patricia Arnez, and Lance Taylor. 1984. Defense spending, economic structure and growth: evidence among countries and over time. *Economic Development and Cultural Change* 32: 487–98.

Fontanel, Jacques. 1982. *Military Expenditure and Economic Growth: France, Morocco*. New York: United Nations.

Frederiksen, Peter C. and Robert E. Looney. 1982. Defense expenditures and economic growth in developing countries: some further empirical evidence. *Journal of Economic Development*: 113–24.

Frederiksen, Peter C. and Robert E. Looney. 1983. Defense expenditures and economic growth in developing countries. *Armed Forces and Society* 9: 633–45.

Friedman, Samuel R. 1974. An alternative model to Szymanski. *American Journal of Sociology* 79: 1459–62.

Garnier, Maurice A. and Lawrende E. Hazelrigg. 1977. Military organization and distributional inequality. *Journal of Political and Military Sociology* 5: 17–33.

Gilpin, Robert. 1975. *U.S. Power and the Multinational Corporations*. New York: Basic Books.

Gleditsch, Nils P., Olav Bjerkholt, and Ådne Cappelen. 1988. Military R & D and economic growth in industrialized market economies. In Peter Wallerstein (ed.), *Peace Research: Achievements and Challenges*, pp. 198–215. Boulder, Colo.: Westview.

Goertz, Gary and Paul F. Diehl. 1986. Measuring military allocations: a comparison of different approaches. *Journal of Conflict Resolution* 30: 553–81.

Gold, David. 1990. *The Impact of Defense Spending on Investment, Productivity and Economic Growth*. Defense Budget Project, Washington, D.C., monograph.

Goldstein, Joshua. 1985. Kondratieff waves as war cycles. *International Studies Quarterly* 29: 411–41.

Goldstein, Walter, 1981. The opportunity costs of acting as a super power: U.S. military strategy in the 1980s. *Journal of Peace Research* 18: 241–60.

Gothheil, Fred M. 1974. An economic assessment of the military burden in the Middle East. *Journal of Conflict Resolution* 18: 502–13.

Green, Donald W. and Christopher J. Higgins. 1977. *SOVMOD I: A Macroeconometric Model of the Soviet Union*. New York: Academic Press.

Grobar, Lisa M. and Richard C. Porter. 1989. Benoit revisited: defense spending and economic growth in LDCs. *Journal of Conflict Resolution* 33: 318–45.

Hagen, Everett E. 1972. An observation on the Benoit and Dorfman analyses. *International Development Review* 14: 14–15.

Halperin, Morton H., Jacob A. Stockfisch, and Murray L. Weidenbaum. 1973. *The Political Economy of the Military–Industrial Complex*. Berkeley, Calif.: University of California Press.

Hamilton, Earl J. 1977. The role of war in modern inflation. *Journal of Economic History* 37: 13–19.

Hartley, Keith and Pat McLean. 1978. Military expenditure and capitalism: a comment. *Cambridge Journal of Economics* 2: 287–92.
Heisler, Martin O. 1982. Domestic defense expenditures: theoretical considerations in comparative perspective. Presented at the annual meeting of the International Studies Association, Cincinnati, 24–7 March.
Hill, Kim Quaile. 1978. Domestic politics, international linkages, and military expenditures. *Studies in Comparative International Development* 13: 38–59.
Hollenhorst, Jerry and Gary Ault. 1971a. An alternative answer to: 'Who pays for defense?' *American Political Science Review* 65: 760–3.
Hollist, Ladd. 1971. Alternative explanations of competitive arms processes: tests on four pairs of nations. *American Journal of Political Science* 21: 313–40.
Huisken, Ron. 1983. Armament and development. In Helena Tuomi and Raimo Vayrynen (eds.), *Militarization and Arms Production*, pp. 3–25. New York: St. Martin's.
Intriligator, Michael D. and Dagobert L. Brito. 1986. Mayer's alternative to the I–B model. *Journal of Conflict Resolution* 30, 1: 29–31.
Jackman, Robert W. 1976. Politicians in uniform: military governments and social change in the Third World. *American Political Science Review* 70: 1078–97.
Johnson, Paul M. and Robert A. Wells. 1986. Soviet military and civilian resource allocation, 1951–1980. *Journal of Conflict Resolution* 30: 195–219.
Jolly, R. (ed.). 1978. *Disarmament and World Development*. Oxford: Pergamon.
Kennedy, Gavin. 1974. *The Military in the Third World*. New York: Charles Scribner's Sons.
Kennedy, Gavin. 1975. *The Economics of Defense*. Totowa, NJ.: Rowman & Littlefield.
Kennedy, Gavin. 1983. *Defense Economics*. London: Duckworth.
Kick, Edward and Ban Dev Sharda. 1986. Third World militarization and development. *Journal of Developing Societies* 2: 49–67.
Kidron, Michael, 1970. *Western Capitalism since the War*. London: Weidenfeld & Nicholson.
Kindleberger, Charles P. 1973. *The World in Depression: 1929–1939*. Berkeley, Calif.: University of California Press.
Kindleberger, Charles P. 1981. Dominance and leadership in the international economy. *International Studies Quarterly* 25: 242–54.
Kinsella, David. 1989. Defense spending and economic performance in the United States: a causal analysis. Yale University, New Haven, Conn., mimeograph.
Korb, Lawrence J. 1980. The FY 1981–1985 defense program: issues and trends. *AEI Foreign Policy and Defense Review*, Vol. 2, No. 2. Washington, D.C.: American Enterprises Institute.
Krasner, Stephen D. 1976. State power and the structure of international trade. *World Politics* 28: 317–47.
Kriesberg, Louis and Ross Klein. 1980. Changes in public support for U.S. military spending. *Journal of Conflict Resolution* 24: 79–111.
Lebovic, James H. and Ashfaq Ishaq. 1987. Military burden, security needs, and economic growth in the Middle East. *Journal of Conflict Resolution* 31: 106–38.
Lee, Jong Ryool. 1973. Changing national priorities in the United States. In Bruce M. Russett and Alfred Stepan (eds.), *Military Force and American Society*, pp. 61–105. New York: Harper & Row.
Leidy, Michael P. and Robert W. Staiger. 1985. Economic issues and methodology in arms race analysis. *Journal of Conflict Resolution* 29: 503–30.
Leontief, Wassily and Faye Duchin. 1980. *Worldwide Economic Implications of a Limitation on Military Spending*. A Report for the U.N. Group of Governmental Experts on the Relationship Between Disarmament and Development.

Lim, David. 1983. Another look at growth and defense in less developed countries. *Economic Development and Cultural Change* 31: 377–84.
Lindgren, Goran. 1984a. Armaments and economic performance. *Journal of Peace Research* 21: 375–87.
Lindgren, Goran. 1984b. Military and civilian research and development. Presented at the annual meeting of the International Studies Association, Atlanta, 27–31 March.
Looney, Robert E. and Peter C. Frederiksen. 1988. Economic determinants of Latin American defense expenditures. *Armed Forces and Society* 14: 459–71.
Lucier, Charles E. 1979. Changes in the values of arms race parameters. *Journal of Conflict Resolution* 23: 17–39.
Lyttkens, Carl Hampus and Claudio Vedovato. 1984. Opportunity costs of defense: a comment on Dabelko and McCormick. *Journal of Peace Research* 21: 389–94.
Mayer, Thomas F. 1986. Arms races and war initiation: some alternatives to the Intriligator–Brito model. *Journal of Conflict Resolution* 30: 3–28.
McKinlay, R.D. and A. S. Cohan. 1976. The economic performance of military regime: a cross-national aggregate study. *British Journal of Political Science* 6: 291–310.
Melman, Seymour. 1970. *Pentagon Capitalism: The Political Economy of War*. New York: McGraw-Hill.
Melman, Seymour. 1972. Ten propositions on the war economy. *American Economic Review* 62: 312–18.
Melman, Seymour. 1974. *The Permanent War Economy: American Capitalism in Decline*. New York: Simon & Schuster.
Mintz, Alex. 1989. 'Guns' vs. 'butter': a disaggregated analysis. *American Political Science Review* 83: 1285–93.
Mintz, Alex and Chi Huang. 1991. 'Guns' vs. 'butter': the indirect link. *American Journal of Political Science* 35: 738–57.
Modelski, George, 1987a. *Long Cycles in World Politics*. Seattle: University of Washington Press.
Modelski, George (ed.). 1987b. *Exploring Long Cycles*. Boulder, Colo.: Rienner.
Moon, Bruce E. and William J. Dixon. 1985. Politics, the state, and basic human needs: a cross-national study. *American Journal of Political Science* 29: 661–94.
Morris, Morris D. 1979. *Measuring the Conditions of the World's Poor: The Physical Quality of Life Index*. New York: Pergamon.
Morrow, James D. 1989. A twist of truth: a reexamination of the effects of arms races on the occurrence of war. *Journal of Conflict Resolution* 33: 500–29.
Nabe, O. 1983. Military expenditures and industrialization in Africa. *Journal of Economic Issues* 17: 575–87.
Nardinelli, Clark and Gary B. Ackerman. 1976. Defense expenditures and the survival of American capitalism: a note. *Armed Forces and Society* 3: 13–16.
Neuman, Stephanie. 1978. Security, military expenditures and socioeconomic development: reflections of Iran. *ORBIS* 22: 569–94.
Neuman, Stephanie. 1979. In reply. *ORBIS* 23: 477–80.
Neuman, Stephanie. 1984. International stratification and Third World military industries. *International Organization* 38: 167–97.
Nyangoro, Julius E. 1984. Military expenditure and economic performance in African countries. Presented at the annual meeting of the International Studies Association, Atlanta, 27–31 March.
Organski, A. F. K. and Jacek Kugler. 1980. *The War Ledger*. Chicago: University of Chicago Press.
Peroff, Katheleen. 1977. The warfare–welfare tradeoff: health, public aid and housing. *Journal of Sociology and Social Welfare* 4: 366–81.
Peroff, Katheleen and Margaret Podolak-Warren. 1979. Does spending on defense

cut spending on health? A time series analysis of the U.S. economy 1929–1974. *British Journal of Political Science* 9: 21–40.

Pryor, Frederick. 1968. *Public Expenditure in Communist and Capitalist Countries*. Homewood, Ill.: Irwin.

Rasler, Karen A. and William R. Thompson. 1985a. War and the economic growth of major powers. *American Journal of Political Science* 29: 513–38.

Rasler, Karen A. and William R. Thompson. 1985b. War-making and state-making: governmental expenditures, tax revenues, and global wars. *American Political Science Review* 79: 491–507.

Rasler, Karen A. and William R. Thompson. 1988. Defense burdens, capital formation, and economic growth: the systemic leader case. *Journal of Conflict Resolution* 32: 61–86.

Rothschild, Kurt W. 1973. Military expenditure, exports and growth. *Kyklos* 26: 804–14.

Russett, Bruce M. 1970. *What Price Vigilance? The Burdens of National Defense*. New Haven, Conn.: Yale University Press.

Russett, Bruce M. 1971. Some decisions in the regression analysis of time series data. In James F. Herndon and Joseph L. Bernd (eds.), *Mathematical Applications in Political Science*, Vol. 5, pp. 29–50. Charlottesville, Virg.: University of Virginia Press.

Russett, Bruce M. 1972. The revolt of the masses: public opinion on military expenditures. In Bruce M. Russett (ed.), *Peace, War, and Numbers*, pp. 299–319. Beverly Hills, Calif.: Sage.

Russett, Bruce M. 1982. Defense expenditures and national well-being. *American Political Science Review* 76: 767–77.

Smith, Dan and Ron Smith. 1979. Reflections on Neuman. *ORBIS* 23: 471–7.

Smith, Dan and Ron Smith. 1980. Military expenditure, resources and development. Birkbeck College, London, mimeograph.

Smith, Ron P. 1977. Military expenditure and capitalism. *Cambridge Journal of Economics* 1: 61–76.

Smith, Ron P. 1978. Military expenditure and capitalism: a reply. *Cambridge Journal of Economics* 2: 299–304.

Smith, Ron P. 1980. Military expenditure and investment in OECD countries, 1954–1973. *Journal of Comparative Economics* 4: 19–32.

Smith, Ron P. and George Georgiou. 1983. Assessing the effect of military expenditure on OECD economies: a survey. *Arms Control* 4: 3–15.

Starr, Harvey, Francis W. Hoole, Jeffrey A. Hart, and John R. Freeman. 1984. The relationship between defense spending and inflation. *Journal of Conflict Resolution* 26: 103–22.

Stein, Arthur A. 1980. *The Nation at War*. Baltimore: Johns Hopkins University Press.

Stevenson, Paul. 1974. A defense of Baran and Sweezy. *American Journal of Sociology* 79: 1452–6.

Stoll, Richard J. 1982. Let the researcher beware: the use of the Richardson equations to estimate the parameters of a dyadic arms acquisition process. *American Journal of Political Science* 26: 77–89.

Szymanski, Albert. 1973. Military spending and economic stagnation. *American Journal of Sociology* 79: 1–14.

Szymanski, Albert. 1974. A Reply to Friedman, Stevenson, and Zeitlin. *American Journal of Sociology* 79: 1462–77.

Taylor, Lance. 1981. Military economics in the Third World. The Massachusetts Institute of Technology, Cambridge, Mass., mimeograph.

Terhal, P. 1981. Guns or grain: macro-economic costs of Indian defence, 1960–1970. *Economic and Political Weekly* 16: 1998–2003.

Thompson, William R., Robert D. Duval, and Ahmed Dia. 1979. Wars, alliances, and military expenditures: two pendulum hypotheses. *Journal of Conflict Resolution* 23: 629–54.

Tufte, Edward R. 1978. *Political Control of the Economy*. Princeton, NJ.: Princeton University Press.

United Nations. 1973. *Disarmament and Development*. New York.

United Nations. 1978. *Economic and Social Consequences of Arms Race and of Military Expenditures*. New York.

United States Arms Control and Disarmament Agency. 1978. Military expenditure reporting and limitations. In *World Military Expenditures and Arms Transfers: 1967–1976*, pp. 13–15. Washington, D.C.

United States Arms Control and Disarmament Agency. 1980. Conversion rates for international expenditure comparisons. In *World Military Expenditures and Arms Transfers: 1969–1978*, pp. 15–17. Washington, D.C.

United States Congressional Budget Office. 1983. *Defense Spending and the Economy*. Washington, D.C.

Wallace, Michael D. 1979. Arms races and escalation: some new evidence. *Journal of Conflict Resolution* 23: 3–16.

Wallace, Michael D. 1980. Some persisting findings: a reply to Professor Weede. *Journal of Conflict Resolution* 24: 289–92.

Wallace, Michael D. 1982. Armaments and escalation: two competing hypotheses. *International Studies Quarterly* 26: 37–56.

Wallace, Michael D. and Judy M. Wilson. 1978. Non-linear arms race models. *Journal of Peace Research* 15: 175–92.

Weede, Erich. 1980a. Arms races and escalation: some persisting doubts. *Journal of Conflict Resolution* 24: 285–7.

Weede, Erich. 1980b. Beyond misspecification in sociological analyses of income inequality. *American Sociological Review* 45: 497–501.

Weede, Erich. 1983. Military participation ratios, human capital formation, and economic growth: a cross-national analysis. *Journal of Political and Military Sociology* 11: 11–19.

Weede, Erich and Horst Tiefenbach. 1981. Some recent explanations of income inequality. *International Studies Quarterly* 25: 255–82.

Weidenbaum, Murray L. 1974. *The Economics of Peacetime Defense*. New York: Praeger.

Zeitlin, Maurice. 1974. On 'Military spending and economic stagnation'. *American Journal of Sociology* 79: 1452–6.

2 Defense spending and economic performance: a disaggregated analysis[1]

Alex Mintz, Chi Huang, and Uk Heo
Texas A & M University

There is serious disagreement among scholars of defense economics and politics on the impact of military spending on economic performance. Some scholars found military expenditures to have a dampening impact on the economy, others found a positive correlation between military spending and various indicators of economic performance, while still others were unable to find any evidence for a defense–growth tradeoff (see Chan 1985; Gold 1990; and Lindgren 1984 for comprehensive reviews of the literature). Stephanie Neuman (1979, 470) has therefore concluded that, 'despite the volume of writing on the subject, we still do not know whether there is a causal relationship between military expenditures [and economic performance], much less what that relationship is.'

Previous studies have all focused on the relationship between total military spending and specific indicators of economic performance (inflation, unemployment, investment, growth, interest rates, and so on – see DeGrasse *et al.* 1983; Gold 1990; Huisken 1982; Kinsella 1990; Mintz and Huang 1990; Mosley 1985; Rasler and Thompson 1988; Smith 1977, 1980; Starr *et al.* 1984 to name just a few). This chapter analyzes the relationship between various components of the U.S. defense budget (personnel, procurement, operation and maintenance (O & M), and research development testing and evaluation) and two important indicators of the state of the economy: inflation and unemployment.

In an article published elsewhere, one of the authors of this chapter (Mintz 1989) explained the need to disaggregate total military spending into major subcomponents of the military budget in an analysis of the guns–butter tradeoff: there is no reason to expect the impact on welfare spending of allocations to the procurement of weapon systems to be similar to the impact of spending for operation and maintenance programs or salaries and benefits of over 2 million active uniformed personnel. He hypothesized (1989, 1287) that while allocations to capital-intensive programs such as procurement or research and development (R & D) may 'take resources away from welfare programs, allocations to labor-intensive programs [such as personnel] may ease the task of the government's health and education sectors rather than lead to a tradeoff.' Estimating Russett's equations

(1982) with disaggregated data, Mintz found no evidence for a guns–butter tradeoff in the pre-Reagan era but strong evidence for tradeoffs between procurement/R & D expenditures and education expenditures during the Reagan years. He pointed out (1989, 1290) that procurement and R & D expenditures 'grew every year during that period by an average of more than 10 percent, while education expenditures were cut (in constant prices) in five out of the seven years by an average of almost 5 percent (1.3 percent if 1982 is excluded). Military personnel and O & M outlays rose, on average, by only 3.8 percent and 3.6 percent respectively.'

Finding no evidence for a defense–welfare tradeoff at the aggregate level 'seems to imply either that no sub-category of defense expenditure affects welfare spending or that subcategories of defense spending have positive and negative impacts essentially canceling one another out' (Mintz 1989, 1287). The same can be said about the analysis of the guns–growth tradeoff. But, while we expect variations in the impact of the different components of the defense budget on economic performance, the explanations for these variations are obviously different from those presented by Mintz (1989) in his analysis of tradeoffs between 'guns' and 'butter.'

The purpose of this chapter is to analyze the relationship between defense spending and economic performance at a less aggregated level than has been done previously. Most studies evaluated the effect of military spending on economic performance (see, for example, Mintz and Huang 1990, 1991). The neo-Keynesian approach (see, for example, Griffin *et al.* 1982a, 1982b) reverses the direction of causality in guns–butter research by arguing (based on the work of Baran and Sweezy (1966); and O'Connor (1973)) that policy-makers use military expenditures as a counter-cyclical instrument in response to the performance of the economy. According to this perspective, increased levels of military spending are necessary to ensure continuous economic growth. Governments often use military spending as a macro-management tool since it is largely controllable (relative to other governmental programs), is easy to justify to the public in view of the arms race, and is one of the very few governmental policies conservatives advocate. According to this perspective then, poor economic performance motivates policy-makers to increase military spending (Baran and Sweezy 1966; Griffin *et al.* 1982a, 1982b; Smith 1977, 1978). Liberal political economists are interested, in contrast, in the *impact* of military spending on economic performance (Kinsella 1990), while realists are interested in the impact of military spending on the power of nations and the distribution of power in the international system. We now turn to explain the links between the various components of the defense budget and unemployment and inflation.

EMPLOYMENT

Defense-related employment reached 6.68 million or 5.68 percent of the total labor force during the Reagan years in the White House (Cusack

1991). The Pentagon supports 2.1 million uniformed personnel, over 1 million defense civilians, more than 1 million military reservists, and more than 2 million in the defense industry. A common argument against disarmament, therefore, is that it will create unemployment (Lindgren 1984, 380). Department of Defense (DoD) data show, however, that the employment effects of various types of military spending (such as procurement, research and development, and personnel) are very different. For example, allocations of 1 billion dollars to military personnel programs support 49,000 individuals while allocations of a similar amount to defense nonpay programs create only 35,000 jobs (U.S. Department of Defense 1983).

DeGrasse *et al.* (1983) and Gansler (1980) pointed out that labor in the defense industry is highly skilled and relatively well paid. 'A very low proportion of blue-collar workers and a very high proportion of engineers and scientists are involved in the development and production of weapons systems' (Mintz 1989, 1287). Allocations of funds to military R & D and procurement programs are largely directed at the capital- and technology-intensive sectors of industry (Huisken 1982, 8). Military personnel expenditures go in contrast to finance the pay of soldiers and retired military personnel. Part of the operation and maintenance budget supports civilian employees in the Department of Defense. In contrast to labor in the defense *industry*, the armed forces recruit disproportionately from lower income groups. The same amount of funds creates considerably more jobs when allocated to the military personnel subcategory of the budget than to the R & D or procurement subcategories.

There is also considerable disagreement among scholars on the employment effects of defense versus *civilian* spending. According to DeGrasse *et al.* (1983, 12), military purchases from the private sector create fewer jobs than most other forms of private spending. According to calculations made by the Public Interest Research Group in Michigan and the Center for Defense Information and reported in Nincic and Cusack (1979, 111), military spending creates fewer jobs than many forms of civilian spending. Huisken (1982, 8) claimed that military expenditure is 'among the least efficient types of expenditures from the standpoint of creating employment; that is, per unit of expenditure, most plausible patterns of expenditure for civilian goods and services require more workers than does military expenditure.' Gansler (1980, 13) argued, in contrast, that defense expenditures may be a more effective stimulant than expenditures in other areas of government, because defense creates a greater economic multiplier for the dollars invested.

The empirical evidence for the employment effects of military spending is mixed (see, Chester 1978; Smith 1977; Smith and Georgiou 1983; Szymanski 1973). Szymanski found that high military spending reduces unemployment. Smith (1977) also tested the hypothesis that high levels of military expenditure lead to low levels of unemployment and found (1977, 67–8) that 'the U.S. has provided the most evidence in support of the contention that military expenditure has been used to offset tendencies towards stagnation. . . . if there is under-utilization of resources, an increment in military expenditure will expand output and reduce unemployment.' Chester (1978) and Smith and Georgiou (1983) found, in contrast, no association between military expenditure and unemployment. A more complete review of the empirical findings can be found in Kinsella (1990).

Military expenditures can be used by policy-makers as a countercyclical instrument for combating high levels of unemployment (Griffin *et al.* 1982a; Mayer 1991; Mintz and Hicks 1984). A quick 'fix' might be in the form of enlarging the size of the armed forces. Another possibility is, of course, to use military contract awards to fight unemployment (see Mayer 1991); but as has been pointed out by many scholars (see, for example, DeGrasse *et al.* 1983; Gansler 1980) highly skilled labor in the defense industry might be in a lesser need to be supported during periods of economic decline and rising unemployment. So the bottom line is that the countercyclical response of the government to poor economic performance may take different forms by using different components of the defense budget.

INFLATION

Starr *et al.* (1984) studied the relationship between military spending and inflation in four Western countries – the United States, the United Kingdom, France, and West Germany – in the time period 1956–79. They found no evidence for a statistically significant relationship in the U.S. and the U.K., but did find a two-way relationship between military spending and inflation in France and West Germany. According to Starr *et al.* (1984), the U.S. could export its inflation by using the status of the dollar as a key currency with running balance-of-payment deficits in the 1950s and 1960s (see also Calleo 1981). These results are consistent with those reported by Smith (1977) who correlated the share of military expenditure of the gross domestic product and the average rate of inflation in Organization for Economic Cooperation and Development (OECD) countries for the period 1960–70. Smith has also found no significant correlation between his measure of military expenditures and the rate of inflation in the majority of the cases.

Defense is a multifaceted phenomenon. The effects of different components of defense spending on the economy are not necessarily identical. Chan (1985, 424) argued that 'the impact of military personnel costs is similar to that of the governments' civilian programs of income transfer.' According to Chan (1985) these programs 'should be separated from other types of defense spending.' Allocations earmarked for the development and production of weapons systems are expected to have inflationary effects different from those of military personnel programs.

Different patterns of allocation of resources may also have different impacts on the inflation rate for civilian products, which results as a partial spinoff effect of military spending. For example, the influx of capital to defense projects such as the MX intercontinental ballistic missile system was estimated to bring about an increase at a rate of 0.1 percent in the consumer price index, while a project such as a five-year buildup of 167 ships has the estimated effect of a 0.12 percent increase in inflation (Korb 1980).

Melman (1985) found defense spending to be more inflationary than other forms of spending. Gansler (1980) explained that the inflationary impact of military spending is not just in terms of 'program inefficiencies' but also a result of the increasing cost of weapons systems. According to Gansler (1980, 15) there is continuous demand on the defense industry 'for increasing performance at almost any cost.' Consequently, unit production costs have continuously risen.

According to Griffin *et al.* (1982a), the state's ability to finance its expenditures depends overwhelmingly on revenues from the monopoly sector of the economy. If the non-competitive, monopoly sector is economically depressed or stagnating, the state is likely to come to its aid by increasing spending (Griffin *et al.* 1982a, 1982b). Increased levels of military spending have often led to an increase in demand for monopoly products and inflationary pressures.

Inflationary pressures may force the government in some instances to cut spending, including military spending. Griffin *et al.* (1982a) found inflation to have a negative impact on military spending. The obvious candidate for such cuts is the military personnel component of the budget. Wildavsky (1988) pointed out that defense is a people-oriented activity. Almost half of the DoD budget is earmarked for personnel activity. The defense industry and other components of the so-called military–industrial complex may in contrast resist cuts in weapons systems (Kurth 1989). *Newsweek* has recently reported that Congress has approved funding for several weapons systems (such as the V-22 Osprey) despite claims by the Joint Chiefs and the Pentagon of the lack of need for these systems. Defense affects the economic well-being of certain geographical areas in the country and of certain powerful corporations. One-sixth of all contract awards are typically granted to California while Texas and New York account together for another sixth of all contract awards (U.S. Department of Commerce, annually). On the other hand, R & D and O & M programs are typically adjusted upward to account for increasing prices. The inflation rate for weapons systems is often higher than the inflation rate for consumer goods. And payments to military personnel cannot lag too far behind inflation.

Mintz and Hicks (1984) examined the impact of several indicators of economic performance on the components of the defense budget but did not analyze the effect of military spending on economic performance.

DATA ANALYSIS

Lindgren (1984, 381) recently claimed that the relationship between military expenditure and economic performance is too complex to be captured by correlation or regression methods. Kinsella (1990) and Chan and Davis (1991) used Granger causality analysis. Both Chan (1985) and Ward (1987) have recommended the use of longitudinal design. According to Chan (1985, 407),

> The results based on cross-sectional designs are less trustworthy, as this approach is inherently limited in its ability to inform us about causal relationships. To tackle questions such as the impact of military spending on economic performance, we need dynamic analysis to determine temporal leads and lags, the reciprocal influences among the variables, and the over-time changes in the empirical parameters.

Due to the complexity of the relationships among the four components of defense spending and inflation and unemployment, and the unsettled controversies in the literature about their causal direction, it is almost impossible to specify a dynamic structural-equation model without *a priori* imposing some arbitrary restrictions. Since, given the current state of knowledge about this topic, such a model is likely to be misspecified, its statistical estimates are likely to be biased and the causal inferences will be misleading.

The lack of sound and commonly accepted theories of defense–growth tradeoffs demands a methodology which relies less on prior information in model specification and yet allows for tests of competing hypotheses about causal ordering among variables. Granger (1969) provided a useful definition of causality which can be tested with standard time-series methods. Granger's causality is based on an intuitively plausible notion that the past can cause the future while the future cannot cause the past. It can be described as follows. Let Y_t be a stationary series which has information up to and including period t. If Y_t can be predicted more accurately by using all available past information of X_t than by using all available information apart from X_t, then X causes Y (see Freeman 1983; Granger 1969). Furthermore, if X improves the predictability of Y and Y improves the predictability of X, then feedback is occurring between the two variables (Granger 1969, 428–9).

Granger's idea of bivariate causality can be generalized to multivariate situations in the context of vector autoregression (VAR). Following Sargent and Sims (1977), a VAR model relates current values of a group, or *vector*, of two or more variables to past values of that vector. Since all variables in a VAR model are allowed to interact with their own and each other's past values, the distinction between exogenous and endogenous variables in VAR models is blurred. This implies that a VAR model does not require us to specify causal paths on *a priori* grounds and, therefore, it fits with the idea of interconnectedness among the six variables examined in this study. On the other hand, VAR models still allow us to examine if the various causal links, which can be expressed by zero restrictions of blocks of coefficients, suggested by the competing theories are indeed consistent with empirical data. Although the individual coefficient estimates in a VAR model are not as accurate as in a *correctly specified* structural-equation model, the causal inferences based on a VAR model are more accurate than that based on a misspecified structural-equation model (Freeman *et al.* 1989). The choice of a VAR model for this study thus reflects our interest in exploring the causal linkages among the six variables in the political economy of military spending.

Taking all of this into account resulted in the specification of the following six-equation VAR system:

$$\begin{bmatrix} X_{1t} \\ X_{2t} \\ X_{3t} \\ X_{4t} \\ X_{5t} \\ X_{6t} \end{bmatrix} = \begin{bmatrix} \mu_1 \\ \mu_2 \\ \mu_3 \\ \mu_4 \\ \mu_5 \\ \mu_6 \end{bmatrix} + \sum_{i=1}^{P} \begin{bmatrix} \alpha_{11i} & \alpha_{12i} & \alpha_{13i} & \alpha_{14i} & \alpha_{15i} & \alpha_{16i} \\ \alpha_{21i} & \alpha_{22i} & \alpha_{23i} & \alpha_{24i} & \alpha_{25i} & \alpha_{26i} \\ \alpha_{31i} & \alpha_{32i} & \alpha_{33i} & \alpha_{34i} & \alpha_{35i} & \alpha_{36i} \\ \alpha_{41i} & \alpha_{42i} & \alpha_{43i} & \alpha_{44i} & \alpha_{45i} & \alpha_{46i} \\ \alpha_{51i} & \alpha_{52i} & \alpha_{53i} & \alpha_{54i} & \alpha_{55i} & \alpha_{56i} \\ \alpha_{61i} & \alpha_{62i} & \alpha_{63i} & \alpha_{64i} & \alpha_{65i} & \alpha_{66i} \end{bmatrix} \begin{bmatrix} X_{1,t-i} \\ X_{2,t-i} \\ X_{3,t-i} \\ X_{4,t-i} \\ X_{5,t-i} \\ X_{6,t-i} \end{bmatrix} + \begin{bmatrix} v_{1t} \\ v_{2t} \\ v_{3t} \\ v_{4t} \\ v_{5t} \\ v_{6t} \end{bmatrix}$$

where X_1 through X_4 are the change rates of the four major components of military spending (in fiscal year 1982 constant dollars): personnel, O & M, procurement, and R & D; and X_5 and X_6 refer to the unemployment rate and the inflation rate, respectively. v_l ($l = 1, \ldots, 6$) is a white-noise error term which represents other factors not included in the equation.

Data on the four components of military spending were obtained from *The Budget of the United States* (various years) and *The Statistical Abstract of the United States* (various years). The time period covered in this study is 1955 to 1988.

Since all the published annual data on unemployment and inflation rates are reported on a calendar year basis, they are not compatible with the fiscal-year-based data of military spending reported by the Department of Defense. In this study, the inflation rate in a fiscal year is reconstructed from the monthly consumer price index (CPI) published by *Business Statistics* (1977, 1986) and *Monthly Labor Review* (March and September 1988, December 1989). It reflects the change rate in the CPI from the first month of each fiscal year (July prior to FY 1977, and October afterwards) to the first month of the next fiscal year.

The unemployment rate in a fiscal year is computed from monthly unemployment data published by *Business Statistics* (1977, 1986) and *Employment and Earnings* (December 1988). It reflects the average unemployment rate during the 12-month period of a fiscal year. The

Table 2.1 Defence spending and economic performance, 1955–88

FY	Personnel	O & M	Procurement	R & D	Inflation	Unemployment
1955	10643	7905	12997	1391	–0.4	5.1
1956	10666	8519	12182	1491	2.0	4.1
1957	10384	9214	13649	1686	3.3	4.1
1958	10440	9113	14677	1742	2.5	5.7
1959	11801	10384	14410	2859	0.8	6.2
1960	11738	10223	13334	4710	1.4	5.3
1961	12085	10611	13095	6131	1.4	6.4
1962	16331	11594	14532	6319	1.2	6.0
1963	16256	11874	16632	6376	1.0	5.7
1964	17422	11932	15351	7021	1.5	5.4
1965	17913	12349	11839	6236	1.1	4.9
1966	20009	14710	14339	6259	1.8	4.0
1967	22952	19000	19012	7160	2.7	3.8
1968	25118	20578	23283	7747	2.9	3.8
1969	26914	22227	23988	7457	4.3	3.4
1970	29032	21609	21584	7166	5.5	4.0
1971	29079	20491	18858	7303	5.9	5.7
1972	29571	21675	17131	7881	4.4	5.9
1973	29773	21069	15654	8157	3.0	5.2
1974	30409	22478	15241	8582	5.7	5.0
1975	32162	26297	16042	8866	11.5	7.3
1976	32546	27837	15964	8923	9.7	8.0
1977	33672	30587	18178	9795	5.4	7.3
1978	35553	33580	19976	10508	6.5	6.3
1979	37345	36440	25404	11152	8.9	5.8
1980	40897	44788	29021	13127	12.2	6.8
1981	47941	51885	35191	15278	12.6	7.4
1982	55170	59695	43271	17729	10.2	9.1
1983	60886	64932	53624	20554	5.1	10.1
1984	64158	67388	61879	23117	4.2	7.8
1985	67842	72371	70381	27103	3.2	7.3
1986	71511	75288	76517	32283	1.5	7.0
1987	72020	76205	80744	33596	4.5	6.4
1988	76337	84475	77166	34792	4.3	5.6

transitional quarter (that is, July to September of the calendar year of 1976) from the old fiscal year to the new fiscal year is not included in our analysis to ensure that all the data are based on 12-month units. Data on the four components of the defense spending and inflation and unemployment rates are reported in Table 2.1.

Since each of these variables has distributed lags on the right-hand side of the equation, multicollinearity is likely to be a problem. Multicollinearity inflates the variances of coefficient estimates and makes some individual α's statistically insignificant. This should not affect our causal inferences, however, since they are not based on a *t*-test of individual estimates but on *F*-tests of joint hypotheses of *blocks* of coefficients attached to lagged variables (Freeman 1983, 346).

Before testing the causal ordering among the six variables, we have to first determine a finite lag order, p, of our VAR model. Since no reliable prior information about lag length is available, we decided to rely on two popular objective information criteria suggested by Akaike (1974) and Schwarz (1978), that is, *AIC* and *SC*, to determine the lag order of our VAR model. Applying the general forms of Akaike's and Schwarz's information-theoretic criteria to the choice of the lag order of a VAR model, the *AIC* and *SC* for $VAR(j)$ are

$$AIC(j) = T \ln|\hat{\Sigma}_j| + 2k^2 j$$
$$SC(j) = T \ln|\hat{\Sigma}_j| + \ln(T)\, k^2 j$$

where $\hat{\Sigma}_j$ is the maximum likelihood estimate of the disturbance covariance matrix computed under the assumption that $VAR(j)$ is the best model, and k is the dimension of the VAR model. The 'optimal' (in an information sense) lag length p is chosen such that AIC(p) numerically minimizes $AIC(j)$ and $SC(p)$ numerically minimizes SC(j), for $j=m, m+1, \ldots, n-1, n$, where m and n are the lower and upper bound for the VAR order, respectively. The lower bound, m, may be zero unless there are reasons to suggest otherwise.

Following the procedures recommended by Huang (1989), we first have to specify a range, with the lower bound at zero and the upper bound at n, that contains the true lag order. In theory, the maximum order, n, can be any positive integer which is large enough to include the true order. In reality, of course, n is limited by the total number of observations, N, which is 33 in our case. Since 'the maximum order n cannot be greater than the ratio of the total number of observations minus one to the total number of variables in the system plus one' (Huang 1989, 5), the maximum number of lags we can consider in this six-equation VAR system is four. However, if we set n at four, there will be only a few degrees of freedom left in each equation while calculating $SC(4)$ and $AIC(4)$ and the statistical results would not be trusted. Thus, we set the upper bound of lag order at three, while computing $SC(j)$ and $AIC(j)$, where j refers to the lag lengths ranging from zero to three.

Table 2.2 Determination of VAR order based on Schwarz's and Akaike's information criteria

VAR order j	$SC(j)$	$AIC(j)$
0	1315.4244	1315.4244
1	577.7687*	527.3256
2	602.9278	502.0416
3	579.6038	428.2745*

Note: * denotes minimum value.

Table 2.3 F-tests for causal relations among variables based on one lag

Equation	Coefficients	*F* (1,23)	Significance level
Personnel	Personnel	1.55	0.23
	O & M	1.21	0.28
	Procurement	0.49	0.49
	R & D	0.22	0.64
	Unemployment	0.04	0.85
	Inflation	2.95*	0.10
O & M	Personnel	1.11	0.30
	O & M	1.54	0.23
	Procurement	0.64	0.43
	R & D	0.18	0.67
	Unemployment	0.01	0.95
	Inflation	0.28	0.60
Procurement	Personnel	0.04	0.85
	O & M	7.25**	0.013
	Procurement	0.41	0.53
	R & D	0.60	0.45
	Unemployment	4.35**	0.048
	Inflation	0.01	0.94
R & D	Personnel	0.85	0.37
	O & M	0.08	0.78
	Procurement	0.70	0.41
	R & D	8.81***	0.01
	Unemployment	0.20	0.66
	Inflation	0.86	0.36
Unemployment	Personnel	1.49	0.23
	O & M	2.31	0.14
	Procurement	0.001	0.97
	R & D	2.68	0.11
	Unemployment	62.16***	0.01
	Inflation	19.41***	0.01
Inflation	Personnel	0.24	0.63
	O & M	0.02	0.89
	Procurement	0.08	0.78
	R & D	0.07	0.80
	Unemployment	0.57	0.46
	Inflation	24.97***	0.01

* Statistically significant at the 0.1 level.
** Statistically significant at the 0.05 level.
*** Statistically significant at the 0.01 level.

Table 2.4 F-tests for causal relations among variables based on three lags

Equation	Block of coefficients	*F* (3,11)	Significance level
Personnel	Personnel	2.30	0.13
	O & M	2.63	0.10
	Procurement	0.29	0.83
	R & D	3.30*	0.06
	Unemployment	0.25	0.86
	Inflation	0.81	0.52
O & M	Personnel	0.25	0.86
	O & M	1.09	0.39
	Procurement	1.82	0.20
	R & D	0.21	0.89
	Unemployment	0.53	0.67
	Inflation	0.78	0.53
Procurement	Personnel	1.08	0.40
	O & M	2.82*	0.09
	Procurement	0.96	0.45
	R & D	0.60	0.63
	Unemployment	1.47	0.28
	Inflation	0.10	0.96
R & D	Personnel	4.99**	0.02
	O & M	0.55	0.66
	Procurement	1.35	0.31
	R & D	2.38	0.13
	Unemployment	0.39	0.76
	Inflation	3.80**	0.04
Unemployment	Personnel	1.16	0.37
	O & M	1.90	0.19
	Procurement	0.78	0.53
	R & D	2.12	0.16
	Unemployment	2.20	0.15
	Inflation	6.20***	0.01
Inflation	Personnel	0.58	0.64
	O & M	0.16	0.90
	Procurement	1.09	0.39
	R & D	0.30	0.82
	Unemployment	1.00	0.43
	Inflation	6.78***	0.01

* Statistically significant at the 0.1 level.
** Statistically significant at the 0.05 level.
*** Statistically significant at the 0.01 level.

As is shown in Table 2.2, Schwarz's information criterion (*SC*) reaches minimum at lag length of one, while Akaike's criterion (*AIC*) reaches minimum at three. The three-lag model has the advantage of taking into account the interrelationships among variables over a longer time period. But given the limited number of observations available, it may use up too many degrees of freedom. The one-lag model, on the other hand, saves twelve degrees of freedom for each equation. But it may fail to capture the longer-term effects of some variables. Acknowledging the problems associated with both models, we report results of both *VAR*(1) and *VAR*(3) models in Tables 2.3 and 2.4, respectively.

RESULTS

Granger causality analysis of the four components of the defense budget and the two important indicators of economic performance revealed (Table 2.3) that unemployment at $t-1$ affects procurement at t, that inflation at $t-1$ affects military personnel spending at t, the expected impact of inflation at $t-1$ on inflation at t and the expected effect of inflation and unemployment at t–1 on unemployment at t. The analysis has also revealed no evidence for a significant impact of personnel, procurement, operation and maintenance, or research and development expenditures on either inflation or unemployment, and no impact of economic performance (at $t-1$) on O & M or R & D spending. Whereas the interpretation of the impact of inflation on personnel expenditures is straightforward (personnel payments are adjusted upward to account for the increase in the cost of living), the impact of unemployment on the procurement of weapons systems is less trivial and more important, since it shows that the government uses procurement spending as a counter-cyclical economic tool to regulate unemployment.

The impact of military spending on economic performance is also not evident based on the Granger causality analysis of three-year lags (Table 2.4). The impact of the four components of the defense budget on both unemployment and inflation are insignificant even at the 0.10 level. The significant impact of inflation on military personnel and that of unemployment on procurement (found based on the analysis of one-year lag) have washed out in the analysis of three-year lags (the impact of unemployment on allocations to procurement are still significant with two-year lags – results not shown here – but not with three-year lags). The impact of the inflation rate (with three-year lags) on research and development is significant, however.

CONCLUSIONS

This study focused on the relationship between military spending and economic performance at a less aggregated level than was done previously. The analysis revealed three important findings:

(a) There is strong empirical evidence to suggest Keynesian counter-cyclical use of procurement spending to combat unemployment. Whereas Kinsella (1990) and many other scholars have reported (based on an aggregate analysis of the defense–growth tradeoff) that there is no evidence that defense spending is affected by unemployment, our disaggregated analysis revealed that policy-makers use procurement expenditures to regulate unemployment. Allocations to weapons systems increase when unemployment rises and decrease when unemployment declines. There is no evidence to suggest that other defense programs (personnel, operation and maintenance) are also used to regulate unemployment.

(b) Policy-makers' response to poor economic conditions, such as rising unemployment, is quick. It does not last long, however. The impact of unemployment on allocations to procurement programs is evident with a one-year lag and with a two-year lag, but it becomes insignificant when a three-year lag is introduced. Politicians are obviously more concerned about the current economic situation than about past performance of the economy.

(c) The impact of military spending on the economy is not immediate but delayed (Mintz and Huang 1990, 1991). Our analysis of lags of one, two and three years revealed no significant impact of military spending on the economy. In a previous study (Mintz and Huang 1990), we showed a delayed effect (of five years) of military spending on investment. We conclude, therefore, that whereas the state of the economy influences defense expenditures *instantaneously*, defense spending has a *delayed* long-term effect on the economy.

NOTE

1 Mintz's participation in this project was supported, in part, by Grant No. SES–8911030 from the National Science Foundation.

REFERENCES

Akaike, Hirotugu. 1974. A new look at the statistical model identification. *IEEE Transactions on Automatic Control* AC-19: 716–23.

Baran, Paul A. and Paul M. Sweezy 1966. *Monopoly Capital: An Essay on the American Economic and Social Order*. New York: Monthly Review Press.

Calleo, D. P. 1981. Inflation and American power. *Foreign Affairs* 59: 781–812.

Cappelen, Ådne, Nils Petter Gleditsch, and Olav Bjerkholt. 1984. Military spending and economic growth in the OECD countries. *Journal of Peace Research* 21: 361–73.

Chan, Steve. 1985. The impact of defense spending on economic performance: a survey of evidence and problems. *ORBIS* 29: 403–34.

Chan, Steve and David R. Davis. 1991. Defense allocation, inflation, and unemployment in South Korea and Taiwan: A Granger analysis. *Korean Journal of Defense Analysis* 3: forthcoming.

Chester, E. 1978. Military spending and capitalist stability. *Cambridge Journal of Economics* 2: 293–8.

Cusack, Thomas 1991. On the domestic political-economic sources of American military spending. In Alex Mintz (ed.), *The Political Economy of Military Spending in the United States*. London: Routledge.

DeGrasse, Robert W. Jr with Elizabeth McGuinness and William Roger. 1983. *Military Expansion, Economic Decline: The Impact of Military Spending on U.S. Economic Performance*. Armonk, NY: Sharpe.

Freeman, John R. 1983. Granger causality and time series analysis of political relationships. *American Journal of Political Science* 27: 327–58.

Freeman, John R., John T. Williams, and Tse-min Lin. 1989. Vector autoregression and the study of politics. *American Journal of Political Science* 33: 842–77.

Gansler, Jacques S. 1980. *The Defense Industry*. Cambridge, Mass. and London: MIT Press.

Gold, David. 1990. *The Impact of Defense Spending on Investment, Productivity, and Economic Growth*. Washington, D. C.: Defense Budget Project.

Granger, C. W. J. 1969. Investigating causal relations by econometric models and cross-spectral methods. *Econometrica* 37: 424–38.

Griffin, Larry J., Joel A. Devine, and Michael Wallace. 1982a. Monopoly capital, organized labor, and military expenditures in the United States, 1949–1976. *American Journal of Sociology* 88. Supplement: 113–53.

Griffin, Larry J., Michael Wallace, and Joel A. Devine. 1982b. The political economy of military spending: evidence from the United States. *Cambridge Journal of Economics* 6: 1–14.

Huang, Chi. 1989. Determining the lag order of a vector autoregressive process: some guidelines for political studies. Paper presented at the annual meeting of the American Political Science Association.

Huisken, Ron. 1982. Armaments and development. In Helena Tuomi and Raimo Vayrynen (eds.), *Militarization and Arms Production*, pp. 3–25. New York: St. Martin's Press.

Kennedy, Gavin. 1983. *Defense Economics*. New York: St. Martin's Press.

Kinsella, David. 1990. Defense spending and economic performance in the United States: a causal analysis. *Defence Economics* 1: 295–309.

Korb, Lawrence J. 1980. *The FY 1981–1985 Defense Program: Issues and Trends*. Washington, D.C.: American Enterprise Institute for Public Policy Research.

Kurth, James R. 1989. The military–industrial complex revisited. In Joseph Kruzel (ed.), *American Defense Annual, 1989–1990*, pp. 195–215. Lexington, Mass.: Lexington Books.

Lindgren, Goran. 1984. Review essay: Armaments and economic performance in industrialized market economies. *Journal of Peace Research* 21: 375–87.

Mayer, Kenneth R. 1991. Elections, business cycles, and the timing of defense contract awards in the United States, 1954–1986. In Alex Mintz (ed.), *The Political Economy of Military Spending in the United States*. London: Routledge.

Melman, Seymour. 1985. *The Permanent War Economy: American Capitalism in Decline* (revised version). New York: Simon & Schuster.

Mintz, Alex. 1989. Guns versus butter: a disaggregated analysis. *American Political Science Review* 83: 1285–93.

Mintz, Alex and Alexander M. Hicks. 1984. Military Keynesianism in the United States, 1949–1979: disaggregating military expenditures and their determination. *American Journal of Sociology* 90: 411–17.

Mintz, Alex and Chi Huang. 1990. Defense expenditures, economic growth and the 'peace dividend'. *American Political Science Review* 84: 1283–93.

Mintz, Alex and Chi Huang. 1991. 'Guns' vs. 'butter': the indirect link. *American Journal of Political Science* 35: 738–57.

Mosley, Hugh G. 1985. *The Arms Race: Economic and Social Consequences*. Lexington, Mass. and Toronto: D.C. Heath.

Neuman, Stephanie. 1978. Security, military expenditures and socioeconomic development: reflections on Iran. *ORBIS* 22: 569–94.

Neuman, Stephanie. 1979. In reply. *ORBIS* 23: 477–80.

Nincic, Miroslav and Thomas R. Cusack. 1979. The political economy of U.S. military spending. *Journal of Peace Research* 16: 101–15.

O'Conner, James. 1973. *The Fiscal Crisis of the State*. New York: St. Martin's.

Rasler, Karen and William R. Thompson. 1988. Defense burdens, capital formation, and economic growth: the systemic leader case. *Journal of Conflict Resolution* 32: 61–86.

Russett, Bruce M. 1982. Defense expenditures and national well-being. *American Political Science Review* 76: 767–77.

Sargent, Thomas J. and Christopher A. Sims. 1977. Business cycle modeling without pretending to have too much a priori economic theory. In Christopher A. Sims (ed.), *New Methods in Business Cycle Research: Proceedings from a Conference*, pp. 45–109. Minneapolis: Federal Reserve Bank of Minneapolis.

Schwarz, Gideon. 1978. Estimating the dimension of a model. *The Annals of Statistics* 6: 461–4.

Sheehan, Richard and Robin Grieves. 1982. Sunspots and cycles: a test of causation. *Southern Economic Journal* 48: 775–7.

Smith, Ronald P. 1977. Military expenditure and capitalism. *Cambridge Journal of Economics* 1: 61–76.

Smith, Ronald P. 1978. Military expenditure and capitalism: a reply. *Cambridge Journal of Economics* 2: 299–304.

Smith, Ronald P. 1980. Military expenditure and investment in OECD countries, 1953–1973. *Journal of Comparative Economics* 4: 19–32.

Smith, Ronald P. and George Georgiou. 1983. Assessing the effect of military expenditure on OECD economies: a survey. *Arms Control* 4: 3–15.

Starr, Harvey, Francis W. Hoole, Jeffrey A. Hart, and John R. Freeman. 1984. The relationship between defense spending and inflation. *Journal of Conflict Resolution* 28: 103–22.

Szymanski, Albert. 1973. Military spending and economic stagnation. *American Journal of Sociology* 79: 1–14.

U.S. Department of Commerce, Bureau of Economic Analysis (annual). *Business Statistics*. Washington, D.C.: Government Printing Office.

U.S. Department of Labor, Bureau of Labor Statistics (monthly). *Employment and Earnings*. Washington, D.C.: U.S. Government Printing Office.

U.S. Department of Labor, Bureau of Labor Statistics (monthly). *Monthly Labor Review*. Washington, D.C.: U.S. Government Printing Office.

U.S. Office of Management and Budget. Various years. *Budget of the U.S. Government*. Washington, D.C.: U.S. Government Printing Office.

Ward, Michael D. 1987. Cargo cult social science and eight fallacies of comparative political research. *International Studies Notes* 13: 75–7.

Wildavsky, Aaron B. 1988. *The New Politics of the Budgetary Process*. Glenview, Ill.: Scott, Foresman.

3 Political–economic tradeoffs and British relative decline

Karen A. Rasler and William R. Thompson
Indiana University

Modeling the influence and interaction of key variables in national political economies has attracted increasing attention in the past few years. With the expansion of interest has come a proliferation of questions, contexts in which to ask them, and, inevitably, conclusions that are not always compatible. Do military regimes allocate resources differently than civilian regimes? Do parties of the left spend differently when they are in power than parties of the right? Is the political business cycle a persistent feature of electoral systems or simply an intermittently on–off phenomenon? How do political decision-makers respond to political–economic crises? How do political economies respond to political decision-makers who create domestic crises through over- or underspending? The questions are numerous and the answers that are produced will always depend to some extent on how the questions are posed. For example, a cross-sectional analysis of 20, 40, 80, or 160 political economies is likely to yield a different statistical outcome each time the number of cases is changed. A longitudinal analysis is also likely to produce different answers depending on how long the time series are. Considerations such as these underscore the need to be as explicit as possible at the outset about what sort of investigation is being undertaken.

Thematically, we are interested in the political economy of relative decline. Relative decline occurs when a state's economy grows more slowly than its competitors' and/or when economic growth falters compared to the state's own historical record. The most interesting cases of relative decline are those few states that have reached the very pinnacle of the world economy's pecking order. When these preeminently successful states ultimately enter phases of relative decline, both types of decline (the comparative and the historical) are apt to be manifested simultaneously. Exactly why these states tend to experience relative decline remains unclear but two of the more popular explanations concern 'excessive' state spending on military and welfare functions. Thus, as in the other chapters of this volume, we too will be examining the possible effects of defense and welfare on economic growth. Unlike the other chapters, however, any answers that we manage to produce will be restricted by design to a rather rarefied universe – the world economy's lead economies of the past five centuries.

Our goals are modest in this chapter. As one part of a larger project on the relative decline of preeminent system leaders, we have been exploring models that place emphasis on the role of tradeoffs between consumption and investment/economic growth. Our accumulated findings to date suggest that the role of consumption–investment tradeoffs is somewhat secondary to the onset of relative decline. However, our tests so far have focused either on contrasting system leaders with non–system leaders at similar points in time, in comparing a nineteenth-century leader (Britain) with a twentieth-century leader (the United States), or in comparing two brief, before and after intervals within the ongoing U.S. twentieth-century case. What we have not yet investigated is the comparison of a period of system-leadership decline with a subsequent period in that state's history, after the question of leadership has long since been resolved.

The global political economy has not experienced very many lead economies in the past 500 years.[1] Portugal and the United Provinces of the Netherlands represent the two earliest cases but the opportunities for empirical modeling are extremely limited. The ongoing U.S. case is just that – still ongoing and therefore not yet eligible for a decline and extended postdecline comparison. That leaves Britain. But even if we are forced to examine Britain by default, it remains an excellent choice for several reasons.

Least important in the substantive sense but methodologically indispensable, we have access to a respectable amount of data on Britain extending back easily to the beginning of the nineteenth century and even earlier in a number of cases. We thus have data that encompass Britain's systemic heyday and a lengthy slice of the aftermath of its preeminence.

A second factor is that Britain's claim to nineteenth-century preeminence is not all that controversial. It is true that it did not have the system's largest population or army. Yet it did possess the most dynamic and efficient economy as reflected in its pioneering role in modern industrialization techniques and production. It did become the world's most prominent trading state, monopolizing at times a third or more of the world's trade. It did develop into the world's financial center and leading creditor state. It probably is more accurate to say that the pound sterling carried the gold standard than the other way around. Equally uncontroversial is Britain's claim to leadership in the instruments of global reach as exemplified by naval power.

We also have a fairly good idea of the pace of Britain's decline. The plots in Figures 3.1, 3.2, and 3.3 chart Britain's and its successor's relative positions in terms of their naval power, leading-sector production, and trade participation.[2] Britain's leading-sector position plummeted after 1870. Britain's naval position declined immediately after World War I and continued to erode between the wars. During this same interwar period,

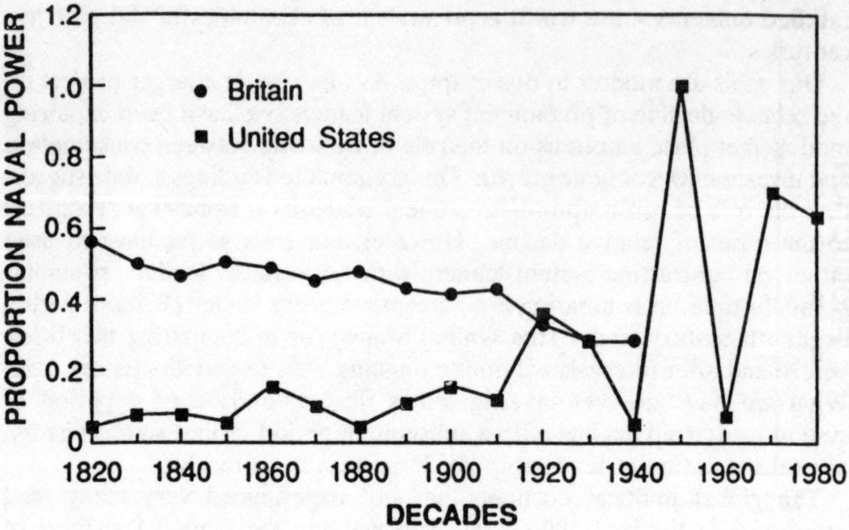

Figure 3.1 British and American naval power transitions
Source: Modelski and Thompson (1988).

the United States surpassed the British position. Of the three dimensions, Britain's lead in trade lasted the longest period of time. Until World War II, it managed to retain an increasingly slim lead.

The basic lesson of the three plots is that Britain's lead status in a number of dimensions ended prior to or during World War I. The period between the two world wars was characterized by continuing British relative decline and an uneven and rather hesitant U.S. ascent. By the end of World War II, Britain had emerged on the winning side but only a very few British decision-makers dared dream about a return to their former level of political–military–industrial preeminence.

Thus, with no fear of contradiction, we can stipulate that Britain after World War I and even more clearly after World War II was no longer engaged in systemic leadership decline per se. This statement is not meant to suggest that Britain ceased to experience relative decline. Positional erosion continued but the question of systemic leadership was no longer involved.

Nevertheless, more than one economic historian has confessed to feelings of *déjà vu* when confronted with analyzing British political economy developments since the late 1940s. As Kirby (1981, 105–6) puts it:

> The literature on Britain's postwar economic ills is vast: managerial weaknesses, excessive trade union power and restrictive practices, an anachronistic social structure, an inadequate education system, the rising tide of government expenditure and weaknesses in government economic policy generally – all of these hypotheses and more have their

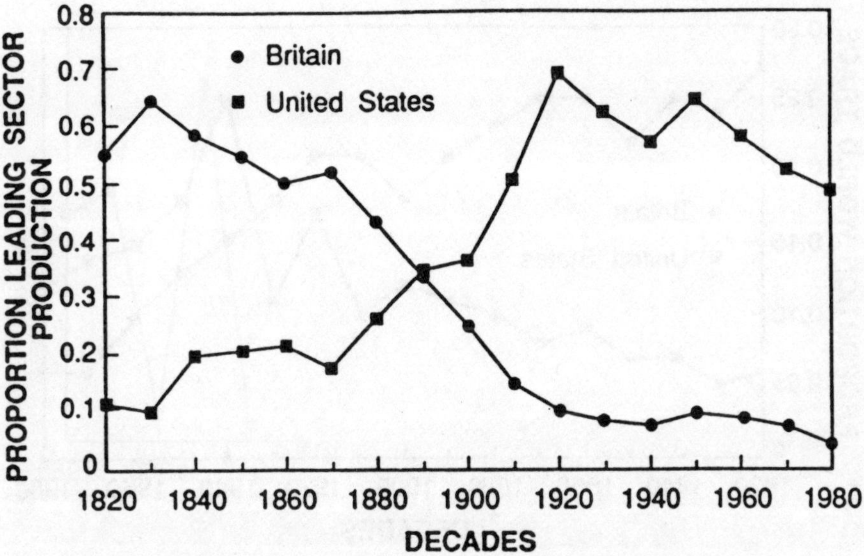

Figure 3.2 British and American leading-sector production transition
Source: Thompson (1988).

> supporters and all of them, either singly or in some combination, are regarded as primarily responsible for Britain's alleged failures as an industrial and trading actor. The element of *déjà vu* lies in the fact that a substantially similar list of weaknesses can and . . . has been applied to the British economy in the 1870–1914 period.

Kirby goes on to suggest that a number of post–World War II analyses of Britain's problems are ahistorical in the sense that the direct link between post-1945 policy problems and pre-1914 problem origins is too often overlooked. That is to say, Britain's post–World War II relative decline is a continuation of processes that began in the nineteenth century. No doubt, Kirby is correct and this is all the more reason to conduct a more extended analysis encompassing a period of systemic leadership and its aftermath.[3] It provides an excellent opportunity to investigate whether the processes of relative decline undergo substantial change as the state in question slides down the system's political–military hierarchy and technological gradient.

As we shall see, the models that we explore in this chapter raise questions about the timing of the causes of Britain's decline. Some causes may in fact be more accurately perceived as consequences of decline. Consumption–investment tradeoffs may offer one of the better examples we have. These types of factors may facilitate further decline and in that sense may deserve the causal label. But we need to distinguish as best we can the second-order causes from the roots of relative decline.

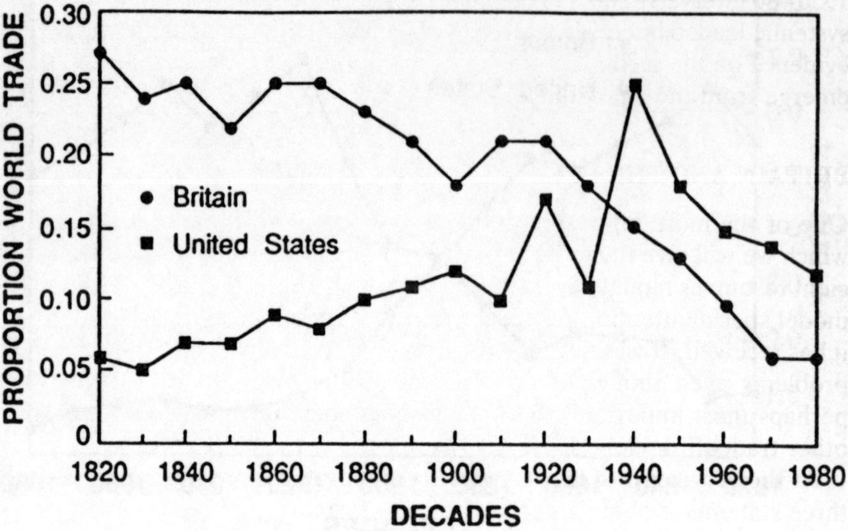

Figure 3.3 British and American trading transition
Sources: Rostow (1970), Banks (1971), and U.S. ACDA (1985).

Only in this fashion can we cobble together a strong explanation of decline and perhaps also draw conclusions about how best to address its policy manifestations.

Still another reason for an extended analysis is the opportunity to assess the role of intervening structural changes. In economic systems, there are some historical tendencies for systems to move from a predominantly agrarian orientation to a primarily industrial structure before moving into an increasingly service-oriented economy. In politics, there has been a related tendency to move toward greater political participation and more service-oriented political systems. Both tendencies have been markedly under way during Britain's fall from preeminence. Given the temporal overlaps, it is tempting to connect the political–economic structural shifts and decline. Whether the shift in political structure was a primary or secondary factor in Britain's decline is one of the specific questions to be addressed in this examination.

We would do well to pause at this point and introduce some explicit theoretical considerations before seeking any answers to questions about the etiology of decline. After discussing three models – the Sprout and Sprout model of rising demands and insufficient resources, Gilpin's hegemonic decline model, and Smith's hegemonic protection costs model – some empirically testable implications are derived and applied to modeling British domestic political–economic interactions in the 1831–1913 and

1950–80 intervals. The outcome does not lead to a comprehensive model of systemic leadership decline. However, some additional and fairly concrete evidence on the secondary role of consumption–investment tradeoffs does emerge from the analysis.

BRITAIN AND THE PROBLEM OF TRADEOFFS

One of the more interesting models in the tradeoff literature and one to which we will give the most attention initially is the rising demands/insufficient resources model developed by Sprout and Sprout (1968). We give the model special attention for three reasons. It deserves more attention than it has received. It was developed specifically for British political–economic problems even though it does possess wider applicability. Finally and perhaps most important, the model offers some intriguing contrasts with other tradeoff models.

At the very heart of the rising demands/insufficient resources model are three statements about trends in political systems. First, there exists some variable ensemble of goods and services. The amount of goods and services that are actually available at any given time will fluctuate. The amount that is available is also likely to increase over-time even though the rate of growth may not be all that rapid.

A second tendency describes the likely behavior of a system's set of commitments. The flavor or the biases of these commitments will vary from system to system but in all systems, authorities will choose to allocate resources to meet the perceived needs of the system and some proportion of its membership. Once the allocations are decided upon, they do not tend to fluctuate nor are they likely to be constant over-time. Instead, they are most likely to expand in scale and in terms of the proportion of the population encompassed.

A leading reason for the proliferation of commitments has to do with a third tendency. The demands placed upon the political system by its members are likely to escalate. Old demands may or may not be translated into ongoing commitments but new demands are sure to be made. Environmental changes create new problems. Expectations rise. New groups emerge as politically significant actors. All three factors work together to guarantee the escalation of political demands.

The political dilemma implied by the three trends is clear. The odds are that ongoing commitments plus new demands will tend to surpass the aggregate resources available for meeting commitments and demands. Something has to give. Either more resources must be generated or commitments and demands must be suppressed or altered. Neither option is particularly attractive to politicians who must seek reelection.

Precisely how this process is played out will vary from system to system, depending in part on the types of political economies involved, the degree of consensus on collective goods, and the quality of the prevailing public order. In the specific case of Britain, the pertinent facts include its lengthy history as a major power and the associated extensive and expensive commitments to foreign-policy objectives and military security. Concurrently, and especially since the late nineteenth/early twentieth century, Britain is a relatively open political system with an expanding electorate. Electoral victories have increasingly depended on what the Sprouts quaintly referred to as government 'giving more heed to the demands of less favored constituents.'

In addition, Britain has become an increasingly import-dependent society. To pay for a large number of imports, a large number of competitive exports are required. To generate these competitive goods, a steady flow of new fixed-capital investment is essential to maintain the efficiency of British production equipment and methods. Investment funds, however, must compete with societal consumption propensities. Private consumption, military consumption, and nonmilitary governmental consumption have the potential to reduce the availability of investment funds. Moreover, all of the various types of consumption compound the problem by leading directly or indirectly to greater import dependence which, in turn, raises the need for more exports. And since many exports require imported ingredients, the import–export spiral is made all the more vicious.

Post-World War II British decision-makers have experienced an acute form of this dilemma of rising demands and insufficient resources. According to the Sprouts, domestic capital formation and exports earned the highest political priority in order to keep the economy functioning. Private consumption and social services (nonmilitary governmental spending) also received high priority to ensure governmental tenures. Much lower priorities were assigned to foreign commitments and military spending. In sum, to maintain fixed-capital investment, private consumption, and nonmilitary public spending, the proportion of resources allocated to military consumption has been reduced. To reduce the other components of gross national product simply would not be very politically expedient.

The Sprouts' model is parsimonious and straightforward. Note, however, that it is not so much a generic model of decline but is rather an explanation for political expedience and, in the case of Britain, a diminishing international profile. Given finite resources and rising demands, decision-makers will opt for the choices that are more rewarding politically. Proportional cuts in investment, private consumption, or social services, therefore, are more likely to be avoided than are proportional cuts in defense and foreign-policy commitments. As a consequence, Britain has been priced out of the great-power league.

The end result is, of course, a relative decline in Britain's international political–military standing. In that respect, the Sprouts do offer an explanation for decline but it is envisioned to be a second-order form of decline. The original sources of British decline, according to the Sprouts, are four in number. Nineteenth-century technological innovations brought about radical changes in naval engineering that had the general effect of reducing the political–military significance of naval power and, derivatively, the significance of the world's leading naval power.

A second change that is highlighted is labeled change in geopolitical structure and scale. Structure in this case refers to the number of important competitors. The late-nineteenth-century emergence of Germany, the United States, and Japan made the great-power playing field more crowded. Some of the new players also enjoyed access to more impressive resource bases (scale) in raw materials, populations, and the size of the domestic market. Unless Britain could somehow bring about a political–territorial amalgamation of its far-flung empire, it would find itself gradually eclipsed by the emergence of these new powers.

Presumably both a cause and an effect of this eclipse process was the erosion of Britain's industrial, commercial, and financial primacy, the Sprouts' third factor. While it seems rather awkward to try to explain decline by decline, it should be kept in mind that the Sprouts were attempting to describe the contextual antecedents for subsequent foreign–domestic commitment tradeoffs. The erosion of primacy suggests a major qualitative change in the aggregate resources available to competing political claimants.

Finally, a fourth factor emphasized by the Sprouts is the development of lower-class political mobilization at home and abroad. At home, political mobilization meant increased demands for governmental services. Abroad, political mobilization made it increasingly unlikely that the metropole could continue to dominate the imperial periphery as in the past. Alternatively put, domestic political demands were rising while access to external resources was experiencing increasing challenges.

It is certainly possible to quarrel with some aspects of these four sources of decline. The nineteenth-century geopolitical changes are inescapable in any inventory of factors involved in Britain's relative decline. The implications of technological change in naval engineering are far more debatable. Sorely missing are the consequences of technological change (or the relative lack thereof in Britain for a critical period) for the erosion of British economic preeminence.

Despite the disagreements, our analytical emphasis should remain on the causal layering explicit in the Sprouts' model of rising demands and insufficient resources. General background conditions and environmental changes are seen as setting up a situation in which demands are more likely to be escalating while the available set of resources is more likely to be found less than optimally satisfactory. Choices have to be made. The central question is which set of preferences is most likely to predominate.

Contrast this approach with the generic decline model for hegemons designed by Gilpin. Most of the ingredients are the same.[4] Gilpin (1981) divides gross national product into four principal components: investment, protection costs (spending on defense and foreign commitments), nonmilitary public consumption, and private consumption. The three types of consumption are described as tending to rise proportionally over time. To the extent that one or more consumption type increases proportionally without an equivalent reduction in another type of consumption, the proportion of GNP allocated to investment must diminish. Diminished investment leads to future erosion in efficiency, productivity, and international competitiveness. Equally eroded are the prospects for underwriting hegemonic political–military activities.

Which way do decline processes work? Do processes of decline lead to tradeoffs among consumption and investment as the Sprouts' model suggests? Or is decline basically caused by choices, implicit or explicit, made among types of consumption and investment as in Gilpin's model? Of course, this theoretical question need not be an either/or proposition. First-order tradeoffs could easily lead to consequent, second-order tradeoffs. Nor is it clear that all preeminent powers must experience the exact same processes of decline. What is first-order for one case may be a second-order consideration in another setting.

PREVIOUS FINDINGS

We have been pursuing these questions for some time now. The empirical outcomes are not always fully congruent, but definite answers to the questions raised above are emerging with some clarity. In Rasler and Thompson (1988), we explored the question of tradeoffs between defense spending and capital formation and the implications for economic growth. Our theoretical focus in that study was Smith's (1977) argument that could be said to represent (albeit implicitly) a compromise between the models advanced by the Sprouts and Gilpin.[5]

Smith assumes that resources devoted to military purposes can be extracted from economic growth or by diverting resources from consumption and/or investment. Which tradeoffs are pursued is a function of the nature of the state in question. Advanced capitalist states, Smith contends in much the same vein as the Sprouts, are not likely to interfere with private consumption or the welfare component of public consumption. Such interference would be too unpopular and politically costly. Increases in military spending are thus likely to occur at the expense of investment as in the Gilpin model. Moreover, the systemic protection costs assumed by the hegemon or system leader are guaranteed to raise military costs for that state. Yet by providing a defense umbrella for other states, the incentives to engage in free-riding on the part of the protected states are increased. Thus, the system leader incurs relatively high economic costs for engaging in the leadership role that nonleaders are able to evade. The central irony of the process is that the way in which the system is protected tends to undermine that same system by chipping away at the capabilities of the leading state.

To test this argument, we analyzed two sets of regression equations. The first set was restricted to the pre-1914 era and contrasted Britain's longitudinal behavior (1831–1913) with serial outcomes recorded for France, the United States, Germany, and Japan. For all five countries, defense burdens (military spending/GNP), controlling for economic growth (GDP per capita), were regressed against investment (fixed capital investment/GNP). In none of the five cases did significant evidence emerge for a tradeoff between defense spending and investment.

The second set of regressions examined the same five states. In this test, however, the time period was post-1945 and the emphasis was placed on comparing the outcome for the U.S., the post-World War II system leader, with the results associated with the other four states. The contemporary results diverged dramatically from the results for the nineteenth century. A statistically significant defense–investment tradeoff emerged only in the U.S. equation. While the examination was highly restrictive in the small numbers of variables examined, the results suggested that the role of military costs as a factor in leadership decline is not particularly uniform. It seemed to be discernible in the U.S. case but not at all in the earlier British case.[6]

Rasler (1990) is also concerned with investment tradeoffs, but in this analysis the examination is restricted to the post-World War II U.S. case. The types of consumption examined, however, were broadened to include defense, welfare, and total governmental and deficit spending. The literature to which the analysis is responding continued to include the leadership decline arguments, but was broadened to include conservative and radical critiques of welfare spending as a major source of public consumption that crowds out investment and profits. Another relevant subset of the literature that is encompassed can be labeled the 'political crisis of advanced industrialism.' In one version, industrialization led to expanded public participation which, as in the Sprouts' argument, has led to public demands on governments that exceed economic capabilities to respond but which also accord greater priority to consumption over investment. A second, neo-Marxist version emphasizes fiscal crises and military/welfare spending as an outgrowth of capitalist states pursuing legitimation by attempting to respond to demands for full employment and social services at the expense of sustained economic growth.[7]

Two central empirical questions guided the 1990 study. First, is there evidence for the hypothesis of tradeoffs discussed in the paragraph above? Second, is the evidence temporally consistent with the causal arguments? If one looks at a 1948–86 period, does the tradeoff evidence persist throughout the nearly 40-year period or is it limited to some portion of the time span under investigation. More specifically, if the tradeoffs are found only in the latter half of the 1948–86 period, after the U.S. productivity downturn began, it may be rather difficult to sustain the causal effect of public consumption in bringing about relative decline.

A more obvious explanation is that the economic stagnation exacerbates spending-related tradeoffs rather than the other way around.

Although a number of equations were examined that involve different mixes of types of public consumption and investment, a consistent pattern emerged. The relationships between investment and military, welfare, total governmental, and deficit spending were negative as a number of analysts have argued. However, the parameter estimates tended to be larger and were more likely to be statistically significant after 1966–1970 than before. Since the evidence for a public consumption–investment squeeze failed to precede the actual downturn in productivity, it is extremely difficult to blame the downturn on public consumption. On the other hand, it is fairly easy to observe that downturns make tradeoffs more difficult and more likely.

Finally, Rasler and Thompson (1990) reviewed historical conceptualizations of overconsumption explanations of decline. Variations are found in Greek, Roman, and medieval writings that continue to be expressed in contemporary models. Turning to the more contemporary expressions, particular stress was placed on explaining the implications of two models elaborated by Cipolla (1970) and Gilpin (1981). We have already mentioned what is at stake in Gilpin's argument. Cipolla's argument presents an interesting contrast in that we interpret him as saying that the relative decline probably is a function not so much of increased consumption but rather declining productivity. If consumption increases in the context of declining productivity, decline will accelerate and social tensions will be aggravated. And one manifestation of social tensions is an intensified competition between consumption and investment.

Again, the central analytical tension is one of cause and effect. Gilpin's cause is Cipolla's effect. To this basic disagreement, we add several observations linked to the distinctive nature of system leaders. First, the Cipolla and Gilpin models are based on the histories of empires. The system leaders with which we are concerned, however, have sought control over the transoceanic, global political economy as opposed to the conventional territorial expansion of traditional empires. Therefore, we should be careful not to mix imperial apples with system-leader oranges. If they operate on different premises, they may experience decline in different ways as well.

A related observation is that the priority given to economic growth and commerce has placed significant restrictions on the scale of system leaders' public consumption. With the exception of wartime spending, the domestic political culture of system leaders has stressed limited governmental activities and budgets to match (Rasler and Thompson 1983). Moreover, we know a fair amount about the actual consumption propensities of Britain and the United States. Proportionately speaking, private consumption has declined since the nineteenth century. Nonmilitary public consumption has increased, but only in the twentieth century. Military consumption in both cases is also greater in the twentieth century than it was in the nineteenth, but there is also a fair amount of fluctuation (as opposed to a monotonic, positive trend) in military spending. The superficial case for public consumption playing a significant role in Britain's pre–World War I decline is not very appealing. Nor do Rasler's (1990) findings help the case for public consumption applying to the ongoing U.S. case of relative decline.

These observations lead to the conclusion that consumption–investment tradeoffs are more likely to be a derivative phenomenon of decline processes, as opposed to fundamental causal factors in the etiology of decline. Such a conclusion does not rule out the possibility that tradeoffs can facilitate further decline once decline is under way due to other processes.

Rasler and Thompson (1990) investigate these arguments by comparing Granger causality relationships among types of consumption, investment, and economic growth in the pre-1914 British and post-1945 U.S. cases. The basic question was whether evidence could be uncovered to determine whether consumption led to investment growth problems or whether the causal arrows pointed in the opposite direction – investment/growth problems leading to consumption problems. A third possibility is that the causal arrows point in both directions suggesting reciprocal relationships between consumption and investment/growth. Naturally, a further possibility is that no evidence for causality might be discernible.

In the British 1831–1913 case, a number of causal arrows (see Figure 3.4 below) were found. However, none of them pointed from the various types of consumption to investment or economic growth. In the U.S. case, only one causal path from a consumption variable to an economic performance variable was uncovered. Private consumption influenced economic growth. Thus, in neither case did public consumption demonstrate an observable impact on either investment or economic growth.

The findings of Rasler and Thompson (1988, 1990) and Rasler (1990) do not support the argument that consumption-driven investment tradeoffs are critical to an understanding of the relative decline of system leaders. The evidence suggests that they are derivative phenomena of decline. What is still not clear, however, is the extent to which these tradeoffs act as second-order influences on continuing decline. There is some suggestion of this in Rasler's (1990) findings based on dividing the U.S. case into two temporal segments (before and after the onset of productivity decline). But the U.S. case is still under way and therefore awkward to analyze. It may be too soon to develop reliable findings on the relative decline of the United States. Alternatively, future developments, conceivably, could turn around the U.S. decline. What we need is a case with a longer history and one in which the question of relative decline is no longer controversial. A third requirement is that we be able to model the relationships between the kinds of variables that we have been discussing. Only the British case satisfies all three of these criteria.

We have examined previously the relationships among consumption, investment, and economic growth in the British 1831–1913 setting. Our assumption has been that the era of British systemic leadership had ended by the onset of World War I, if not earlier. To explain the erosion of British preeminence, as opposed to its consequences, we needed to focus on the period preceding World War I. But what happened after World War I? More specifically, did the Granger relationships observed to describe the 1831–1913 period continue to characterize the British political economy after 1918? If consumption–investment tradeoffs are indeed second-order influences on decline, we should expect to find more evidence for tradeoffs in the more contemporary period even though, or especially since, we found no evidence of tradeoffs in the nineteenth century. In the interests of minimizing the nature of the modeling problems involved, we will avoid the increasingly chaotic behavior in the interwar years and concentrate on the period after World War II.

Our specific prediction is that we should expect to find the relationships observed in 1831–1913 at work in the 1950–80 period as well. In addition, however, we expect to see the emergence of some consumption-driven investment tradeoffs in the 1950–80 period that were nonexistent in the 1831–1913 period. However, if the Sprouts were right in 1968, we may find causal arrows pointing from investment and growth to military consumption but we should not expect to find any reciprocal relationships or causal arrows pointing from military consumption to investment and growth.

Whether we should anticipate nonmilitary-public-consumption-driven tradeoffs with economic performance variables is less clear. The Sprouts argued only that investment and social-service spending enjoyed higher priority than military spending. They did not discuss which of the two – investment or social-service spending – enjoyed the more politically significant constituency. At the same time, there is no compelling reason to suppose that these particular priorities or the significance of their constituencies have remained constant across Labour and Conservative regimes. This observation alone would suggest, at the least, the potential for the development of reciprocal relations among nonmilitary public consumption and investment and economic growth in the post–World War II era. Moreover, to the extent that nonmilitary forms of consumption receive higher priority, we should also expect their economic impact or significance to expand as well.

GRANGER TESTS OF ANTECEDENCE

It is difficult to divorce causality implications from the tradeoff arguments presented by the Sprouts, Gilpin and Smith. An increase in some type of consumption means a decrease in investment or military spending. If it is investment that suffers, somewhere down the road, the prospects for economic growth will have been diminished. Unfortunately, social scientists have had a difficult time documenting and modeling causal paths. One of the techniques that is proving increasingly useful in this regard is the Granger test of antecedence (see Chan *et al.* 1990; Freeman 1983; Freeman and Duvall 1984; Goldstein 1988; Hoole and Huang 1989; Majeski and Jones 1981; Starr *et al.* 1984; Yantek 1984). The causality question is transformed into the more technical question of whether or not one variable can be said to explain the subsequent path of a second variable.

Given two variables, *X* and *Y*, with past histories that have influenced their current values, two models are conceivable:

$$X_t = f(X_{t-1}, X_{t-2}, \ldots, X_{t-n}); \tag{3.1}$$

$$X_t = f(X_{t-1}, X_{t-2}, \ldots, X_{t-n}, Y_{t-1}, Y_{t-2}, \ldots, Y_{t-n}). \tag{3.2}$$

In Equation 3.1, X_t is a function solely of its own previous values. In Equation 3.2, X_t is a function of both its past history and the past history of Y_t. If the additional previous values of Y_t in Equation 3.2 yield a statistically significant reduction in the unexplained variation in X_t beyond the residual variation in model 3.1, Y_t is said to antecede or 'Granger cause' X_t. Similarly, if the addition of the X_t and Y_t past values contribute to a statistically significant reduction in the error variance of Y_t relative to the error variance attributed solely to the previous values of Y_t, *X* Granger causes *Y*. If both *X* and *Y* Granger cause one another, the relationship is reciprocal.

Another possibility is 'instantaneous' Granger causality: *Y* is said to cause *X* instantaneously if the reduced error variation in model 3.3 is significantly smaller than the error variation in model 3.2:

$$X_t = f(X_{t-1}, X_{t-2}, \ldots, X_{t-n}, Y_t, Y_{t-1}, Y_{t-2}, \ldots, Y_{t-n}). \tag{3.3}$$

If it is the current values of Y_t that improve an analyst's ability to predict X_t after taking into consideration the past values of both X_t and Y_t, then X_t and Y_t are considered to be interdependent only in the current period.

Thus, there are four possibilities. *X* and *Y* may be independent of one another. *X* or *Y* may antecede *Y* or *X* respectively. Alternatively, *X* and *Y* may prove to be mutually antecedent and, therefore, reciprocally related. Or, *X* or *Y* may be limited to an instantaneous relationship. All four possibilities still fall short of 'proving' causality beyond a shadow of doubt. But if an analyst is attempting to ascertain whether changes in one variable systematically impact upon other variables, these statistical tests should prove quite useful in choosing between the various available tradeoff arguments and interpretations. For example, if nonmilitary government spending is the 'culprit' in reducing investment as critics of welfare programs suggest, we should expect to find at the very least nonmilitary

Table 3.1 Granger tests of antecedence in the British case, 1831–1913 and 1950–80 (quasi-*F* statistics)

Independent variables	*Dependent variables* Military consumption	Nonmilitary Public consumption	Private consumption	Investment	Economic growth
1831–1913					
Military consumption	–	3.7*	0.65	0.90	0.96
Nonmilitary public consumption	3.1*	–	2.3*	1.0	0.46
Private consumption	1.4	1.2	–	1.0	0.88
Investment	1.3	0.98	4.0*	–	5.1*
Economic growth	1.2	1.4	1.4	9.6*	–
1950–80[a]					
Military consumption	–	1.8	1.9	0.01	1.0
Nonmilitary public consumption	3.3*	–	1.8	1.5	0.97
Private consumption	1.1	3.1*	–	2.7*	2.3
Investment	8.1*	2.9*	2.4	–	4.0*[b]
Economic growth	6.0*	6.9*	2.8*	3.5[b]	–

Note: * signifies statistical significance at 0.05; lag structure = 2,6; (a) denotes that the 1950–80 relationships were estimated from 1953–80 data due to outliers in military spending from 1950 to 1952; (b) indicates that the reported quasi-*F* test outcomes are based on instantaneous tests of antecedence.

governmental spending anteceding domestic fixed-capital formation. If there is no evidence of antecedence, a necessary criterion for an assertion of causality is visibly absent.

DATA ANALYSIS

Table 3.1 and Figure 3.4 display the outcome of our analysis of central relationships in Britain's political economy. Keep in mind that our principal interest concerns whether the forms of consumption, and which forms of consumption, antecede investment and economic growth.[8] We are also asking whether this relationship changes over time, particularly when relative decline has been experienced for quite some time.

Table 3.1 reports which of the twenty possible paths of antecedence are statistically significant in the 1831–1913 and 1950–80 eras.[9] Six significant paths are demarcated for the first period. Ten paths are disclosed in the

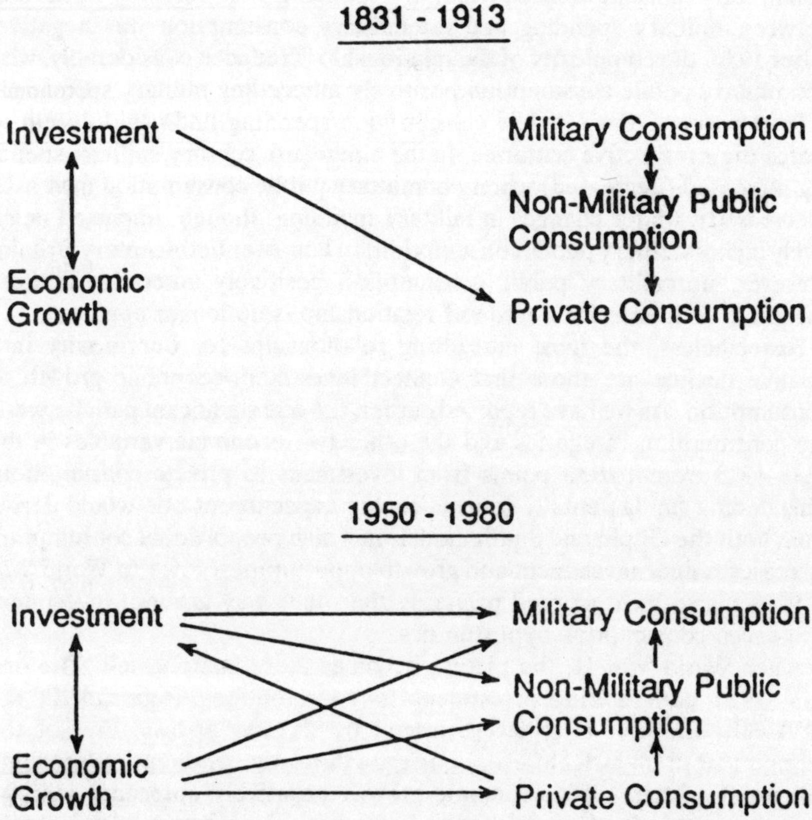

Figure 3.4 British paths of antecedence, 1831–1913 and 1950–80

more recent period. Figure 3.4 helps clarify which variables are predictors and in which direction they predict. While it is less critical to questions involving antecedence as opposed to tradeoffs, an Appendix table lists the respective coefficients and their relationship signs.

In both cases, investment and economic growth are related reciprocally and positively. The two forms of public consumption also are interdependent in both time periods as are nonmilitary public and private consumption. The signs of the consumption interrelationships, however, appear to have changed over time. Before 1913, nonmilitary public consumption negatively anteceded private consumption. After 1950, the direction of antecedence reversed itself and changed sign as well. Before 1913, military spending and nonmilitary public consumption were related reciprocally but the relationship signs were curiously dissimilar. The relationship between nonmilitary consumption and military spending was positive, while that between military spending and nonmilitary consumption was negative. After 1950, the complexity of the relationship is reduced considerably, with nonmilitary public consumption positively anteceding military spending.

In retrospect, these public consumption/spending findings do seem to match their respective centuries. In the nineteenth century, military spending increased (decreased) when nonmilitary public consumption increased (decreased). Major changes in military spending, though, impacted negatively on nonmilitary public consumption. In late-twentieth-century Britain, however, nonmilitary public consumption positively antecedes military spending. Evidence for a tradeoff relationship is no longer apparent.

Nevertheless, the most interesting relationships for our inquiry into relative decline are those that connect investment/economic growth to consumption. As we have reported earlier, the one significant path between the consumption categories and the other two economic variables in the 1831–1913 examination points from investment to private consumption. This finding fundamentally contradicts the expectations one would derive from both the Gilpin and Smith models in which proportional consumption increases reduce investment and growth opportunities. Prior to World War I, it seems to have worked primarily the other way around: investment influenced consumption opportunities.

After World War II, the picture becomes more complicated. The one 1831–1913 path linking investment to consumption disappears in the 1950–80 period. It is replaced instead by six new arrows. Five of the six point from investment/economic growth to the consumption/spending categories. After 1950, economic growth negatively antecedes military spending and private consumption and positively antecedes nonmilitary public consumption. Similarly, investment negatively antecedes military spending and positively antecedes nonmilitary public consumption. The one arrow from the consumption side of the 1950–80 portion of Figure 3.4 links private consumption to investment. The relationship, nevertheless, is positively signed.

What do these findings mean in terms of the alternative models discussed earlier? First, we find no evidence for military spending crowding out investment in either period. All the arrows point the wrong way. Thus Smith's model is not supported by this British examination.

Gilpin's model is not very helpful in the 1831–1913 period. Again, all of the important arrows point the wrong way. No consumption variables predict to investment/economic growth. This is not quite the case in the 1950–80 period. But the sign of the solitary exception is mispredicted. No consumption-driven tradeoffs emerge among the five variables after 1950.

The Sprout and Sprout model never argued that protection costs had undermined British hegemony. Nor did the Sprouts discuss consumption as a first- or second-order cause of relative decline. What they did say was

Table 3.2 Proportional central government expenditure, by function, 1890–1975

		Functions			
Year	Defense	Administration/ justice	Economics/ environment	Social services	Other
1890	43.4	15.5	1.2	9.8	30.1
1900	74.2	6.3	0.8	7.4	11.3
1910	52.4	10.9	1.3	20.4	15.0
1920	40.8	4.9	10.0	18.7	25.7
1930	16.4	4.9	2.4	35.9	40.3
1938	44.4	4.1	3.4	27.6	20.4
1950	24.0	4.0	12.7	39.6	19.7
1960	24.1	3.5	9.3	36.3	26.8
1970	17.3	3.8	9.2	44.9	24.8
1975	14.7	4.7	11.2	44.2	25.2

Data source: Flora *et al.* (1983: 444–5).

that the nature of British political economy had evolved in a direction that gave highest priority to investment/growth, private consumption, and nonmilitary public consumption. From this we deduced that military spending was more likely to be influenced by changes in the allocations to the high-priority agenda items than the other way around. For the most part, this approximates what we found. Investment and economic growth predict to military spending after 1950. The 'only' influence military consumption projects in our simple five-variable model is to nonmilitary public consumption. The degree to which this intra–public consumption tradeoff has become simplified with the passage of time and political-economy developments presumably supports the Sprouts' argument.

The degree to which the outcome matches the Sprouts' prediction (or, more accurately, our interpretation of what that prediction might have been) is less than perfect in at least one sense. The Sprouts' arguments were predicated to a great extent on assumptions about the effects of an expanding electorate and their rising demands for social services. Other things being equal, as social services expanded, military spending would have to be curtailed. We know that proportional allocations to social services have indeed expanded and military spending has declined in Britain. We certainly do not wish to contest this fact. Table 3.2 provides ample support for this observation. Yet it is largely a twentieth-century phenomenon, as is graphically illustrated in Figure 3.5.

Our reservation at this juncture is that the evidence for major changes, vis-à-vis the implications of the Sprouts' arguments, in how the British political-economy influence map works from one time period to the next is mixed. The electorate expanded, demands rose, and governmental services grew between the pre-World War I and post-World War II eras. Priorities clearly changed. Yet even though military spending once had a higher

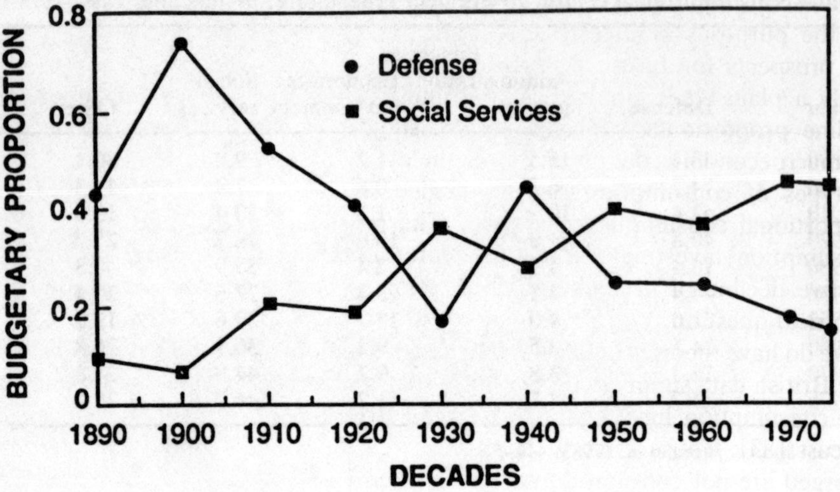

Figure 3.5 British defense and social-services spending
Source: Flora *et al.* 1983.

priority in the British policy-preference schedule, there is no evidence that it once had a greater impact on the political economy.[10] Partly as a consequence, the influence of military spending does not become less visible in 1950–80; it stays about the same.[11] The two other types of consumption, on the other hand, have become more influential and this development is certainly in accord with these categories' improved priorities. Perhaps we should simply be content with two out of three predictions, a record which is not all that bad by social-science criteria.

CONCLUSION

The political economy of relative decline can be a complex process. Observers and participants alike will continue to dispute the very existence of decline until it no longer matters. Those who accept its existence provide a bewildering array of explanations for the phenomenon. Despite several hundreds, if not thousands, of years of data, impressions, and prominent cases, we still do not have much consensus on why and how preeminence erodes. One reason for this absence of consensus is the marked tendency for hypotheses to be developed and assessed without reference to rigorous empirical scrutiny. To be sure, only a few cases of preeminence decline lend themselves readily to systematic data analysis. This is all the more reason to utilize the opportunity that they represent.

A reasonably popular argument about the sources of relative decline revolves around the effects of consumption–investment tradeoffs. Military spending, spending on welfare services, and/or the more generic type of private consumption are said to reduce what is left of the societal pie for the purposes of investment. If the investment proportion declines, the prospects for future economic growth are made bleaker. It is certainly a plausible argument. If consumption increases, investment must decline proportionally. This equation, subject to some caveats, is true by macroeconomic definition. Nonetheless, it is less clear that specific subtypes of consumption can be singled out as systematic sources of proportional consumption increases. The possibility exists, but whether consumption–investment tradeoffs represent a significant cause of the relative decline of preeminent states remains both a theoretical and an empirical question.

We do have theories of decline that assign a major role to these tradeoffs. The British data simply do not confirm that tradeoffs involving investment and consumption have characterized the British political economy since at least 1831. Those tradeoffs (negatively signed relationships) that have emerged are not consumption-driven and only appear in the most recent period. If they are related to decline, the timing of their appearance would suggest that they are more effects than causes of relative decline.

To what extent the changes in the nature of consumption–investment relationships are attributable to parallel changes in the political priorities assigned to some forms of consumption is more difficult to gauge. The findings suggest that post-1950 military spending is subordinated to investment as well as economic growth and nonmilitary public consumption, and not the other way around. It may also be fair to say that post-1950 military spending has become increasingly subordinated in comparison to the pre-1913 situation. Yet given the extreme difficulties in disentangling the process of relative decline from the implications of an expanding electorate in the British case, we might do just as well to adopt the perspective embodied in the Sprouts' fusion of the twin trends. Rising demands in the context of insufficient resources due in considerable part to a century of relative decline are responsible for the nature of consumption–investment squeezes and other policy problems in post–World War II Britain's political economy.

APPENDIX: COEFFICIENTS DERIVED FROM BIVARIATE VECTOR AUTOREGRESSIONS FOR BRITAIN, 1831–1913 AND 1950–80

		Dependent variable				
Independent variable		*EG*	*I*	*PC*	*NMPC*	*M*[a]
				1831–1913		
EG	(lag 1)	—	2.00*	0.06	0.88	0.88
	(lag 2)	—	0.00	0.08	0.53	0.62
	(lag 3)	—	−0.27	0.04	0.05	0.53
	(lag 4)	—	0.04	0.03	1.50*	0.61
	(lag 5)	—	−1.80	0.14	0.17	0.47
	(lag 6)	—	0.16	0.09	1.20	−0.18
I	(lag 1)	0.08*	—	−0.01	0.01	−0.02
	(lag 2)	−0.02	—	0.00	0.02	0.01
	(lag 3)	−0.05*	—	0.01	0.03	0.06
	(lag 4)	0.01	—	0.02*	−0.03	0.09
	(lag 5)	0.01	—	0.00	0.07	−0.04
	(lag 6)	0.01	—	−0.01	0.03	−0.04
PC	(lag 1)	−0.21	−0.11	—	1.60	−1.60
	(lag 2)	0.06	−1.90	—	2.20	−0.62
	(lag 3)	0.06	1.60	—	0.39	0.25
	(lag 4)	0.15	0.58	—	0.55	−0.12
	(lag 5)	0.04	0.22	—	−1.20	0.01
	(lag 6)	−0.06	−0.71	—	−9.20	0.82
NMPC	(lag 1)	0.00	−0.11	−0.02	—	0.29*
	(lag 2)	0.00	−0.09	−0.02	—	0.24*
	(lag 3)	0.01	0.04	−0.01	—	0.19*
	(lag 4)	−0.01	−0.19	−0.03*	—	0.04
	(lag 5)	0.00	0.17	−0.03	—	−0.08
	(lag 6)	0.02	0.39	−0.03*	—	0.01
M	(lag 1)	0.02	−0.16	0.02	−0.61*	—
	(lag 2)	−0.02	0.14	0.01	−0.34	—
	(lag 3)	0.01	−0.08	−0.00	0.16	—
	(lag 4)	0.01	−0.02	0.02	0.13	—
	(lag 5)	0.01	0.08	−0.02	−0.08	—
	(lag 6)	0.00	−0.29	0.02	−0.03	—
				1950–80		
EG	(lag 0)[b]	—	1.39*			
	(lag 1)	—	1.63*	0.17	0.39	0.16
	(lag 2)	—	0.88	−0.06	1.58*	−0.13
	(lag 3)	—	0.95	−0.09	−0.05	−0.15
	(lag 4)	—	0.53	0.06	0.63	−0.73
	(lag 5)	—	0.43	−0.19*	−0.49	−1.42*
	(lag 6)	—	0.26	0.09	0.21	−1.05*
I	(lag 0)[b]	0.44*	—			
	(lag 1)	−0.36	—	0.02	0.39*	0.19
	(lag 2)	−0.06	—	−0.05	0.65*	−0.21

		EG	*I*	*PC*	*NMPC*	*M*[a]
	(lag 3)	0.18	—	−0.09	−0.21	−0.01
	(lag 4)	0.10	—	0.03	−0.05	−0.87*
	(lag 5)	0.23	—	0.01	−0.71*	−0.81*
	(lag 6)	0.09	—	0.09	−0.15	−0.23
PC	(lag 1)	0.65	0.78	—	1.04	1.09
	(lag 2)	0.78	2.47*	—	1.94*	0.76
	(lag 3)	−0.51	−0.54	—	2.20*	1.75
	(lag 4)	0.80	0.74	—	0.89	−0.83
	(lag 5)	0.32	0.16	—	−0.44	1.72
	(lag 6)	0.76	0.66	—	−0.14	−1.68
NMPC	(lag 1)	0.09	0.15	−0.06	—	0.13
	(lag 2)	−0.08	−0.27	−0.04	—	0.03
	(lag 3)	0.07	−0.08	0.01	—	−0.26
	(lag 4)	0.05	−0.22	0.00	—	−0.04
	(lag 5)	−0.05	0.09	0.03	—	0.37*
	(lag 6)	−0.07	−0.33	0.00	—	0.58*
M	(lag 1)	−0.01	−0.09	−0.04	0.17	—
	(lag 2)	−0.06	−0.11	−0.01	−0.42	—
	(lag 3)	−0.02	−0.12	−0.06	0.00	—
	(lag 4)	−0.08	−0.05	−0.04	−0.02	—
	(lag 5)	0.02	−0.04	−0.01	0.01	—
	(lag 6)	−0.07	−0.01	−0.01	−0.16	—

Note: * = p 0.05; lag structure = 2,6; *EG* = economic growth, *I* = investment, *PC* = private consumption, *NMPC* = nonmilitary public consumption, *M* = military spending; (a) denotes that relationships involving military spending are based on 1953–80 data; (b) coefficients for lag 0 are used for instantaneous tests of antecedence – only significant coefficients are displayed.

NOTES

1 The authors wish to thank Richard Eichenberg for his comments on an earlier version of this paper. The concept and history of systemic leadership are discussed in Modelski (1987) and Thompson (1988).

2 The leading-sector production data are based on an index system developed primarily by Rostow (1978) for different purposes. The share data and the appropriate sources are reported in Thompson (1988, 133–44). Shares of naval power are based on a complicated indicator system encompassing a range between armed warships to SLBM (Submarine-Launched Ballistic Missile) accuracy, depending on the time period and the nature of capital-ship technology. Details and data are provided in Modelski and Thompson (1988). Proportion of world-trade data are based on information reported in Banks (1971), Rostow (1978), and U.S. Arms Control and Disarmament Agency (1985).

3 The historical continuity emphasis on British decline problems is not unique to Kirby. Adams (1982), Eatwell (1982), Gamble (1981), and Wiener (1981) also take this approach in a variety of ways. For alternative views, see Pollard (1982, 1989) and Barnett (1986).

4 The Gilpin model combines the investment–consumption tradeoff with external threat considerations, structural changes in the economy, and technological

innovation. See Gilpin (1981, 1987), Rasler and Thompson (1990), and Thompson (1988) for further discussions of the model.

5 In addition to Smith (1977), see the exchange among Chester (1978), Hartley and McLean (1978), and Smith (1978, 1980). See as well Cappelen *et al.* (1984).

6 The literature on military spending tradeoffs is fairly extensive. Useful reviews may be found in Chan (1985), Gold (1990), and Lindgren (1984).

7 Some examples of the welfare-spending tradeoff literature include Brittan (1975), Domke *et al.* (1983), Gilpin (1981), O'Connor (1973), Rose (1975), and Wright (1979).

8 The three consumption indicators are expressed annually as proportions of GNP (Mitchell, 1988). Investment, from the same source, is fixed domestic capital as a proportion of GNP. Economic growth is measured in terms of GDP per capita (Maddison 1979, 1982, 1987).

9 Each variable is logged and first-differenced. In the absence of specific theoretical guidance, analysts have some discretion in examining four lagged values of each variable per equation and then evaluating relationships at six- and eight-year lags. The findings reported in this paper represent a structure involving six values of the antecedent variable linked to two values of the variable to which it is predicting. Somewhat different results will be associated with different lag structures. Naturally, analysts are not at liberty to select the most 'favorable' results, but a selection as to which results are the most appropriate to report nevertheless must be made. We look for significant antecedent paths that are safe to anticipate as illustrated by the relationship between investment and economic growth. We also prefer to use isomorphic lag structures for different countries/time periods that are being compared. Once a choice is made as to which results should be reported, it is our responsibility to note any major deviations associated with different lag structures. We have none to report. Finally, the separate tests for instantaneous relationships revealed new information in only two cases. Consequently, we report only the two exceptions.

10 The easiest explanation for the limited impact of British military spending prior to World War I is the British exploitation of inexpensive Indian troops for many of its imperial undertakings. The topic is discussed further in Thompson and Zuk (1986).

11 More extensive modeling along the lines of structural equations, of course, might force some reconsideration of this conclusion.

REFERENCES

Adams, Richard N. 1982. *Paradoxical Harvest: Energy and Explanation in British History, 1870–1914*. Cambridge: Cambridge University Press.

Banks, Arthur S. 1971. *Cross-Polity Time-Series Data*. Cambridge, Mass.: MIT Press.

Barnett, Correlli. 1986. *The Pride and the Fall: The Dream and Illusion of Britain as a Great Nation*. New York: Free Press.

Brittan, Samuel. 1975. The economic contradictions of democracy. *British Journal of Political Science* 15: 129–59.

Cappelen, Ådne, Nils P. Gleditsch, and Olav Bjerkholt. 1984. Military spending and economic growth in the OECD countries. *Journal of Peace Research* 21: 361–73.

Chan, Steve. 1985. The impact of defense spending on economic performance: a survey of evidence and problems. *ORBIS* 29: 403–34.

Chan, Steve, Cal Clark, and David R. Davis. 1990. State entrepreneurship, foreign investment, export expansion, and Taiwan's economic growth. *Journal of Conflict Resolution* 34: 102–29.

Chester, E. 1978. Military spending and capitalist stability. *Cambridge Journal of Economics* 2: 293–8.

Cipolla, Carlo M. 1970. Editor's Introduction. In C.M. Cipolla (ed.), *The Economic Decline of Empires*. London: Methuen.

Domke, William K., Richard C. Eichenberg, and Catherine M. Kelleher. 1983. The illusion of choice: defense and welfare in advanced industrial democracies, 1948–1978. *American Political Science Review* 77: 19–35.

Eatwell, John. 1982. *Whatever Happened to Britain? The Economics of Decline*. New York: Oxford University Press.

Flora, Peter, Jens Alber, Richard Eichenberg, Jurgen Kohl, Franz Kraus, Winified Pfenning, and Kurt Seebohm. 1983. *State, Economy and Society in Western Europe, 1815–1975*, Vol. 1. Chicago: St. James Press.

Freeman, John R. 1983. Granger causality and the time series analysis of political relationships. *American Journal of Political Science* 27: 327–58.

Freeman, John R. and Raymond D. Duvall. 1984. International economic relations and the entrepreneurial state. *Economic Development and Cultural Change* 32: 373–400.

Gamble, Andrew. 1981. *Britain in Decline: Economic Policy, Political Strategy and the British State*. Boston: Beacon Press.

Gilpin, Robert. 1981. *War and Change in World Politics*. Cambridge: Cambridge University Press.

Gilpin, Robert, 1987. *The Political Economy of International Relations*. Princeton, N.J.: Princeton University Press.

Gold, David. 1990. *The Impact of Defense Spending on Investment, Productivity and Economic Growth*. Washington, D.C.: Defense Budget Project.

Goldstein, Joshua S. 1988. *Long Cycles: Prosperity and War in the Modern Age*. New Haven, Conn.: Yale University Press.

Hartley, K. and P. McLean 1978. Military expenditure and capitalism: a comment. *Cambridge Journal of Economics* 2: 287–92.

Hoole, Frank W. and Chi Huang. 1989. The global conflict process. *Journal of Conflict Resolution* 33: 142–63.

Kirby, M. W. 1981. *The Decline of British Economic Power since 1870*. London: Allen & Unwin.

Lindgren, Goran. 1984. Review essay: Armaments and economic performance in industrialized economies. *Journal of Peace Research* 21: 375–87.

Maddison, Angus. 1979. Per capita output in the long run. *Kyklos* 32: 412–25.

Maddison, Angus. 1982. *Phases of Capitalist Development*. New York: Oxford University Press.

Maddison, Angus, 1987. Growth and slowdown in advanced capitalist economies: techniques of quantitative assessment. *Journal of Economic Literature* 25: 649–98.

Majeski, Stephen J. and David L. Jones. 1981. Arms race modeling: causality analysis and model specification. *Journal of Conflict Resolution* 25: 259–88.

Mitchell, Brian R. 1988. *British Historical Statistics*. Cambridge: Cambridge University Press.

Modelski, George. 1987. *Long Cycles in World Politics*. Seattle: University of Washington Press.

Modelski, George and William R. Thompson. 1988. *Sea Power and Global Politics since 1494*. Seattle: University of Washington Press.

O'Connor, James. 1973. *The Fiscal Crisis of the State*. New York: St. Martin's Press.

Pollard, Sidney. 1982. *The Wasting of the British Economy: British Economic Policy, 1945 to the Present*. London: Croom Helm.
Pollard, Sidney. 1989. *Britain's Prime and Britain's Decline: The British Economy, 1870–1914*. London: Edward Arnold.
Rasler, Karen. 1990. Spending, deficits and welfare–investment tradeoffs: cause or effect of leadership decline? In D.P. Rapkin (ed.), *World Leadership and Hegemony*. Boulder, Colo.: Lynne Rienner.
Rasler, Karen and William R. Thompson. 1983. Global wars, public debts and the long cycle. *World Politics* 35: 489–516.
Rasler, Karen and William R. Thompson. 1988. Defense burdens, capital formation, and economic growth: the systemic leader case. *Journal of Conflict Resolution* 32: 61–86.
Rasler, Karen and William R. Thompson. 1990. Relative decline and the overconsumption–underinvestment hypothesis. Unpublished manuscript.
Rose, Richard. 1975. Overloaded government: the problem outlined. *European Studies Newsletter* 5: 13–18.
Rostow, Walt W. 1978. *The World Economy: History and Prospect*. Austin: University of Texas Press.
Smith, Ron P. 1977. Military expenditures and capitalism. *Cambridge Journal of Economics* 1: 61–76.
Smith, Ron P. 1978. Military expenditures and capitalism: a reply. *Cambridge Journal of Economics* 2: 299–304.
Smith, Ron P. 1980. Military spending and investment in OECD countries, 1954–1973. *Journal of Comparative Economics* 4: 19–32.
Sprout, Harold and Margaret Sprout. 1968. The dilemma of rising demands and insufficient resources. *World Politics* 20: 660–93.
Starr, Harvey, Francis W. Hoole, Jeffrey A. Hart, and John R. Freeman. 1984. The relationship between defense spending and inflation. *Journal of Conflict Resolution* 26: 103–22.
Thompson, William R. 1988. *On Global War: Historical–Structural Approaches to World Politics*. Columbia: University of South Carolina Press.
Thompson, William R. and Gary Zuk. 1986. World power and the strategic trap of territorial commitments. *International Studies Quarterly* 30: 249–67.
U.S. ACDA (Arms Control and Disarmament Agency). 1985. *World Military Expenditures and Arms Transfers*. Washington, D.C.: U.S. Arms Control and Disarmament Agency.
Wiener, Martin J. 1981. *English Culture and the Decline of the Industrial Spirit, 1850–1980*. Cambridge: Cambridge University Press.
Wright, Erik Olin. 1979. *Class, Crisis and the State*. London: Verso Press.
Yantek, Thom. 1984. Box-Jenkins Transfer Function Analysis. *Political Methodology* 10: 377–411.

4 Guns, butter, and growth: the case of Norway

Ådne Cappelen, Nils Petter Gleditsch, and Olav Bjerkholt
Central Bureau of Statistics of Norway
and International Peace Research Institute, Oslo

THE ECONOMICS OF WAR AND PEACE

Major changes in international relations in recent years have once again put the question of conversion of resources expended in the arms race on the political agenda. The past three decades have seen numerous expressions of public concern about the costs of the arms race, as well as academic research on the economic consequences of disarmament.[1] However, this research has had limited political impact, mainly because even the modest disarmament scenarios in these studies have seemed unrealistic, except in a very distant future. Today this is no longer true. The superpowers have taken the first steps in the elimination of particularly threatening weapons systems. There is progress across the board in global as well as regional European arms control and disarmament negotiations. Several nations have announced unilateral cutbacks in military forces, and others are imposing a de facto freeze on defense spending.[2]

Regional conflicts remain a threat to peace in the Middle East and elsewhere, and ethnic and other internal conflicts appear to be increasing to the point where they might endanger international stability. Moreover, so far it is only in Europe that regional arms control and disarmament is making progress. And even in Europe older conflicts, temporarily suppressed by the Cold War, are reemerging. Yet, this is overshadowed by the fact that the structural and ideological bases of the East–West conflict in Europe have largely disappeared. It now seems highly unlikely that the two superpowers will engage in serious rivalry over local conflicts in other areas; rather, they have started to work together to contain such conflicts. While there may well be serious regional wars in the years to come, the wealthiest forty or so countries have refrained from war among themselves for over 30 years.

Few countries will be prepared at short notice to dispense entirely with the option of threatening military force in self-defense as a last resort. Few if any are likely to join the ranks of Iceland and Costa Rica, which have no domestic military forces. But among those countries affected by the East–West conflict, and particularly in Europe, the size of the military establishment is going to come under very serious discussion. Increasingly, pressing public and private needs will compete with national security requirements for public funds: social welfare, care for the increasing cohorts of the aged, responsible environmental policies, more efficient and less polluting means of transportation, effective antidrug policies. Many of these civilian priorities will even be formulated in terms of security – as in the relatively new notion of 'environmental security' – with the deliberate purpose of signaling to policy-makers that protection against environmental and other threats to industrial societies is as important as national security in the traditional sense. In Eastern Europe and the Soviet Union, consumers will be pushing hard for improved standards of consumer goods, and public funding will be needed to ease the transition towards a market economy.

Much of the writing on the economics of defense conversion emphasizes various *problems* involved in the transition. Resources cannot always be transferred from one sector to the other; plants involved in specialized defense production may have to be closed down when the demand for weapons disappears; employees in the defense sector may have to be retrained or seek early retirement; entrenched interests, whether representing labor, capital, or local communities with tax revenues from firms and defense employees, may resist disarmament – as epitomized in the concept of a 'military-industrial complex.' In the study of single industries, scholars have frequently chosen the more challenging and difficult cases, and this may have led to an overly dim view of the prospects. More recently, some research on conversion has focused on the high cost of weapons destruction (as with chemical weapons) or verification (as in the case of the agreement to ban intermediate-range nuclear forces).

Yet most available research also indicates that, regardless of transition problems, the effects of conversion in the medium to long term are clearly positive, for employment as well as for economic growth. For instance, various studies have investigated the competitive relationship between 'guns' and 'butter' – that is, between military spending and domestic welfare spending (see, for example, Davis and Chan 1990; Harris *et al.* 1988; Russett 1982; and extensive reviews in several other chapters in this volume). In this chapter, we shall examine the Norwegian military sector in the light of the 'guns' versus 'butter' hypothesis. We begin with a description of the Norwegian military sector. Then we go on to a critique of the modeling found in most studies in this area; next we analyze some new empirical results; and in the final section we discuss the consequences.

THE NORWEGIAN MILITARY SECTOR

Norway has a military sector relatively typical of small industrialized countries in Western Europe. The absolute size of the military establishment is very limited in terms of the total armed forces in the East–West confrontation: in 1987 Norway's military spending[3] accounted for 0.3 percent of the global spending, or 0.6 percent of NATO spending.[4] In

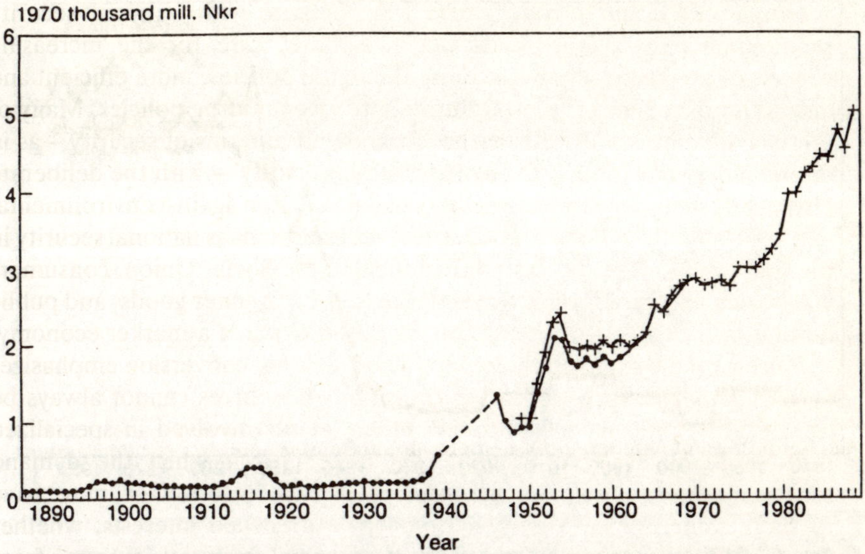

Figure 4.1 Norwegian military consumption 1887–1989, thousand million NKr, fixed 1970 prices
Sources: National account publications of the Central Bureau of Statistics, Oslo. There are two nonoverlapping curves for the period 1949–69, due to a change in definitions in the national accounts. There are no meaningful data for the period of the German occupation (1940–5).

domestic terms, military spending can nevertheless be seen as a major project, regularly consuming about 3 percent of the Norwegian national product. On the other hand, this is very far from a wartime economy, in which a country might spend 40–50 percent of its national product on the military sector.

Figures 4.1–4.4 provide a long-term view of the Norwegian military sector. Figure 4.1 gives the absolute level of military consumption over the past 100 years in constant prices. It shows that World War II represented a turning point, with important consequences for military spending in peacetime. From about 1895 until the mid-1930s we can note no long-term trend, neither upwards nor downwards, in military spending. With World War I there is a marked hump: the emergency measures of a neutral country. After World War II followed an initial period of disarmament. Norway's joining NATO in 1949 did not have any immediate effect; but after the outbreak of the Korean War, military spending rose very rapidly. After the Korean War military spending decreased and then leveled out until the mid-1960s, but at a level unprecedented prior to Korea. Since then there has been a long-term increase in military spending, with somewhat uneven variations. In 1978 the NATO heads of government agreed to increase military spending by 3 percent per annum in real terms, and Norway has adhered to this decision, through changing governments and

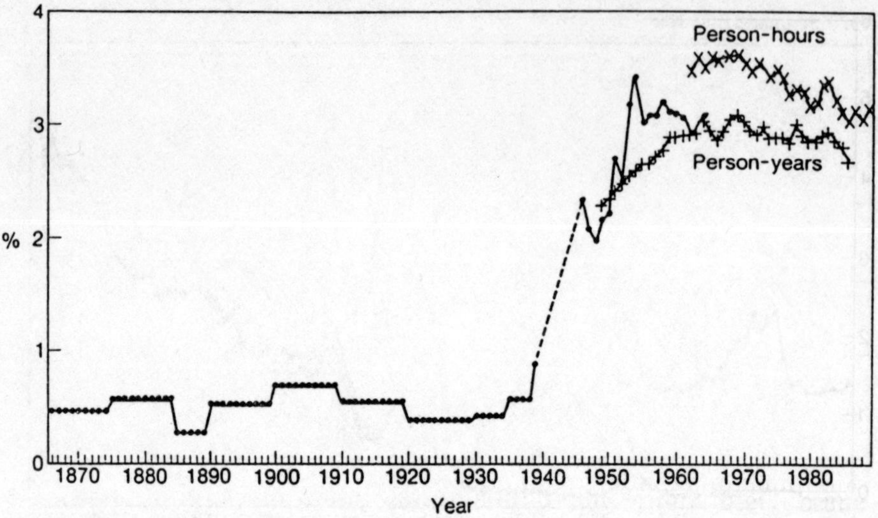

Figure 4.2 Military employment as a share of total employment, 1865–1989, percentages

Sources: See Figure 4.1. For the years 1865–1930 we only have data for five- or ten-year intervals. The figure assumes that the level is constant between these years. The curves for 1865–1964 and 1949–86 are based on data for person-years, while the curve for 1962–89 is based on person-hours. The difference between the first two is due to a change in the definitions in the national accounts. A curve based on the number of employees – not shown here – would fall in between the ones based on person-hours and person-years. There are no meaningful data for the period of the German occupation (1940–5).

shifting economic fortunes. In the late 1980s the Norwegian Labor Party adjusted the growth rate to 2.5 percent, an adjustment left unchanged by the most recent nonsocialist government, which held office from September 1989 to November 1990. For 1991, however, there is wide agreement on a zero-growth defense budget.[5] The cuts, relative to what might have been undertaken under the assumption of 'business as usual,' concern both labor and equipment costs. On the equipment side, a decision has been made not to replace fighters that crash, so the Norwegian F-16 fleet (originally 72 were purchased) is slowly being depleted. At the same time, preparedness has been lowered, a decision which mainly reduces labor costs. Shorter and more intensified training has been introduced for parts of the conscript force, as an experiment.

Figure 4.2 depicts – for an even longer time-period – the use of labor resources by the military, in percentage of the labor force. Military use of manpower accompanied the rise in military spending after World War II, but leveled off after the Korean War. Over the past three decades it has remained fairly constant, although the trend now points downwards.

One reason why there is a contrast between Figures 4.1 and 4.2 is

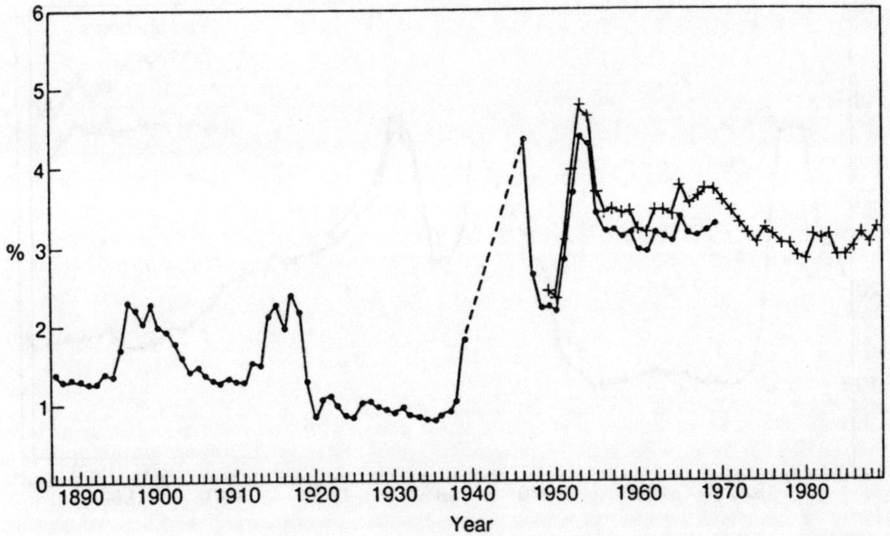

Figure 4.3 Norwegian military consumption 1887–1989 as a share of GDP, percentages

that military spending is an absolute measure, while the military use of manpower is depicted relative to total employment. However, the absolute size of manpower consumed by the armed forces also stopped rising in 1952 and has stayed about level since then.

As far as military spending is concerned, the absolute and relative measures differ more. Figures 4.3 and 4.4 give two commonly used relative measures for military spending. They show military consumption as a share of the national product has stagnated, while military consumption as a share of general government consumption has decreased since the 1950s, and is now almost as low as in the period between the World Wars.

We lack thorough analyses of the long-term determinants of Norwegian military spending. However, a visual inspection of the curves indicates that external determinants have played a major role. A long-term influence is the East–West conflict; short-term influences are the events leading to Norway's secession from the union with Sweden in 1905, the World Wars, and the Korean War – possibly also the Indochina War and the new Cold War in the early 1980s. Norway was not an active combatant in the traditional sense in any of these wars. During World War II Norway's conventional military role in defending itself against the German invasion ended within two months and gave way to a five-year occupation. In the other wars Norway did not participate at all. In 1905, war was a real threat, but was averted. On the other hand, because Norway has been a close ally of the United States since World War II, even remote wars may have been perceived as indirect threats, in that they might escalate into worldwide conflict.

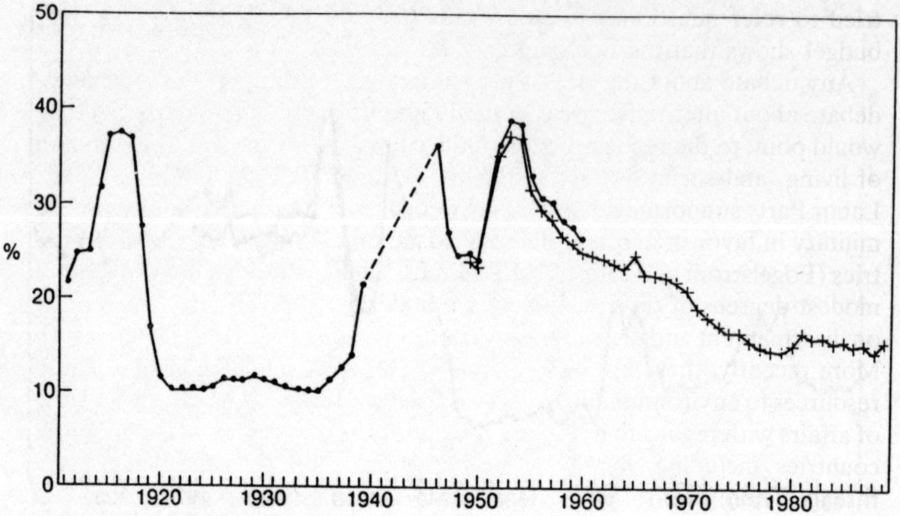

Figure 4.4 Norwegian military consumption 1911–89 as a share of general government consumption, percentages
Sources: See Figure 4.1. The change in definitions corresponds to that in Figure 4.1. General government consumption includes expenditure at the local levels. There are no meaningful data for the period of the German occupation (1940–5).

The rapid rise of military spending in the early 1950s was accompanied by considerable debate. Nevertheless, opposition to high military spending came mainly from the relatively far left and did not give rise to any mass movement. (Such a movement did arise later, however, on issues relating to nuclear weapons.) Annual real increases in military spending became the order of the day in the thriving Norwegian economy, with relatively feeble opposition. Not till the 1980s did the issue of military spending cause any divergence between the major parties, with the Labor Party favoring 2.5 percent annual increases in real terms and the nonsocialist coalition parties (which ruled in the period 1981–6 and again in 1989–90) sticking to 3 percent. Today, for the first time since World War II, there seems to be broad consensus that the defense budget should be cut. It remains to be seen if this sentiment will lead to a long-term reduction; or simply peter out; or result in a one-time cut, to be followed by new annual increases. The military establishment argues consistently that Norway has a 'minimum defense,' which cannot be reduced without irreparable harm to the defense effort. However, such national perceived minima tend to adjust to the actual level of spending, and in the future the military establishment will have to come up with an improved rationale for continued high spending if it is to be heard. In late 1989 the Norwegian government appointed a broadly composed Defense Commission (only the third such commission after World War II), due to report in early 1992. Initially the government tried to refer questions of defense cuts to the Commission, but the 1991 budget shows that the tide could not be stemmed.

Any debate about the size of the military establishment is usually also a debate about alternative uses. In the 1950s critics of high military spending would point to the reconstruction of the country after the war, the standard of living, and social welfare programs. Around 1960 the left wing of the Labor Party supported an idea from Swedish public debate of abolishing the military in favor of a 'moral defense' based on aid to the developing countries (Fogelström and Morell 1959). Similar ideas, although involving more modest degrees of disarmament, have underlain the various U.N. reports on disarmament and development (United Nations 1972, 1982, 1985, 1986). More recently, there has been increased emphasis on channeling released resources to environmental projects in Eastern Europe. The disastrous state of affairs with regard to pollution in Eastern Europe is seen by neighboring countries, including Norway, as a threat comparable to traditional military threats. Therefore – in pure self-interest – it may be appropriate to redirect resources from the traditional type of defense to environmental protection.

A strong competitor to the environment is care for the aged. Like many other Organization for Economic Cooperation and Development (OECD) countries, Norway faces a major demographic decline in the relative size of the working population early in the next century. At the same time, increased consciousness and organization among the elderly has led to the emergence of a small but vocal group of 'gray panthers,' who – at least temporarily – have succeeded in putting strong pressure on the government for heeding their obligations to the older population.

Several previous studies, by ourselves and others, have investigated the economic impact of reduced defense spending. For instance, Andreassen (1972), Bjerkholt (1967), and Bjerkholt *et al.* (1980) have undertaken studies of the national effects of various cuts in military spending, ranging from general and complete disarmament to minor reductions. Generally, these studies have concluded that with a suitable set of countermeasures, the economic adjustment problems can be overcome without major economic dislocations. Local adjustment problems are somewhat more severe (Gleditsch 1987; Skomsvold *et al.* 1987). A separate study of the economic effects of international disarmament (Cappelen *et al.* 1982) concluded that Norway was likely to experience a net gain from an international policy of lowering defense budgets and increasing allocations to development assistance, mainly because of Norway's low level of arms exports.

MODELING THE TRADEOFFS BETWEEN MILITARY AND CIVILIAN SPENDING

Two separate issues are raised in studies on the economic consequences of military spending. One concerns effects on the size and composition of government spending as a result of changes in military spending. If total public consumption is budget-constrained, any increase in military spending will obviously come at the expense of some other part of public consumption, such as health or education. There is a large body of studies analyzing such tradeoffs between different parts of government spending.

A second issue concerns the consequences of changes in military spending on the national economy. Several econometric studies using widely differing modeling approaches have concluded that military spending 'crowds out' investment. Thus even if a direct tradeoff between military and civilian government spending is rejected, the negative effect on investment (and thereby economic growth) implies a tradeoff in the long run because income will be lower as a result of 'unproductive' military spending.

In a process difficult to formalize, society allocates certain parts of national income to various categories of government consumption. One way of modeling the tradeoffs between different categories of government spending favored by economists is to make use of analogous assumptions of rational behavior, as in microeconomic models of the individual consumer. In this analogy it is assumed that resources are allocated to different consumption categories (such as military, health, education, and private consumption) according to what maximizes welfare, as defined by a societal preference function. It is then possible to derive 'demand' functions for each consumption category which will depend on

- the size of the budget or total spending
- relative prices of different consumption categories
- sociodemographic characteristics
- parameters of the preference function, including variables such as military threat and other 'political' variables.

Many models of military spending have been developed along these lines (see Smith 1989 for a recent study with a number of references).

A more common and simple-minded approach, however, is to estimate models to explain the spending on civilian purposes (health, education) using military spending as an explanatory variable. Frequently categories of public spending are used to explain each other. For this to be a consistent framework, a simultaneous-equation approach is required. It is not meaningful to specify a model where all categories of public spending enter the same equation and where one switches between having, say, military spending as endogenous in one equation and exogenous in another, as long as one uses ordinary least squares when estimating the parameters of the model.

If the current détente between the United States and the Soviet Union continues, the relevance of such models as a basis for forecasts of the future composition of public spending is also questionable, to say the least. In any case, the future development of military spending in a small country like Norway is not likely to be determined by relations estimated from historical data in the present circumstances. We have chosen instead to take military spending as an exogenous variable in our study, and to analyze the consequences for the national economy of alternative uses of the resources used by the military sector. Our present study will be confined to an analysis of the effects of national disarmament only.

EFFECTS OF MILITARY SPENDING ON THE NORWEGIAN ECONOMY

Surprisingly few studies of the economic effects of military spending have used existing econometric models that have been developed, for instance, for purposes of national economic planning. Instead, most studies have used very simple, ad hoc econometric models with few equations. In this section we present the results from simulations on a disaggregated input–output-based econometric model of the Norwegian economy (MODAG).

MODAG is a disaggregated input–output-based model used for medium-term macroeconomic planning and policy analysis by various government bodies in Norway (Cappelen and Longva 1987). MODAG has about 250 stochastic equations, and 1050 nonstochastic equations and identities. The total number of variables is about 1750. The model has 40 commodities, and each commodity may in principle have three different prices depending on origin and use: import price, export price, and domestic price (price of Norwegian goods delivered to the home market). Import prices are exogenous, as is the exchange rate. Most other prices are determined by unit costs by sector, as well as the competing import price and an index of capacity utilization. Unit costs are determined by the input–output structure. The unit wage costs depend on productivity, which again is given by factor demand equations where the number of hours by sector depends on relative factor prices, output, and the capital stock. The capital stock is determined via investment equations where output is the most important factor, but where profitability is also included. Exports are determined mainly by demand equations relying on the Armington (1969) approach. These equations contain an indication of world market activity and relative export/import prices. However, exports of oil, gas, and net receipts from shipping services – which constitute one-third of Norwegian total export revenues in 1990 – are exogenous. Imports are determined by import shares for each commodity, which depend on relative domestic/import prices. Import shares differ between domestic users. Consumer demand depends on household income disaggregated by socioeconomic groups as well as credit supply. Total consumption is then disaggregated using a linear expenditure system. Labor supply is disaggregated by sex and age, and is fairly inelastic with regard to real wages adjusted for taxes. Wage growth by sector is determined by equations where unemployment enters in a nonlinear way. Additional explanatory variables are taxes, productivity, and prices. Changes in prices and productivity are – after a lag of three years at most – fully reflected in wages.

Table 4.1 Macroeconomic development in the reference scenario, 1990–2007

	Levels in 1990 current prices (Thousand million NKr)	Average annual growth (percentages)				
		1990–5	1995–8	1998–2001	2001–4	2004–7
Private consumption	336	2.4	2.1	2.5	2.4	2.4
Public consumption	138	2.9	2.9	2.9	2.8	2.8
Civilian	116	2.8	2.8	2.8	2.7	2.7
Military	22	3.0	3.0	3.0	3.0	3.0
Gross investment[a]	108	3.6	2.0	1.9	1.5	2.0
Exports[a]	150	4.0	5.4	5.7	5.4	4.6
Imports[a]	212	4.0	2.4	4.5	3.1	3.1
GDP[a]	565	3.0	2.3	2.9	2.7	2.6
Employment	–	1.5	0.9	1.3	1.0	1.0
Unemployment rate[b]	5.2	3.2	3.3	2.7	2.5	2.0
Consumer prices	–	3.4	3.0	2.9	3.0	3.2
Wage rate	–	4.0	3.2	3.7	4.0	4.8
Current account[b]	13	14	12	6	24	40
PSBR[b,c]	8	1	11	11	13	14

Notes:
(a) All these variables exclude oil, gas, and shipping-related activities.
(b) Underlined figures denote level in the final year of each period.
(c) PSBR = public sector borrowing requirement (that is, 'the deficit').

MODAG is mainly Keynesian in character in the short and medium term, although its multipliers are fairly small due to the openness of the Norwegian economy and the high marginal tax rates for households. In the long run more neoclassical results emerge, mainly due to the NAIRU (nonaccelerating inflationary rate of unemployment)[6] which is implied by the wage equations.

MODAG disaggregates government spending into four sectors: Military, Health and social services, Education, and Administration and miscellaneous. The latter three groups are subdivided into central and local government. Military spending is divided into three categories: wage costs, procurement of equipment, and operating costs. This disaggregation enables us to analyze changes in the overall level of military spending as well as changes in the cost structure of the military sector. The three cost categories differ with regard to import content. Major weapons system are mainly imported, operating costs have import shares around 0.4–0.5, while labor remuneration has no direct effect on imports. (Military wages and salaries do, of course, generate imports via changes in household income and consumer demand, but no more than other wages and salaries.) In 1990, wages and salaries made up only one third of military spending while the corresponding figure for civilian government consumption was approximately two thirds. Thus, a switch from military to civilian consumption spending has a pronounced direct impact on labor demand.

In our reference scenario total military spending is assumed to grow by 3 percent annually in line with the 1978 NATO decision. The overall growth in military spending in the reference scenario is assumed *not* to increase employment. Overall military employment has by and large been constant for many years.

Table 4.1 presents the developments in some important macroeconomic variables in the reference scenario. We shall not discuss these numbers in detail, but would only point out that the gradual lowering of the unemployment rate during the simulation period makes the results of alternative scenarios quite dependent on how large are the changes we assume will take place. This is due to the nonlinear character of the wage equations which is important at low unemployment levels (in the 2–3 percent range). The average unemployment rate from 1970–90 is slightly above 2 percent. Clearly the 1990 figure (5.2 percent) is a very high one by Norwegian standards, as was the observed unemployment level for 1989 (4.9 percent).

The two disarmament scenarios we study in this chapter are designed to illustrate what happens if military spending is replaced by increased spending for high-priority civilian government consumption or by reduced tax rates. Both alternatives – or a combination – may be considered realistic under the present circumstances. In both our disarmament scenarios we have assumed military employment to remain constant at the current (1990) level, as in the reference scenario. In view of the stability of military employment over the years, this assumption does not seem too unreasonable, at least for moderate levels of disarmament. The disarmament that takes place from 1990 to 2007 (the last year in our calculations) is quite moderate, as military spending is reduced by 1.2 percent annually. The difference in military spending compared to the reference scenario increases over time, of course, and by 2007 the reduction exceeds 50 percent in the two disarmament scenarios (see Table 4.2). Disarmament is assumed to reduce operating costs and procurement of equipment by the same proportions.

In the first disarmament scenario the alternative public-sector use is an increased spending on health and social services equivalent to the reduction in military spending. Thus the ex ante change in the budget balance is nil. However, military spending will have effects on the Norwegian economy different from those of spending an equal amount on health and social services. Thus, the final effects on the public-sector borrowing requirement (PSBR) (or 'budget balance') will be nonzero. In this scenario – called HEALTH – total public consumption in constant prices will be the same as in the reference scenario; we simply assume a change in allocation between different sectors.

In our second disarmament scenario, direct taxes on personal income are reduced by an amount which in inflation-adjusted terms equals – prior

Table 4.2 Macroeconomic effects of disarmament/conversion: deviations from reference scenario (percentages)

	1992		1995		2001		2007	
	HEALTH	TAX	H	T	H	T	H	T
Variables in constant prices:								
Private consumption	0.2	0.5	0.4	1.2	0.8	2.6	1.3	4.1
Civilian	2.2	0.0	4.3	0.0	7.2	0.0	10.3	0.0
Military	−11.3		−21.7		−39.1		−52.9	
Gross investment[a]	0.1	0.1	−0.1	0.4	−0.7	0.8	−1.7	1.0
Exports[a]	0.0	0.1	−0.1	0.4	−0.7	0.6	−1.7	0.5
Imports[a]	−0.5	−0.3	−0.8	0.5	−1.4	−0.7	−1.5	−0.8
GDP[a]	0.3	0.0	0.5	0.2	0.5	0.5	0.3	0.7
Employment	0.4	0.0	0.7	0.2	0.6	0.5	0.1	0.4
Unemployment rate[b]	−0.2	0.0	−0.4	−0.1	−0.4	−0.2	−0.2	−0.1
Variables in current prices:								
Consumer prices	0.0	−0.2	0.2	−0.5	1.0	−0.8	3.0	−0.7
Wage rate	0.0	−0.7	0.5	−1.5	3.3	−2.3	7.0	−1.6
Current account[c]	0.1	0.1	0.2	0.1	0.6	0.3	0.7	0.4
PSBR[c]	−0.1	0.1	−0.3	0.1	−0.7	0.3	−1.0	0.4

Notes:
(a) All these variables exclude oil, gas, and shipping.
(b) Change in levels in percentages.
(c) Changes in percentage points of nominal GDP in the reference scenario.

to income changes as a result of conversion – the reduction in military spending. Personal taxes are levied at varying rates depending on type of income and socioeconomic characteristics. To make our calculations as simple as possible, we have in the TAX scenario adjusted the 'add factors' in the tax equations rather than the tax rates. This will not matter much as long as the calculated changes are small, but this procedure will tend to underestimate deviations between the reference scenario and the TAX scenario. The average income tax rate for the household sector is reduced from 34 percent in 2007 in the reference scenario to 31 percent in the TAX scenario, a reduction of 3 percentage points. In 2000 the average tax reduction is 2 percentage points.

The macroeconomic consequences of the two disarmament scenarios described above are presented as percentage deviations from the reference scenario in Table 4.2. Figure 4.5 compares the annual changes in GDP over the simulation period for the two scenarios, relative to the reference scenario. Most of the changes are quite small. The reduction in military spending in both scenarios is more than 50 percent by the year 2007 relative to the reference scenario. However, the share of military spending in GDP in the reference scenario is only 3.7 percent in 2007, so that the shift in demand involved is about 2 percent of GDP in 2007, and less before that.

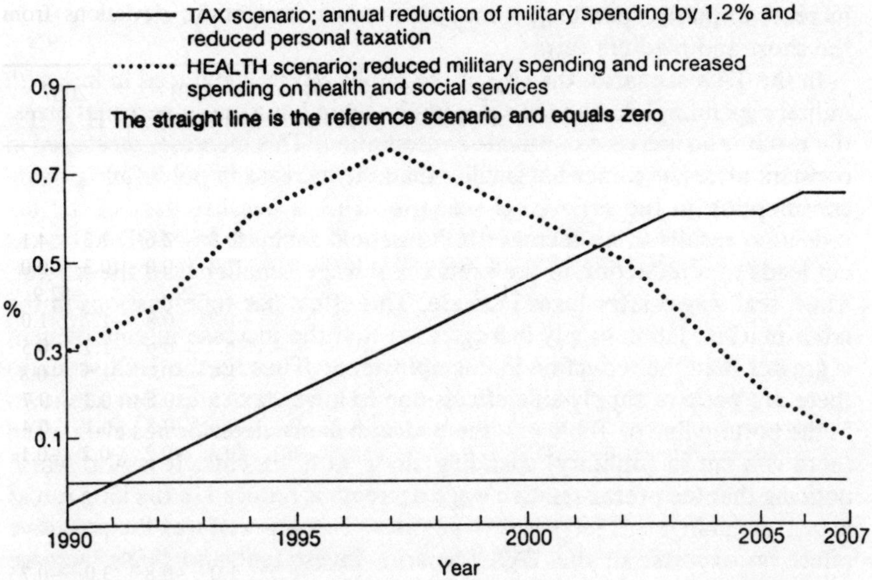

Figure 4.5 Annual changes in GDP under moderate disarmament 1990–2007: deviations from the reference scenario, percentages
Source: Own simulations using MODAG.

In the HEALTH scenario both employment and purchases of goods and services increase, so there is a direct positive impact on labor demand, which reduces unemployment. At the same time the increase in demand increases female labor supply, which in the model partly depends on the sectoral composition of labor demand, an indicator of female job 'opportunities.' Increased employment increases household income and thereby private consumption and housing investment. As unemployment is further reduced (in addition to lower unemployment in the reference scenario), wage rates increase. This leads to increased prices but less than the increase in wages – so the real wage continues to rise and consumption increases further. However, the loss in competitiveness due to increased costs leads to reduced manufacturing output and exports, as well as a reduction in investment due to lower profitability. In spite of this, the current account improves due to lower imports. Norway's imports are much higher than its exports excluding oil, gas, and shipping (which are exogenous in the model). The substantial strengthening of the budget balance as measured by the reduction in the PSBR is mainly due to the increase in employment and wage rates, as most tax revenue derives from wage income. Thus while a cut in military spending results in a moderate loss in taxes, an increase in other public spending increases tax revenue due to the tax on labor costs, income taxes, and VAT (Value Added Tax). Thus it seems reasonable to conclude that not only will a cut in military spending make possible an increase in public spending, it may also reduce budget deficits, at least in the short and medium term.

In the TAX scenario, the size of the public sector is reduced in line with military spending. As the tax cut is implemented as a cut in personal taxes, the result is an increase in private consumption. This increase, measured in constant prices, is somewhat smaller than the increase in public and private consumption in the HEALTH scenario. This is because part of the tax reduction results in an increase in household savings. In MODAG a tax cut leads to a reduction in the pretax real wage, smaller than the tax cut. Thus, real wages after taxes increase. This effect has repercussions in the labor market: labor supply increases, so that the increase in employment is greater than the reduction in unemployment. Thus, in the TAX scenario there are positive supply-side effects due to lower tax rates. But as shown in the bottom line of Table 4.2, the budget balance deteriorates even when there is a cut in (military) spending along with tax cuts. It is also worth noticing that the pretax relative wage decrease is reduced in the long run as lower unemployment increases wage rates. This also reduces the posititive effect on exports. In the TAX scenario, investment and GDP increase gradually. Thus, our model confirms one of the often reported effects of military spending – reducing investment and growth. However, the effect on investment is far less than in some other studies. While it is common to conclude that military spending crowds out investment dollar for dollar (Cappelen *et al.* 1984), the estimate according to the TAX scenario is closer to a 10 percent effect.

As is apparent from Table 4.2, both scenarios improve the current account. In our version of the model, nominal interest rates are constant as well as the exchange rate. The latter assumption is a fairly realistic description of current Norwegian policy. Assuming unchanged nominal interest rates is more dubious but not completely unrealistic, since the current account improves in both scenarios and the inflation rate is not very different from the reference scenario. However, in the TAX scenario when both the current account improves and inflation decreases, one might assume additional positive effects in the economy from a reduction in interest rates.

Another study performed for the Defence Commission (Bowitz and Cappelen 1990) used slightly different scenarios. The reference scenario was approximately the same, although the starting year was adjusted to 1991 and a slightly revised version of the model was used. The disarmament scenario in this study assumed zero growth rather than a slight decrease in military spending; the reduction relative to the reference scenario was assumed to occur only in the purchases of goods and services. In two alternative scenarios the freed resources were used (a) to reduce income taxes on households as in the present analysis, and (b) to increase public spending for educational purposes rather than health. The results of the study by Bowitz and Cappelen are very similar to ours if we take into

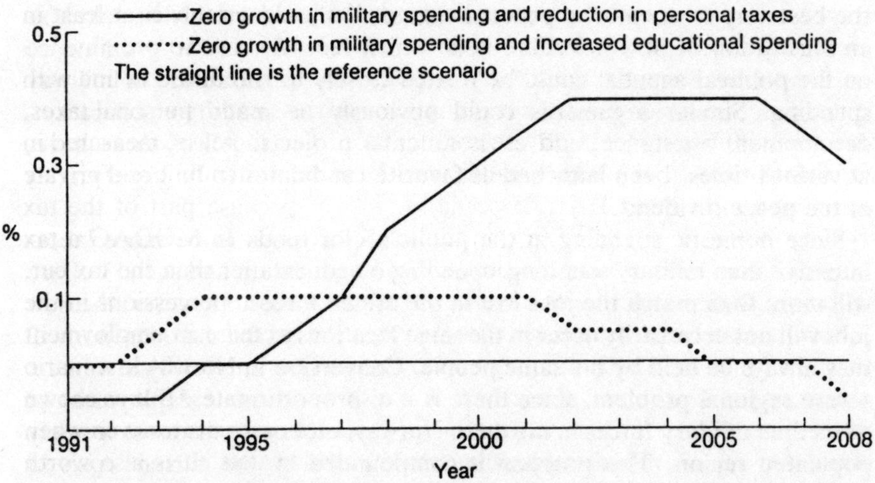

Figure 4.6 Annual changes in GDP under military-spending freeze 1991–2008: deviations from the reference scenario, percentages
Sources: Simulations using MODAG, reported in Bowitz and Cappelen 1990.

account that the present study assumes larger cuts in military spending, cf. Figure 4.6. The changes in real GDP in the two scenarios look very much like those in Figure 4.5, except that they are smaller in absolute value.

CONCLUSIONS

What may seem like a minor disarmament scenario – only 1.2 percent annual reduction – becomes more significant when seen in a longer perspective and compared to a reference scenario of continued 3 percent annual growth. By the year 2007, military spending in the disarmament scenario is down to half of that in the reference scenario. In real terms it is only 18.5 percent lower than the 1990 level, but the 'normal' state of affairs over the past 40 years has been a steady, long-term increase.

Thus, within a 17-year period a considerable 'peace dividend' is accumulated. Various alternative uses could be imagined, all of which would increase domestic welfare. To take but one example: the minor media revolution sponsored by spokespersons for the old-age pensioners quickly generated political support for 'an old-age billion' – that is, increased public spending for old-age care amounting to a total of NKr 1000 million. There was less consensus on where to find the money, and part of the billion ended up as deficit spending. The defense budget did not go unnoticed in the debate. In fact, a slight real decrease in defense spending relative to the 1989 level could have funded most of the 'old-age billion' for 1990. Moreover, similar packages could have been added for each year in the 1990s.

This is not to say that increased spending for old-age care is necessarily the best way to spend the peace dividend; it should merely be taken as an illustration of how a welfare issue which recently rose to prominence on the political agenda, could be related closely to the future of military spending. Similar arguments could obviously be made for education, development assistance, and environmental projects. All of these have, at various times, been launched as favorite candidates to be beneficiaries of the peace dividend.

Since domestic spending in the public sector tends to be more labor-intensive than military spending, spending on education and social welfare will more than match the jobs lost in the armed forces. However, the new jobs will not necessarily occur in the same locations as the old ones, nor will they always be held by the same people. Conversion in Norway involves a severe regional problem, since there is a disproportionate deployment of peacetime military forces in northern Norway, otherwise the most sparsely populated region. This problem is compounded by the current crisis in the fishing industry, which also affects the north most severely. Thus, despite the promise of the new détente and an end to the Cold War, many northern municipalities are anxious to seek Norwegian national prefinancing of projects under NATO's infrastructure program, in order to secure employment for the local construction industry. This is hardly compatible with ideas of a long-term reduction of peacetime arms levels in Europe. On the other hand, education and welfare programs can easily be given a regional slant to provide northern Norway with a larger share of the peace dividend.

Military spending in the smaller NATO countries involves a fairly minor share of the national product. On the other hand, these societies have little freedom of budgetary maneuver. If in the medium term 1–2 percent of the national product can be released for alternative uses, this represents a major opportunity. It does not relieve governments of trying to resolve the structural problems which have caused the present budgetary constraints, nor does it eliminate the necessity of reforms in social-welfare programs to cut costs, while concentrating on the essential services. But the peace dividend may at least provide a breathing space while such reforms are being implemented.

Conscription is an issue rarely discussed in analyses of conversion, or guns-versus-butter tradeoffs. Yet 40 percent of the military employment in Norway (in terms of person-years performed) is derived from the use of conscripts. They are a relatively cheap source of labor supply for the armed forces; it has been calculated that the cost of military manpower would increase by 30–40 percent if conscripts were to be paid at the average salary level of their civilian cohort. The defense budget would increase by 10–14 percent (Christensen and Torvanger 1989; *NOU* 1989). At the moment, conscript labor is abundant, but in the long run it will become scarce because of demographic changes. This is, in a sense, the reverse side of the increasing 'old-age burden,' which makes improved old-age care such a high-priority concern for the next century.

Norway has one of the world's highest rates of mobilization. The peacetime armed forces can be expanded by a factor of 8.6 at full mobilization, to comprise 8 percent of the total population. This percentage is four times higher than in the United States, and seven times higher than in the United Kingdom.[7] Although the military establishment will be reluctant to give up this high degree of mobilization, a long-term disarmament policy will probably make reductions in the rate of mobilization inevitable. This will open up for lower service time (minimum service in the army is today 12 months, plus regular refresher courses up to the age of 45) or a more selective service. At the moment about three-quarters of the male cohort are serving in the armed forces; among the 'losses,' there are three times as many medical exemptions – 12 percent – as conscientious objectors (COs) – 4 percent. Conscription is rooted in the Norwegian Constitution and is firmly established as a democratic foundation for the armed forces. Any weakening of the principle of conscription would meet with strong resistance.

Those accepted as COs perform alternative service equal to the minimum military service plus four months. Since the mid-1960s, COs have increasingly come to be employed in the social services, and currently about 70 percent work in that sector. In a sense then, this part of the conscript force has already been 'converted' to producing 'butter' rather than 'guns.' Most of the other forms of suggested alternative spending can also be found in the alternative service: some COs have served as teachers, and the government and the COs agree in principle that environmental tasks should be a high priority in the future. Development assistance, on the other hand, does not employ COs, although in the mid-1960s there was considerable support for the idea that service in Norway's newly established Peace Corps should be recognized as alternative service.

In a period with a long-term decline in defense spending and declining use for a large number of conscripts in the armed forces, the idea of a comprehensive national service provides an interesting concept for converting some of the resources from military to civilian public consumption, without paying the full price. This is not the place to discuss such concepts in detail (see Gleditsch and Agøy 1991; Moskos 1988). Briefly, however, a comprehensive national service might involve considerable freedom of choice between several forms of service, constrained by the private and public funding available for the different projects. Thus, many who would not ordinarily be COs might spend most of their national service in the social sector or in environmental projects, with possibly a minimum military training to enable them to participate in a mobilization army.

A comprehensive national service would add to the peace dividend by transfering to the civilian sector the cheapest labor resource of the armed forces. In purely financial terms it would represent a relatively marginal addition. However, the symbolic value might be greater in that it would elevate certain new tasks to the same order of importance as national security.

NOTES

1 Cf. Benoit (1967), United Nations (1962, 1972, 1978, 1983, 1989).
2 A recent survey is given in *The 100% Bulletin* published by the British Peace Assembly, London, Summer 1990.
3 We use *military spending* as a generic term. The precise technical terms are *budgeted military expenditure* (the data are found in the annual defense budgets), *military expenditure* (figures in the state accounts), and *military consumption* (from the national accounts). Military consumption excludes money transfers to other organizations, payments in advance or in arrear for goods to be consumed in other years, and includes expenditures for civilian preparedness, budgeted by other ministries as well as military expenditure at the local (municipal) level.
4 Based on data from U.S. Arms Control and Disarmament Agency 1989.
5 In fact, the defense budget increases by 2.4% but this is less than the expected rate of inflation (4%). The Ministry of Defense estimates that the 1991 budget implies a reduction in activity by 1.7% from the 1990 budget and 0.8% from the revised budget.
6 That is, the rate of unemployment which is consistent with nonaccelerating inflation.
7 According to an official white paper to the Norwegian Parliament: 'Om militær verneplikt og sivil tjenesteplikt' [On military conscription and civilian service], *Stortingsmelding* no. 27, 1988–89, p. 8.

REFERENCES

Andreassen, Tormod. 1972. Forsvarets virkninger på norsk økonomi [The effects of military spending on the Norwegian economy]. *Samfunnsøkonomiske studier*, no. 22. Oslo: Central Bureau of Statistics.

Armington, P. 1969. A theory of demand for products distinguished by place of production. *IMF Staff Papers* 16: 159–78.

Benoit, Emile (ed.). 1967. *Disarmament and World Economic Interdependence*. Oslo: Norwegian University Press.

Bjerkholt, Olav. 1967. An analysis of the economic consequences of disarmament in Norway. In Emile Benoit (ed.), *Disarmament and World Economic Interdependence*, pp. 146–53. Oslo: Norwegian University Press.

Bjerkholt, Olav, Ådne Cappelen, Nils Petter Gleditsch, and Knut Moum. 1980. *Disarmament and Development: A Case Study of Norway*. Oslo: International Peace Research Institute, Oslo (PRIO). PRIO Publication no. S-7/80.

Bowitz, Einar and Ådne Cappelen. 1990. Nullvekst i forsvarsutgiftene. En modellbasert analyse [Zero growth in military expenditure. A model-based analysis]. Unpublished paper. Oslo: Central Bureau of Statistics.

Cappelen, Ådne and Svein Longva. 1987. MODAG A: a medium-term macroeconomic model of the Norwegian economy. In Olav Bjerkholt and Jørgen Rosted (eds), *Macroeconomic Medium-Term Models in the Nordic Countries: Contributions to Economic Analysis*, pp. 153–211. Amsterdam: North-Holland. Also in *Reprint series* no. 24. Oslo: Central Bureau of Statistics.

Cappelen, Ådne, Olav Bjerkholt, and Nils Petter Gleditsch. 1982. *Global Conversion from Arms to Development Aid: Macroeconomic Effects in Norway*. Oslo: International Peace Research Institute, Oslo. PRIO Publication no. S-9/82.

Cappelen, Ådne; Nils Petter Gleditsch, and Olav Bjerkholt. 1984. Military spending and economic growth in the OECD countries. *Journal of Peace Research* 21: 361–73.

Christensen, Arne Magnus and Asbjørn Torvanger. 1989. Godtgjeringssystem for vernepliktige mannskap – kva system bør vi velje? [Salary system for military conscripts – what system should we choose?]. *Sosialøkonomen* 43: 12–15.

Davis, David R. and Steve Chan. 1990. The security–welfare relationship: longitudinal evidence from Taiwan. *Journal of Peace Research* 27: 87–100.

Fogelström, Per Anders and Roland Morell. 1959. *Istedenfor atombomben* [Instead of nuclear weapons]. Oslo: Orientering. (Originally published in Sweden in 1958.)

Gleditsch, Nils Petter. 1987. The local impact of reduced military spending. A case study of Norway. In Jürgen Kuhlmann (ed.), Edited Papers from Research Committee 01 'Armed Forces and Conflict Resolution,' XI World Congress of Sociology, New Delhi, August 1986, in *Forum International*, vol. 7. Munich: Sozialwissenschaftliches Institut der Bundeswehr.

Gleditsch, Nils Petter and Nils Ivar Agøy. 1991. From conscientious objection to conversion? The history and sociology of conscientious objection in Norway. Paper presented to the International Symposium on International Perspectives on Conscientious Objection, Utrecht, Netherlands, 23–7 March, 1990. (Forthcoming in a volume edited by Charles Moskos and John Chambers.)

Gleditsch, Nils Petter, Olav Bjerkholt, and Ådne Cappelen. 1983. Conversion: global, national, and local effects. A case study of Norway. *Cooperation and Conflict* 17: 79–95. (Slightly revised edition as 'Conversion effects: a case study of Norway.' In Lloyd J. Dumas and Marek Thee (eds), *Making Peace Possible. The Promise of Economic Conversion*. pp. 231–49. Oxford: Pergamon, 1989.

Gleditsch, Nils Petter, Olav Bjerkholt, and Ådne Cappelen. 1988. Military R & D and economic growth in industrialized market economies. In Peter Wallensteen (ed.), *Peace Research: Achievements and Challenges*, pp. 198–215. Boulder, Colo. and London: Westview. (Longer version as 'Economic incentives to arm: effects of military spending on industrialized market.' *PRIO Report* no. 21, 1986.)

Harris, Geoffrey, Mark Kelly, and Pranowo. 1988. Tradeoffs between defence and education/health expenditures in developing countries. *Journal of Peace Research* 25: 165–77.

Moskos, Charles C. 1988. *A Call to Civic Service: National Service for Country and Community*. New York: Free Press; and London: Collier Macmillan.

NOU. 1989. Godtgjøringssystemet for vernepliktige mannskaper [Salary system for conscripts]. *Norges Offisielle Utredninger*, no. 3. Oslo: Norwegian University Press.

Russett, Bruce M. 1982. Defense expenditures and national well-being. *American Political Science Review* 76: 767–77.

Skomsvold, Rolf, Ådne Cappelen, Nils Petter Gleditsch, and Olav Bjerkholt. 1987. Regionaløkonomiske konsekvenser av nedrustning in Norge [Regional economic consequences of disarmament in Norway]. *Sosiologi i dag* 17: 113–30.

Smith, Ron P. 1989. Models of military expenditure. *Journal of Applied Econometrics* 4: 345–9.

United Nations. 1962. *Economic and Social Consequences of Disarmament*. New York: United Nations.

United Nations. 1972. *Economic and Social Consequences of the Arms Race and of*

Military Expenditures. New York: United Nations. A/32/8469/Rev. 1. E.78.IX.1. (Originally issued in 1971.)

United Nations. 1973. *Disarmament and Development. Report of the Group of Experts on the Economic and Social Consequences of Disarmament*. New York: United Nations. ST/ECA/174. E.73.IX.1. (Originally issued in 1972.)

United Nations. 1978. *Economic and Social Consequences of the Arms Race and of Military Expenditures*. New York: United Nations. A/32/88/Rev. 1. E.72.IX.16. (Originally issued in 1977.)

United Nations. 1982. *The Relationship between Disarmament and Development*. A/36/356. E.82.IX.1. *Study Series*, no. 5. New York: United Nations.

United Nations. 1983. *Economic and Social Consequences of the Arms Race and of Military Expenditures*. New York: United Nations. A/37/386. E.83.IX.2. *Study Series* no. 11. (Originally issued in 1982.)

United Nations. 1985. *Disarmament and Development. Report of the Secretary-General*. New York: United Nations. A/40/618.

United Nations. 1986. *Disarmament and Development. Joint Declaration by the Panel of Eminent Experts in the Field of Disarmament and Development*. New York: United Nations. E.86.IX.5.

United Nations. 1989. *Study on the Economic and Social Consequences of the Arms Race and Military Expenditures*. New York: United Nations. A/43/368. E.89.IX.2. *Study Series* no. 19. (Originally issued in 1983.)

United States Arms Control and Disarmament Agency. 1988. *World Military Expenditures and Arms Transfers 1988*. Washington, DC: U.S. Government Printing Office.

5 Eating your cake and having it too: the Japanese case[1]

Davis B. Bobrow
University of Pittsburgh

Success as a nation with defense, growth, and welfare is enviable. Japan merits examination as a 'proof in principle' demonstration of the nonutopian character of that outcome. What has worked for Japan may or may not be applicable elsewhere, and may or may not be desirable on other grounds. Yet it surely can suggest some conducive conditions and policy measures for serious consideration. As the Japanese might observe, there is a response to foreign achievement other than determined inattention or mechanistic emulation. It is of course to gain knowledge of foreign accomplishments and to adapt them, modify them, to one's own national circumstances.

APPROACH

For predominantly non-Marxist cultures, U.S. and West European analysts surprisingly often invoke relationships of inherent, antagonistic contradiction between 'guns' and 'butter.' Defense resources, usually formulated as budget moneys, are alleged to hurt growth and welfare. The implicit policy prescription is clear – improve growth and welfare by cutting military funds improve defense by cutting welfare. Attempts to demonstrate, refute, and specify these adverse relationships – and deal with variables that may impinge on them – have produced a great many interesting and often technically sophisticated analyses. Unfortunately, the conclusions across studies, countries, and time periods differ as do their policy implications.

Let us take as an example the relationships for 12 major OECD (Organization for Economic Cooperation and Development) countries between defense spending as a share of GNP and two measures of productivity rates of growth – GDP per person employed and manufacturing output per hour. Over the whole period of 1960–86, the correlations are strongly negative. The United States was first on the defense spending measure and last on the productivity measures, while Japan was the opposite. Yet these aggregate findings and the two-nation comparison may conceal as much as they reveal. There also was an underlying trend in which the strongly negative relationships of the 1960s weakened in the 1970s, and were gone for the 1980s. For 1980–6, defense spending/GNP for the 12 countries was in a positive relationship with the value of manufacturing output, and not significantly related to GDP per employed person (Browne 1988). The United States outperformed Japan on average on both measures of productivity growth rate (based on GDP for 1982–6 and on manufacturing for 1980–8), while spending roughly six times more on defense as a share of GNP (Bank of Japan 1989, 35, 139, 142).

Complexity thus rears its ugly head, particularly when the analysis properly focuses on the unique effects of military resources (in contrast, for example, to total government spending). Linear generalizations become tangled thickets when we address the multiple factors lumped under defense, growth, and welfare. Few of us really believe that numbers bought and money spent on weapons are equivalent to defense or even military effort, resources, or accomplishments. Would we find it persuasive to assume that safe streets and law and justice sought and achieved go up with the size of budgets and coercive hardware of police and prison guards? Few would equate large quantities and low costs of consumer nondurable goods with growth or welfare. Further, the variety of national situations threatens to swamp small islands of generalization. Even a general recognition of such complexities warrants skepticism about views such as those which 'explain' strong Japanese growth performance compared to that of the United States by the reverse relationship in defense spending (Makin 1989).

Like many other slogans, that of 'guns' versus 'butter' obscures more than it illuminates if taken as a descriptive rather than symbolic statement. It is of course an extremely materialistic and thus inadequate conception of what defense, growth, and welfare are about. It lends itself to confusing the inherent finiteness of moneys available at any single point in time with the nature of relations between several specific uses of government funds. It overlooks longer-term dynamic possibilities of a 'rising tide' lifting more than one and perhaps even all boats. Most fundamentally, it opens us to capture by a narrowly economic frame of reference that treats policy as sets of microdecisions for cost-effective rationalization, be they annual budget increments or military procurement practices. We can even succumb to treating defense, growth, and welfare as primarily decomposable management problems rather than as ones of ongoing domestic and international macrorelationships of asset accumulation and power, autonomy and dependence, legitimacy and rectitude.

STARTING POINTS

This chapter uses the Japanese case to explore a line which emphasizes political factors and long-run national assets. It tries to provide heuristic stimulation rather than statistical tests of hypotheses. The points of departure emphasize that we distort if we primarily treat: (a) policies as tradeoffs rather than as satisficing; (b) resource stocks and flows as nationally endogenous rather than as having a major international component; and (c) policy processes as economistic rather than as matters of political culture.

First, governments of industrialized democracies are expected to provide defense *and* growth *and* welfare or have a quite persuasive reason for not doing so. Their challenge is to minimize contradiction between these areas of policy and satisfice across them. Better yet, enduring political elites seek positive-sum relations, not just limiting penalties of one on another. That is, they seek ways of providing defense that enhance growth and welfare, ways of providing growth that enhance defense and welfare, and ways of providing welfare that enhance defense and growth. The fundamental policy issues are then not about the particulars of tradeoffs between budget accounts. Those estimates at best provide background information. The real question is how to have it all, or at least the domestic perception of having the best possible deal on all three scoresheets. Success becomes easier with growing amounts of those assets most readily applied to any of the three categories of performance, the assets of wealth, generalized technologies, and skilled people. Accumulation of money, technology, and human capital makes it easier to have more of everything.

Second, relations with foreigners can crucially affect the net value of an action with respect to defense, growth, and welfare. What may look costly in narrowly domestic accounting terms can turn out to be a bargain after taking into account its impact on international transactions. The impacts are of numerous kinds, but all are realistic types. The cost and benefit of, for example, a national budget allocation to defense depends on what it induces foreigners to change or continue about defense provision and posing threats. The same defense allocation can affect growth if it matters for a foreign government's policies on trade, investment, and technology transfer. Particular accomplishments in growth might impose costs on defense by increasing foreign hostility and reducing provision of military security (or by raising the bill). Particular welfare policies might create analogous problems for defense, and growth too. An example might be inefficient dual-economy distribution systems that generate substantial employment but are closed to foreigners.

Several points thus need to be kept in mind. The policy issues facing governments in terms of interactions between defense, welfare, and growth very much include influence on foreigners with whom there are important exchanges. These are usually not avowed enemies. A policy move ostensibly in the domain of defense or growth or welfare can influence foreign behavior that impacts on one of the other domains. This applies to moves of omission and commission. Such complex action–reaction patterns can operate whether or not a government recognizes them. Some governing elites may be more synoptically strategic than others, and better informed about foreigners.

Third, defense–growth–welfare relations are matters of political economy and culture where the political is very important. The political elements that embody and shape those relations are in part inherited and in part purposefully created. At least three types of political elements have substantial, protracted importance – legacies, institutions, and conventions.

Legacies involve widely shared articles of faith among attentive and mass publics that mass media use to monitor politicians and officials. They work to make some policies dangerous to careers and others safe and perhaps rewarding. Most polities have legacies about military matters in relation to growth and welfare, and vice versa. Legacies are violated only by the most self-confident of elites or under the most exigent circumstances. A seemingly cavalier attitude toward legacies endangers elite legitimacy. Guardianship of legacies insures nontrivial credit for rectitude.

Institutions affect the extent to which various resource and bureaucratic turf claims for defense–growth–welfare priorities are advanced, adopted, and implemented. Some insitutional patterns lend themselves to large allocations for military purposes; others inherently impede those allocations. Some insure dominant voice for defense conceptions centered on military matters; others make that very unlikely. Some make it easier to secure at most marginally military public-sector investments under a defense mantle and others make it easier to do so under a growth or welfare mantle. Some facilitate using instruments of one of our domains to advance ends of another, and other institutions work against that.

Conventions are established, repeatedly invoked, and performed as decision rules and routines. They usually have no legal standing but are highly scripted (Kyogoku 1987). That is, policy participants find them familiar and predictable; policy audiences enjoy their details of performance without any need to dwell explicitly on the general rules and roles of the game. The repetitive cycles of budget processes with relatively clear winners and losers lend themselves to conventions.

All political systems have conventions about at least budgetary processes as these affect accounts thought to be central to defense, growth, and welfare. The conventions differ in their resource implications. When major international relationships have gone on for a long time, conventions and even seasonal calendars grow up around them. When distributions of political power are stable, as between contending political parties, conventions flourish for their joint performances. Conventions matter for defense–growth–welfare relations in two ways. First, they in effect determine how these relations are debated and conducted, and much of how the results will be treated. That is true for both domestic and international politics and the bargaining involved. Second, countries with an especially elaborate and well-rooted set of pertinent conventions are more likely to behave in rather sustained and stable ways. Surprises are minimized and the practicality of playing for the long run justified.

Sustained and predictable policies are not necessarily wise ones. Yet it is quite clear that erratic, volatile policies each aborted before any possibility of effective implementation damage defense, growth, and welfare.

RESULTS AND EFFORTS

The argument here only requires a reasonable prima facie case that Japan's achievements in defense, growth, and welfare warrant attention. That argument properly gives as much or more weight to outcomes and results as to measures of government effort. There is no need to assert the optimality or perfection of Japanese policy, or to treat comprehensively contents and measures of defense, growth, and welfare. A simpler approach using widely shared indicators will suffice. In the face of marked success, the burden of proof falls on those who recommend policies different from what was done, not the other way around.

Defense

Japan has incurred no military casualties in the past four decades, regained territory (Okinawa), and in large measure avoided entanglement with one or another side in regional conflicts. Commercial access has been global, with occasional self-imposed and short-lived limitations to avoid offending third parties. A militarily relevant industrial–technology base has been created with few rivals (Defense Science Board 1989; Department of Defense 1989; Agency for Industrial Science and Technology 1988). Moreover, a rate of real growth in military spending greater than that of NATO (North Atlantic Treaty Organization) has been sustained, lending itself to systematic defense planning more than the boom and bust pattern of the U.S. defense budget. The average annual military spending growth rate for the 1960s was 12 percent; that for the 1970s was 16 percent. The compound annual growth rate for 1980–5 was 4.2 percent compared to an average of 2.8 percent for the major NATO military powers (the United States, the United Kingdom, West Germany, France, Italy, and Canada) (Wong 1989, 95–6). Japan now has the world's third largest defense budget, and even before the strong yen it has consistently ranked among the top ten nations globally for many years. Defensive naval forces, emphasizing antisubmarine warfare, are large and sophisticated in terms of regional missions and programmed for further improvements. A similar judgment holds for defense against bomber attack. Licensed coproduction of a best available system (PATRIOT anti-ballistic missile defense missiles) is well under way. Also, much of the threat of ballistic missile attack was removed with the INF (Intermediate-range Nuclear Forces) treaty.

A major foreign power, the United States, has provided an asymmetrically favorable set of defense guarantees, tripwire deployments, and adopted a strategy that made the defense of Japan a U.S. policy priority.

All of this has been done without Japan relinquishing autonomy to a joint (that is, foreign controlled) command. The so-called U.S.–Japanese military 'joint system' has evolved with substantial U.S. dependencies on Japanese hosts. Militarily relevant advanced technology has been transferred by Washington without, until recently, even the formal arrangements for two-way transfer.[2]

All this is to say that Japan has achieved what are thought to be the positive results associated with defense success, and has avoided the negatives. The negatives avoided include triggering others to treat Japan as their principal enemy, and in most cases not even as a current secondary enemy. Soviet, Chinese, Indian, and Korean military buildups have not been taken in response to Japanese policy, nor is Japan viewed so far as the main threat that must be dealt with. Other than purely defensive capabilities in being, Japan's military capacities are ones of enormous potential should political circumstances change, and not ones of war-fighting readiness. We have a case of deterrence by the long shadow of national technology and manufacturing, and by foreign provision.

Defense results are then successful less in pacifist than in conservative, realpolitik terms – what a notable member of the ruling party called sometime ago 'neopacifism' (Kajima 1969). Military policy has been treated as a 'residual' (Calder 1988) except in relation to the United States (and, as we shall see, in domestic politics that bear on relations with the United States). The centrality of the U.S. relationship has been reflected in such diverse ways as direct U.S. intermediation on defense matters with important regional states (such as South Korea), and adapting policy toward the Soviet Union to the tenor of U.S.–Soviet relations.

In effect, Japan has achieved defense success, significant defensive capability, and a long-run military great-power option while at the same time making military effort economically unimportant in aggregate national terms. Costs to growth and welfare have been very small even if one makes the unwarranted assumptions that all defense spending detracts from growth and welfare, and that no defense spending produces offsetting gains in exchanges with foreigners.

Simple indicators include a sustained low allocation of GNP or GDP to the military compared to any member of NATO (by Japanese measures about 1 percent for almost 30 years, by NATO measures about 1.4 percent). Share of the population devoted to the regular military and to the reserve forces is similarly low in relative terms compared to that of the United States and the major European members of NATO. Thus, military personnel have remained low in absolute numbers as well, in spite of Japan's comparatively large population. Data for 1986 are indicative and appear in Table 5.1.

Defense procurements are much less than 1 percent of total industrial production by value – a situation that has persisted for at least three decades. The share of research and development (R & D) under defense auspices, even after the amount has doubled in recent years, was only 5

Table 5.1 Military personnel, 1986

Country	Regulars/ population	Regulars (10,000s)	Reserves/ population	Reserves (10,000s)
Japan	0.002	24.5	0.0004	4.6
U.S.	0.009	216.4	0.005	113.2
U.K.	0.006	32.0	0.006	31.7
FRG	0.008	47.7	0.012	76.2
France	0.008	44.5	0.007	39.1
Italy	0.007	38.8	0.013	76.9

Sources: Military personnel: Defense Agency 1989, 248.
Population (1987): Bank of Japan, 1989. 3–4.

percent of total government funding in FY1989, and less than 1 percent of total national spending on R & D.

Economic growth and strength

Real annual economic growth comparisons for 1984–8, that is, after Japan's high-growth period and including some strong-yen years, show Japan to have marginally exceeded the United States (4.5% to 4.2%) and strongly exceeded the United Kingdom (3.3%), West Germany (2.5%), France (2.2%), and Italy (2.9%) (Bank of Japan 1989, 12).

When we look at changes in performance shown in Table 5.2, Japan stands out for its increases in GNP in total and per capita terms, the growth in automobile production and the sustaining of a ship-construction industry, and the growth in exports and financial reserves. Japan also stands out for decline in household savings, and increases in the tax and social security burdens.

Other aspects of comparison show Japan standing out for dramatically higher rates of domestic capital formation and household savings in 1988 and a decade earlier. Compared to most of the European countries, but not to the United States, the Japanese at the end and the beginning of the period have become a much lower tax and social-security burden. Japan's performance surely is not a function of a relatively balanced government budget, or avoidance of deficit financing burdens on government expenditure. Costs of capital have been kept comparatively low (Bank of Japan 1989, 11–12).

Japan is notable in its investment in future economic performance as measured by investment in productive capacity and R & D. Between 1980 and 1988, the growth rate of real private investment in plants and equipment was 8.7 percent compared to that for OECD as a whole of 4 percent and 2.7 percent for the United States (JETRO 1989, 3). R & D expenditures as a percentage of national income had risen by 1987 to approximate those of the United States and West Germany at something over 3 percent (Science

Table 5.2 Performance changes, 1978–88 (%)

	Japan	U.S.	U.K.	FRG	France	Italy
GNP (US$)	245	127	170	118	128	203
GNP (per capita)	222	105	167	118	117	196
Private final consumption (% GNP)	–1	6	7	–3	–1	0
Government final consumption (% GNP)	–5	9	1	–2	29	9
Gross domestic fixed-capital formation (% GNP)	0	–14	2	–4	–12	7
Household savings rate (% disposable income)	–31	–27	–87	5	–14	–20
Tax burden rate (% national income)	42	–6	12	–7	15	31
Social-security burden rate (% national income)	36	19	12	5	24	–3
Steel production	4	–27	–6	–1	–17	–2
Motor vehicle production	44	–14	–4	7	–13	20
Merchant vessels launched	–5	–99	–89	–13	–85	134
Electrical capacity	9	21	7	25	68	21
Petroleum consumption (per capita)	–20	–19	–21	–14	–25	10
Exports (US$)	172	121	114	127	111	129
Exports (Per capita)	156	101	110	128	103	124
Imports (US$)	136	147	151	106	119	145
Imports (Per capita)	122	125	146	106	110	140
Gold and foreign exchange reserves	196	156	229	17	110	154

Source: Calculated from data in Bank of Japan 1989, 3–4.

and Technology Agency 1989, 23). Nondefense R & D expenditures as a percentage of GNP as of 1985 were 2.8 percent for Japan compared to 1.9 percent for the United States (National Science Foundation 1988, 51). Japanese R & D from 1965 to 1985 increased at a rate of about 150 percent of GNP growth while that of the United States was slightly less than GNP growth. Engineers as a share of the labor force had risen to narrowly exceed that in the United States by 1985 (National Science Foundation 1988, 54). Lest one view these R & D figures as the backdoor appearance of a profound handicap due to emphasis on defense, R & D spending in Japan as of 1985 was only half that in the United States, and the United States had twice as many scientists and engineers as Japan.

Nor has Japan's performance been based on extreme reliance on foreign trade. Indeed Table 5.3 shows much less dependency than for the European comparison countries, and a reduction in that dependency on both the export and import sides. Japan during the decade 1978–88 hardly stands out for export-led growth. What it does stand out for is, first, a reduction in export dependence much less than in import dependence and, second, a sharp growth in the total value of exports relative to

Table 5.3 Trade dependency and value relative to Japan

	Japan	U.S.	U.K.	FRG	France	Italy
Exports/GNP 1978 (%)	10.1	6.8	21.4	22.2	16.7	22.6
Exports/GNP 1988 (%)	9.3	6.6	17.8	26.8	16.9	15.6
Imports/GNP 1978 (%)	8.2	8.6	23.9	18.9	17.2	22.8
Imports/GNP 1988 (%)	6.6	9.5	23.2	20.7	18.0	16.8
Relative export value 1978	1.0	1.5	.7	1.5	.8	.6
Relative export value 1988	1.0	1.2	.5	1.2	.6	.5
Relative import value 1978	1.0	2.3	1.0	1.5	1.0	.7
Relative import value 1988	1.0	2.5	1.0	1.3	1.0	.7

Source: Bank of Japan 1989, 100–1.

many of the European countries and rather average performance on the import side.

Another way of looking at the strength versus dependency associated with trade involves concentration on particular partners. With respect to exports, dependence on the U.S. market has increased greatly from 1982 to 1987 to a remarkable degree of reliance on a single trade partner. European dependence on the EEC (European Economic Community) is nevertheless much more pronounced. An apparent decline in reliance on the oil exporters is largely a function of a not irreversible decline in oil prices. The intra-EEC dependence of the Europeans for imports is even more pronounced than for exports. The United States remains notably diversified with respect to export and import partners (Bank of Japan 1989, 15).

Welfare

In recent years, there are reasonable indications of strong welfare performance defined in terms of the financial resources provided to citizens and at least some important aspects of quality of life. Unemployment and consumer inflation rates have been much lower than in the United States or major West European countries (Keizai Koho Center 1989, 72, 74). National and local income-tax levels were much lower for the vast majority of the population in 1989 than in the United States or the United Kingdom, and the tax rate structure was far more progressive (Keizai Koho Center 1989, 84). The ratio of medical expenses to GNP in the early 1980s was much lower than in the United States, West Germany, France, or Italy, and life expectancy longer (Bank of Japan 1989, 166–7). Acknowledged excellence internationally in precollegiate education was supported by per capita public spending markedly higher in the early 1980s than for the United Kingdom,

West Germany, or Italy, but lower than for the United States. With youth cohorts almost universally completing high school, advancement rates to higher education in the late 1980s were 15 per cent less than the United States but much higher than those for West Germany, the United Kingdom, and France. Social-security benefits in relation to GNP were higher in the same period than in the United States or the United Kingdom (Bank of Japan 1989, 167). Public safety was much better than in most of the counterpart countries with respect to incidence of crime, and arrest rates were higher (Keizai Koho Center 1989, 92).

Less positively, but perhaps not more importantly, prices were notably higher for many consumption items than in the United States or the major West European countries (Bank of Japan 1989, 75). Housing was notably cramped compared to the United States, but not dramatically so compared to West Germany or France. Performance in terms of housing space was impressive when relative population densities are taken into account. In any event, the judgment of most Japanese was that they were middle class.

Interactions

There is then a reasonable case for Japan having found a way to do well in defense, economic growth and strength, and welfare. Doing so seems to have involved less making a particular choice within the set of tradeoffs familiar in U.S. discussions, and more finding ways of skirting them. Even in the scheme of familiar tradeoff choices, the aggregate consequences are not always those assumed in much of American thinking.

The opportunity costs of defense spending can be considered in static and dynamic terms. Static costs treat defense spending as equivalent to a concurrent reduction in some other activity, be it private consumption or another form of government spending.

Static cost data for 1981–8 for Japan, the United States, Germany, France, and the United Kingdom appear in Table 5.4. They deal with private final-consumption expenditure, and central-government spending on social security and education and culture (or the best approximation provided by different national budget systems). While allowance must be made for differences in national budget category definitions, they still indicate the relatively low static opportunity costs imposed on Japanese citizens and society.

Yet the data in Table 5.4 do not warrant a facile leap to the conclusion of relative deprivation because of those static cost differences. Data for the first half of the 1980s on a per capita basis show that social-security benefits in Japan were markedly lower than in West Germany and France, and slightly lower than in the United States. When all public-sector spending on education is considered (central and local government), Japan was markedly lower than the United States and certainly no higher than France (Bank of Japan 1989, 167).

Table 5.4 Static costs of military spending in the 1980s (average %)

Country	Defense GNP	Defense Private final consumption expenditure	Defense Social security	Defense Education and culture
Japan	1.0	1.7	29	33
U.S.	6.0	9.2	59	797
U.K.	4.9	7.4	46	247
FRG	2.8	4.9	58	389
France	3.8	6.3	168	91

Notes: Data for Japan, the United States, and West Germany are for 1981–8 and those for Britain and France are for 1980–7. The base in the social security column is just that for Japan and West Germany. It is 'health and income security' for the United States, 'health and personal social services' for Britain, and 'health and employment' for France. The base in the education and culture column is just that for Japan. It is 'education, training and social services' for the United States, 'education and science' for Britain, 'education, science and culture' for West Germany, and 'culture and education' for France.
Source: Calculated from Bank of Japan 1989, 29, 31, 86.

Dynamic costs estimate the reduction in future private income as a result of prior military spending's effect on private savings and through it on the capital stock. Galenson and Galenson (1986) have found dynamic costs for 1965–82 to be in the range of a tenth to a quarter of 1% of GNP. Their estimates for 1983–94 place these costs in about the same range with 1% of GNP spent on defense, and in the range of a quarter to a half of 1% of GNP were 2% of GNP to be spent on defense. These figures are notionally similar to Okita Saburo's rule of thumb that every 1% of GNP increase in Japanese defense spending would cost a third of 1% of GNP (Okita 1980, 115). Using different methods, Dekle (1989) estimates a relationship for the decade 1961–71 of about 0.14%. Wong (1989) estimates that the compound effect after 15 years of hypothetically higher defense spending for 1970–85 would have been a reduction of 0.9 to 1.3% for each additional percent of GNP spent on defense throughout that period. These are very modest dynamic costs, particularly for a country not troubled by a low propensity for private saving and investment in capital stock.

It is hard to argue that Japan would have been safer or wealthier or provided its citizens with a higher standard of welfare by spending more on defense. There is no compelling case for estimates that the United States would have extended more protection or tolerated a greater amount of Japanese trade surplus or incoming investment. There is little reason to believe that higher Japanese defense spending would have reduced that of the Americans or even the Europeans which were driven by other considerations. There are ample reasons to believe that higher defense spending would have exacerbated Japan's relations with other Asians with adverse security and economic implications, and if anything increased Soviet military measures in the region.

The far greater constraint on military manpower than on military budgets suggests that higher spending would have gone into hardware. (The likelihood of such a consequence is even greater as the age group useful for military service declines in a fast aging society with significant labor scarcity.) That hardware would have tended to cross over from defense into projection forces. The incentives to the private sector associated with much higher procurement budgets would not obviously have led to more efficient development of militarily relevant technologies than through 'spinforward' from debugged commercial applications and U.S. transfers. Nor would such budgets necessarily have led to a much larger defense production base, given 30–50% excess capacity in that achieved anyway.

The benefits of spending less would have been modest in aggregate terms and possibly far outweighed by the different behaviors they might have triggered in terms of less U.S. security provision and economic tolerance. For perspective, in 1988 the trade surplus in Japan's favor amounted to $2.5 for every dollar equivalent spent on the Japanese military, even without deducting military imports from the United States. More speculatively, suppose an unarmed Japan were to then decide that it had to regain military capability associated with a withdrawal of the U.S. Forces (Japan) by an equivalent level of effort (2.2% of GNP) to that of the lowest among the major military members of NATO (Italy). In static 1988 terms this would require spending an additional 1.2% of GNP while saving the subvention for the costs of U.S. Forces (Japan) (on the subvention, see Defense Agency 1988, 184–5). That is, an increase in spending compared to savings of more than 1000 to 1.

EXPLANATIONS

The full explanation of Japan's success in growth and welfare goes well beyond the bounds of this chapter.[3] Since the Pacific War, ruling elites in politics, bureaucracy, and business have persistently refused to opt for unilateral defense effort at the expense of growth and welfare. Yet they have not hesitated to turn to military production when other alternatives for economic vitality were lacking (as in the early 1950s). They also have bent reactively to popular demands on welfare, including the demands of grossly inefficient economic sectors. The motivation to do so may stem from very high rates of incumbent turnover in national elections and very thin individual margins of electoral victory, compared to the United States and the major European democracies (Calder 1988, 66–9). Stable party rule has been combined with individual politicians running scared. Achieving extraordinary stocks of financial, human, and technological resources was probably not especially due to military restraint, but once achieved has multiplied military options as well as ones for growth and welfare.

Both external and internal conditions help to explain Japan's policy performance. Externally, this country surely has been blessed for four decades in its relationship with its primary external ally, the United States, and in some ways with its primary external enemy, the Soviet Union. A set of U.S. proclivities has enabled security to be gained at low cost to defense, growth, and welfare. Those proclivities have arguably turned the net consequences of military spending into growth gains, and, in the past, provided tolerance for social arrangements conducive to some forms of welfare. The Soviet Union 'cooperated' by motivating the United States to extend defense provision and tolerate asymmetric economic relationships. It also cooperated through rigid diplomacy and military bluster. Those contributed to Tokyo's patterns of behavior that would induce Washington to indulge its proclivities.

The importance of these external factors must not be underestimated, but neither must the fact that the opportunities they provided were recognized and used. Substantial credit must go to several generations of Japanese elites intent on being well-informed about the United States, far more experienced in dealing with Americans than the reverse, and networked across indigenous sectors and organizations for dealings with the external world.

The internal factors that enabled Japan to take advantage of its opportunities lie substantially in political legacies, institutions, and conventions. Only some essential points can be noted here (for a lengthier treatment, see Bobrow, in press).

Japan emerged from defeat with four pertinent legacies of substantial continuing importance. These were to never again: (a) rely primarily on the military instrument to achieve major domestic and external goals; (b) have the homeland experience mass-destruction attack; (c) allow the military autonomy let alone dominance over civilian elites; and (d) be in a radically inferior position with respect to technology and high-quality control, mass production of advanced products.

The first two legacies led to a set of self-imposed restraints or conventions from which only minor and implicit deviations would be politically tolerated. Article 9 of the Constitution limited the war option and military capabilities. These restraints also include prohibition against the possession, manufacture, or transit of nuclear weapons, the ban on military exports, and limits on military budgets and uses of national technologies. The same legacies have sustained the security relationship with the United States. The third legacy led to the profound institutional subordination of military institutions, including their civilian element. The final legacy led to techno-economic drives that have yet to reach their culmination. All of these convictions have remarkably and stably dominated public opinion (Bobrow 1989) with the consequence of very limited domestic political incentives to challenge them. They have coexisted with profound suspicion and grievance with regard to the Soviet Union, and thus a reason to tolerate limited violation of the previously mentioned conventions.

Institutionally, attention needs at a minimum to go to parties and politicians, ministries and bureaucrats, and big business – and their connections. The nature and protracted rule (35-plus years) of the Liberal Democratic Party (LDP) make its internal processes far more important than those of the Diet for growth and welfare and, within the limits of the legacies and conventions, for defense. Those processes provide for significantly synoptic allocation of governmental resources at the aggregate level. Good relations with the LDP are essential to ministerial and bureaucratic career success. Big business is the declared partner and banker of the LDP. Substantial numbers of LDP Diet members are ex-bureaucrats. Substantial numbers of LDP Diet members have long experience with defense, growth, and welfare ministries and policies, and pursue them through groupings known as 'tribes.' The LDP is the architect of the prevailing defense–growth–welfare mix. It has long defined itself on the 'platform' of the prevailing relationship with the United States in general and its military aspects in particular. The party works by factions and seniority. The highest positions in the party and the government require many terms of parliamentary experience. Because defense resources are relatively 'small beer,' they are not a primary concern of most politicians and especially of ones with factions to shepherd.

The major opposition party, the Japan Socialist Party (JSP), has defined itself as a party of opposition, in particular to the LDP, having done so much in the military area and in security relations with the United States. The JSP and much of the media then defend the legacies and exact costs for apparent attempts to depart from their implementing conventions. As of the 1980s, the opposition is not against the status quo as a practical matter, only against a more customary military posture for an economic great power. This *de facto* consensus includes the smaller opposition parties as well (except for the Communists). The unidimensional issue character of the JSP in effect constrains one sector of defense policy without posing a threat on the far more important matters of taking control of national politics and policy.

The smooth operations of the political system then benefit from relative inattention to defense. It opens cleavages rather than providing a unifying theme. The incentives to concentrate on other matters are multiplied by a multimember-district Diet electoral system without proportional representation. That system places a premium not on competition between parties on national issues but on competition between individual candidates on what they can do for their district – that is, on economic growth and welfare benefits made manifest locally. Even when the ruling party invokes the rhetoric of national issues and the U.S. relationship, as it did in the 1990 Lower House elections, it does not do so by advocating an upward shift in defense priorities. It rather advocates preserving the larger set of domestic and external lines of policy that have provided adequate defense in the context of surges in growth and welfare. At the same time, the LDP has been and remains the best available option for military organizations, their industrial associates, and U.S. defense-oriented policy-makers.

Politics are about the delivery of tangibles to constituents and organized interests whose political support works on an 'investment' basis (Ike 1978). Defense tangibles are few. Economic efficiency is not then what politics are about but rather the production of benefits or compensation for losses. Nor does the political opposition bother very much about the notable inefficiencies of a defense system marked by very high per-unit costs for hardware, noncompetitive procurement, lack of explicit strategy, and failure to meet planning timetables for force structure. Microefficiency is not the way in which defense–growth–welfare relationships are managed.

Similarities between defense and military institutions and those of other major Western powers are only 'label' deep. The ministry analogue for Japan, the Defense Agency (JDA), is a thoroughly colonized bureaucracy with key posts held by career bureaucrats from ministries far more powerful in their own right and more important for the LDP, big business, and now the United States. The key budget position belongs to the Ministry of Finance; that for international affairs, to the Ministry of Foreign Affairs; that for procurement, to MITI (Ministry of International Trade and Industry). The 'visiting' officials have abundant reason to push policies that conform to those of their home ministries. The JDA fares well as it is helpful to those centers of ministerial power, and is sure to lose if it makes problems for them. That is, the JDA accommodates itself to macroeconomic policy, foreign policy, and industrial policy. Further, it does not even play in issue arenas that often involve defense ministries elsewhere such as arms control, space development, and controls on technology transfer. It is hardly surprising then that defense budget patterns are well predicted by those of macroeconomic policy and the needs of relations with the United States (Bobrow and Hill 1991).

Within the military itself, service rivalry is extraordinarily bitter, with no decisive military arbiter. The U.S. services and industrial contractors are invoked as major lobbyists for the Japanese services be it in Tokyo directly, or indirectly via Washington. The military is plagued by low status relative to civilian elites in government and business, almost universally absent from high-level staffs elsewhere in government, and has been taught that speaking out on defense issues is a quick ticket to retirement. Postservice opportunities are relatively limited with obvious recruitment implications. In short, the military is a fringe rather than a central national institution.

The big-business relationship with defense has several key aspects. First, military business is minor compared to civilian markets. That is true for sales and for R & D. Dependence on defense contracts even for the major defense firms never exceeds 20% of sales and mostly is much less. Second, defense business risks substantial controversy. Third, defense business is stable, profitable, and increasing. Procurement budgets, primarily spent domestically, increased by 50% in the 1984–8 period. Like much of

Japanese government procurement, that for military matters operates through a family system of major firms and even the appearance of competition on weapons or facilities contracts is usually missing or illusory. Fourth, for at least one industry, aircraft, JDA funds are crucial. In sum, the money is good and more is welcome. JDA funds are not, however, worth much in the way of political visibility or diversion from commercial avenues of emphasis.

In sum, legacies, their implementing conventions, and institutional patterns and incentives converge to constrain military emphases. All of these mutually bolstering constraints have demonstrated great endurance. Fittingly for the topic of this chapter, their workings in relation to the economy and thus to growth and welfare are exemplified by the 1% rule adopted in the mid-1970s. The rule, that military spending shall not exceed 1% of GNP, was observed in principle until FY1986. After minor departures since then, it has been reinstated in the budget approved by the Cabinet in December 1989. This rule, even with cheating, makes military spending the tail and not the dog for the allocation of current resources and the shaping of the future national political economy. It effectively bounds the bargaining space with those at home and abroad who want more for defense. Yet in a large and vigorous economy it insures a large and growing defense budget.

LESSONS LEARNED

The Japanese case demonstrates that it is possible to do well in defense while doing well in growth and welfare. The latter performances are not primarily explained by low military spending per se. They also are not explained by some U.S. conservative lore about austere pay-as-you-go financing, or some cost-effectiveness concerns with budgetary efficiency. Nor is defense performance adequately explained by the fact that in absolute terms Japan has long had a large defense budget in international perspective.

The lessons for us are to look beyond those possibilities to the proclivities of foreign powers, to mass public and elite articles of faith, to institutional distributions of power, and to the ongoing presence of a tightly knit, well-informed, and experienced elite. In some circumstances, an effective way to collective national-interest outcomes centers on persistent and opportunistic pursuit and reliable satisfaction of special interests in the public and private sectors. That 'low road' can be far more nationally rewarding than a more romantic, explicit, and inflexible pursuit of grand visions and global objectives.

NOTES

1 The author wishes to acknowledge research support from The Japan–United States Educational Commission, and conducive hosting by the Graduate

School of Policy Science, Saitama University. Views expressed are solely the responsibility of the author.

2 Technology transfer for ostensibly solely military purposes from the United States has a long history. It includes actions following on Article 6 of the Mutual Defense Assistance Agreement of 1954, an agreement to facilitate interchange of patent rights and technical information for purposes of defense of March, 1956; a Data Exchange Arrangements umbrella agreement between the JDA and the Department of Defense in 1962; the creation of a Science and Technology Forum in 1980; and the SDI research and technical secrecy arrangements of 1987–8 (Defense Agency 1988, 331; Phillips 1986). Under the 'three principles on arms exports,' transfer policy was avowedly one way from 1967 until a 1983 exchange of notes enabling Japanese transfer to the United States (Defense Agency 1988, 180, 325–8). Little has flowed out of Japan since then.

3 The roots of strong economic growth arguably well predate the postwar period (Okita 1980, 113–14).

REFERENCES

Agency for Industrial Science and Technology, Ministry of International Trade and Industry. 1988. *Trends and Future Tasks in Industrial Technology: Developing Innovative Technologies to Support the 21st Century* [Summary of the White Paper on Industrial Technology]. Tokyo: mimeograph.

Bank of Japan, Research and Statistics Department. 1989. *Comparative Economic and Financial Statistics Japan and Other Major Countries*. Tokyo: Bank of Japan.

Bobrow, Davis B. 1989. Japan in the world: opinion from defeat to success. *Journal of Conflict Resolution* 33: 571–604.

Bobrow, Davis B. In press. Military Policy. In R. Kent Weaver and Bert A. Rockman (eds), *Do Institutions Matter? Policymaking in Presidential and Parliamentary Systems*. Washington, D.C.: Brookings Institution.

Bobrow, Davis B. and Stephen R. Hill. 1991. Non-Military Determinants of Military Budgets: The Japanese Case. *International Studies Quarterly* 35: 39–62.

Browne, Lynn E. 1988. Defense spending and high technology development: national and state issues. *New England Economic Review* (Sept./Oct.): 3–22.

Calder, Kent. 1988. *Crisis and Compensation: Public Policy and Political Stability in Japan, 1949–1986*. Princeton, N.J.: Princeton University Press.

Defense Agency. 1988. *Defense of Japan 1988*. Tokyo: Japan Times.

Defense Agency. 1989. *Defense of Japan 1989*. Tokyo: Japan Times.

Defense Science Board. 1989. *Defense Industrial Cooperation with Pacific Rim Nations*. Washington, D.C.: Office of the Under Secretary of Defense for Acquisition.

Dekle, Robert. 1989. The relationship between defense spending and economic performance. In John H. Makin and Donald C. Hellmann (eds.), *Sharing World Leadership? A New Era for America and Japan*, pp. 127–49. Washington, D.C.: American Enterprise Institute.

Department of Defense. 1989. *DoD Critical Technologies Plan*. Submitted to the Armed Services Committees (5 May edn.).

Galenson, Walter and David W. Galenson. 1986. Japan and South Korea. In David B. H. Denoon (ed.), *Constraints on Strategy: The Economics of Western Security*, pp. 152–94. McLean, Virg.: Pergamon-Brassey's International Defense Publishers.

Ike, Nobutaka. 1978. *A Theory of Japanese Democracy*. Boulder, Colo.: Westview.
JETRO [Japan External Trade Organization]. 1989. *White Paper on International Trade Japan 1989*. Tokyo: JETRO.
Kajima, Morinosuke. 1969. *Japan's Foreign Policy*. Tokyo: Charles E. Tuttle.
Keizai Koho Center [Japan Institute for Social and Economic Affairs]. 1989. *Japan 1990: An International Comparison*. Tokyo: Keizai Koho Center.
Kyogoku, Jun-ichi. 1987. *The Political Dynamics of Japan*, trans. by Nobutaka Ike. Tokyo: University of Tokyo Press.
Makin, John H. 1989. American economic and military leadership in the postwar period. In John H. Makin and Donald C. Hellmann (eds.), *Sharing World Leadership? A New Era for America and Japan*, pp. 3–40. Washington, D.C.: American Enterprise Institute.
National Science Foundation. 1988. *The Science and Technology Resources of Japan: A Comparison with the United States*. Washington, D.C., NSF 88–318.
Okita, Saburo. 1980. *The Developing Economies and Japan: Lessons in Growth*. Tokyo: University of Tokyo Press.
Phillips, James R. 1986. A history of hi-tech exchange: Japan and the USA. mimeograph.
Science and Technology Agency. 1989. *Indicators of Science and Technology*. Tokyo: Science and Technology Agency.
Wong, Kar-yiu. 1989. National defense and foreign trade: the sweet and sour relationship between the United States and Japan. In John H. Makin and Donald C. Hellmann (eds.), *Sharing World Leadership? A New Era for America and Japan*, pp. 81–126. Washington, D.C.: American Enterprise Institute.

6 Models of military expenditure[1]

Ron P. Smith
Birkbeck College, University of London

SUMMARY

A brief review of the extensive empirical literature devoted to explaining levels of military expenditure indicates a wide variety of unreconciled results. However, comparing the alternative models is not straightforward. This paper uses British postwar military expenditures to illustrate some of the methodological issues involved in model comparison, evaluation and selection. Starting from two published models for the UK, a systematic specification search leads to a new model, which dominates alternative specifications, passes a wide range of misspecification tests, and also fits well to French data.

1 INTRODUCTION

At first glance, defence budgets may not appear the most amenable subject for statistical analysis. Nonetheless, there is now a substantial empirical literature devoted to explaining them. These studies, which are briefly reviewed in Section 2, generally use orthodox regression methods to estimate the parameters of an explicit theoretical model, specified on *a priori* grounds, with military expenditure as the dependent variable. Starting from an explicit theoretical model insures consistency, allows interpretation of the parameters, identifies crucial assumptions, and enables the results to be integrated into a wider body of knowledge. However, there is the familiar problem that the vagaries of nonexperimental data often make it quite easy to obtain empirical results in accord with one's prior theory. As a result, the literature is characterized by a proliferation of models giving conflicting results, each of which is interpreted as justifying the position of the proponent.[2] Since the studies tend not to report either systematic specification searches or misspecification tests, it can be difficult to know exactly why the results differ between studies or the relative statistical performance of the alternative specifications.

This paper will investigate an alternative approach, which has been labeled 'testimation' by Trivedi (1984). Starting from a looser initial specification, competing models are given equal status, and a systematic search is conducted to identify a model which adequately represents the data, in that it passes a wide variety of misspecification tests, and dominates alternatives. This approach, which will be illustrated by an application to UK and French military expenditure, is designed to encourage the data 'to speak for themselves' rather than constrain them within a particular theoretical straitjacket. However, it suffers from a number of problems. For instance, the chosen model may not have an obvious theoretical interpretation. The consistency of the estimated model with extraneous theoretical and institutional information must then be balanced against statistical adequacy and practical relevance in any evaluation. Pesaran and Smith (1985) discuss the interaction of these three criteria. In addition, since the model has been constructed to pass the misspecification tests they merely become design criteria, rather than tests in the strict Neyman–Pearson sense. Proper evaluation of the model requires 'independent' data. Typically these are provided by postsample observations, which can be used *ex post* to evaluate forecasting performance. Postsample observations are not available to assess the model developed here, since one of the design criteria is that it shows no structural breaks over all available data. Instead, the chosen specification will be evaluated by fitting it to French data; on the grounds that an effective model should have wide applicability and be transferable to countries in a similar position.

Section 2 reviews the empirical literature on the explanation of military expenditure, Section 3 reviews the specification issues. The characteristics of the data are an important guide to model development and Section 4 explains the measures used. Section 5 reports the results of the specification search for a UK equation, Section 6 evaluates the model on French data, and Section 7 considers the more general evaluation of both models. Section 8 contains some conclusions.

2 MODELS OF MILITARY EXPENDITURE

Regression models with military expenditure as the dependent variable have been estimated on a variety of different types of data: mainly longitudinal time-series for the industrial world, and cross-country cross-sections for the less developed world, e.g., Maizels and Nissanke (1986); though some studies have used panels pooling time-series and cross-sections, e.g. Chan *et al.* (1982). These studies use a variety of theories about the character of the decision-making process and the relevance of various military, political, and economic influences, operating at domestic, regional, or global levels. These theories are discussed further in Smith (1977).

External influences arise from armed conflicts, arms races, and alliances. Armed conflicts have an obvious effect on military expenditures, as patterns during large wars show. Thus proxy variables for conflict are often included in models. For instance, Kamlet and Mowery (1987) use military war deaths in an explanation of US defence spending, together with a measure of Soviet threat based on signals of noncombat conflict. For cases where there is no direct conflict the standard approach, following Richardson (1960), explains the time-series pattern of military expenditure in terms of arms races: action–reaction accumulations of weapons between antagonists. There is a vast literature on such interactions, in which arms may be measured by physical stocks, e.g., nuclear weapons as in McGuire (1977, 1981) and Desai and Blake (1981); or by military expenditures. Despite their popularity, pure arms-race models of military expenditure have had little empirical success (Schmidt 1987); though Ostrom and Marra (1986) attribute their failure to explain feedback between the superpowers to deficiencies in the Soviet data used. Nonetheless, the military expenditures of potential enemies are an obvious candidate for inclusion in any explanation.

The public good features of military expenditures within alliances have been extensively studied since the classic work of Olson and Zeckhauser (1966). Recent work by Murdoch and Sandler (M&S) provides time-series estimates of the spillover from the military expenditure of allies for NATO countries (M&S 1984) and for various neutrals (M&S 1986). Allies can also provide direct military aid, an important factor in models for Israel, e.g., McGuire (1982, 1987) and Ward and Mintz (1987).

Internal influences include economic, bureaucratic, and political factors. The most direct economic factors are income and prices. National income, within fairly broad limits, constrains what a country can afford, while the relative cost of military provision will influence budgetary choices. Indirect economic factors include the need to stabilize demand, control public expenditure, or subsidize industrial R & D. Bureaucratic explanations emphasize 'incrementalism,' bargaining over the budget starting from the *status quo*, and this idea has been used in models of military expenditure (e.g., Rattinger 1975). Political influences will range from lobbying by the military–industrial complex and other interest groups to the ideological proclivities of the government. One political influence which has attracted attention is the presence of military government, though Zuk and Thompson (1982), in reviewing the empirical results, conclude that, *ceteris paribus*, military governments do not spend more on defence than civilian ones.

In the US the data allow an examination of the complex political process involved in the determination of the defence budget, with distinct roles for President, Armed Services, and Congress. A range of different treatments of the process exist in the literature: Cusack and Ward (1981), Griffin *et al*. (1982), Ostrom (1978). They differ in the way they model the reactive linkages between the different branches of the state, and in the relative weight they attach to geo-strategic factors, domestic lobbying, and considerations of economic management. The role of economic factors is not straightforward. On the one hand, the argument that higher military expenditure increases output has been advanced not only by Keynesians but also by New Classical writers such as Barro (1981). On the other hand, there is the argument that US governments have used variations in military expenditure to manage aggregate demand, Baran and Sweezy (1966). Together these arguments imply mutual feedback: increases in military expenditure raise aggregate demand and deficiencies in aggregate demand prompt countercyclical increases in military expenditure.

Questions about the direction of feedback have been investigated by a number of 'atheoretical' studies using the concept of Granger (1969) 'noncausality.' Chan *et al.* (1982) used the pooled time-series cross-section data of Benoit (1973) for 22 developing countries over the period 1950–67, to analyze the interaction of military expenditure, investment, and GNP. Using the first differences of the logarithms they found military expenditure to be Granger noncausal for investment and GNP, while investment and GNP were Granger noncausal for military expenditure. Georgiou and Smith (1983) also found no Granger causality in either direction between military expenditure and growth, unemployment or profits in the UK and West Germany; but found unemployment and profits to be Granger causal for military expenditure in the US. This might be consistent with the hypothesis that military expenditure has been used for countercyclical policy in the US; though there is also the possibility that, if military expenditure is adjusted optimally to keep output at given target levels in the face of exogenous shocks, there may be no observed correlation. Granger (1988) discusses the issues involved in this case.

Much of the literature treats the determination of military expenditure within a single-equation framework, but there are exceptions. It is determined jointly: with other government expenditures by Dunne *et al.* (1984), Kamlet and Mowery (1987), and Tait and Heller (1987); with other military-related variables by McGuire (1982, 1987) and Ward and Mintz (1987); and with other countries' military expenditures by M&S (1984).

Rather than starting from the bureaucratic or political process, economists have tended to use an extreme 'rational actor' model of the state, in which military expenditure, M, and nondefence expenditure, C, are chosen to maximize a welfare function, which depends on an unobserved variable 'security' or defence output, S, as well as nondefence expenditure, C. Welfare is given by:

$$W = W(S, C, ZP), \tag{6.1}$$

where ZP are exogenous internal political influences which parameterize shifts in the objective function. This is maximized subject to a budget constraint:

$$Y = PM \cdot M + PC \cdot C, \tag{6.2}$$

where Y is aggregate real income and PM and PC are the prices of M and C relative to the income deflator. The other constraint is a 'production function' determining security as a function of the military expenditures of the state concerned, and other security variables, ZS, such as the expenditures of allies and opponents:

$$S = S\,(M, ZS). \tag{6.3}$$

Maximization of (6.1) subject to (6.2) and (6.3) then gives a 'demand function.'

$$M = D\,(Y, PM, PC, ZP, ZS). \tag{6.4}$$

Economic theory would suggest that this function would be homogeneous of degree zero in prices. In addition, the lack of association, across countries and over long periods of time, between the share of military expenditure in income and per capita income suggests the hypothesis of homotheticity.

This optimizing approach has been used to explain military expenditures by: McGuire (1982, 1987) who assumes a Stone–Geary form of objective function; Smith (1980, 1987) who assumes a constant elasticity of substitution form; Dunne *et al.* (1984) who use a Deaton–Muellbauer (1980) functional form and write the budget constraint in terms of total government expenditure rather than national income; and Murdoch and Sandler (1984), who use a general functional form in their theoretical work and a linear demand function for estimation for groups of allies.

3 SPECIFICATION

To illustrate the issues in specification, two models explaining UK military expenditures will be examined in a little more detail. Both are derived from theories of optimizing behaviour by the state. The first model is that given in Smith (1980), 'The demand for military expenditure,' hereafter DME. This paper estimated the equation implied by the first-order condition from the maximization in the previous section:

$$M = F\,(C, PM, PC, ZP, ZS) \tag{6.5}$$

using a log-linear specification. UK military expenditure (deflated by a military price index) is explained by civilian output, the relative price of military to civilian output, and the lagged shares of military expenditure in output in the US and the USSR; together with a lagged dependent variable to represent bureaucratic inertia and decision or implementation lags. There is also a second-order autoregressive process in the residuals to represent the overshooting associated with the UK's repeated defence reviews, in which overambitious plans for expenditures and commitments were cut in response to economic pressures. The equation was estimated for the period 1951–75 by instrumental variables to take account of the possible endogeneity of civilian output.

M&S (1984) use a linear equation explaining UK military expenditure, deflated by a general price index and expressed in dollars, by UK income, and the total military expenditure of the other NATO countries in the previous year. The coefficient of NATO military expenditures is shifted by a dummy variable equal to 0 for 1961–73 and 1 for 1974–9. The dummy is intended to capture the delayed effect of the 1967 switch in NATO strategy from massive retaliation to flexible response. The equation is estimated by generalized least-squares as part of a system of similar equations for the other NATO countries.

Both models obtain coefficient estimates which suggest that the UK 'free rides,' i.e., there is a negative effect of US (NATO) expenditures on UK military expenditures; though the spillover from NATO is reduced after 1973 in the M&S (1984) model. Neither the M&S (1984) nor DME models take much account of politics, partly because many of the political effects emphasized in the US are not equivalent in the UK. For instance, there is very little difference between the budget proposed by the Administration and that enacted by the Legislature, a distinction Kamlet and Mowery (1987) use.[3]

In the exercise below, these two models are used to suggest equations which are evaluated empirically. A full evaluation of these models would require taking account of a range of other considerations such as their more general purpose and their theoretical underpinnings. For instance, the M&S (1984) *a priori* reasoning might not apply to the longer period considered here, and their objective – to model an entire alliance – imposes constraints on data and specification which do not apply to a single-country study.

Despite being closely related, these two models span a large range of possible specifications. Little guidance in choosing between the specifications is provided either by the economic theory, which is derived from optimizing behaviour in both cases, or econometric practice, which is a matter of heated dispute, McAleer *et al.* (1985) and Leamer (1985). The equations differ in functional form, measurement of the dependent variable (deflation by a general or military price index), estimation method, explanatory variables, time period, treatment of possible structural change, dynamics, and stochastic structure. The combination of the difference in measurement and functional form of the dependent variable inhibits the construction of a general model which nests both alternatives, though non-nested tests are available (MacKinnon *et al.* 1983). A decision on any specific issue (e.g., dynamics) can only be made conditional on a particular treatment of the other issues (functional form, etc.). Thus the issues cannot be separated. There are a range of possible design criteria that could be used to select models. These include fit and parsimony, which might be combined in some loss-function-based model selection criterion; theoretical appeal; or passing a battery of diagnostic tests against a range of possible forms of misspecification. Where multiple criteria are used, it is not obvious how they should be traded off. When formal tests are used, it is not obvious what the appropriate size or significance level should be; or how allowance should be made for the joint testing of multiple nonindependent hypotheses. When tests are used to select between models the resulting 'pre-test estimators' are, in general, biased and inadmissible under squared error loss (e.g., Judge *et al.* 1985, 889). Little is known about the power and small sample performance of some of the diagnostic tests. Given that it is not practical to conduct an exhaustive search over the entire space of possible specifications, the order in which the sequence of alternative forms is investigated, and the direction of search, may well influence the choice of preferred specification. The direction of search may be general to specific: simplifying an initial model which includes a large number of potential influences, though there are difficulties in determining the optimal degree of generality for a given sample size. Or it may be specific to general: starting with a simple model and adding factors. Either basis for search may reveal alternative, very different, specifications which perform equally well according to the design criteria.

These factors mean that any search procedure is, to some extent, *ad hoc* and arbitrary. However, the model development procedure adopted here is to start with two competing functional forms and very general specifications, which allow for economic, political, and strategic influences. Then each general model is restricted until an acceptable parsimonious version which passes a range of misspecification tests is found. The four basic tests used are a Lagrange multiplier test for serial correlation, denoted $F_{SC}(1,.)$; a RESET test for functional form, $F_{FF}(1,.)$; a skewness-kurtosis test for normality, $\chi^2_N(2)$; and a RESET test for heteroskedasticity, $F_H(1,.)$. Estimation was done using the Data-FIT program and details of these tests can be found in Pesaran and Pesaran (1989). Finally, a preferred functional form is chosen and the resulting model is subjected to a range of other tests. All the tests will be applied at the 5 percent significance level.

4 THE DATA

In developing a model the characteristics of the data are important, and since the military series used here may be unfamiliar, their characteristics will be discussed at some length.

The main variables used in the specification search are listed below. Logarithms will be denoted by lower case letters, current price values by an asterisk.

Y_t^*	income, gross domestic product (GDP) at current market prices
Y_t	real GDP
$PY_t = Y_t^*/Y_t$	the GDP deflator
M_t^*	UK military expenditure at current prices
M_t	real military expenditure (deflated by its own price index)
$PM_t = M^*{}_t/M_t$	the military expenditure deflator
$SM_t = M_t^*/Y_t^*$	the share of UK military expenditure in income
$C_t = Y_t - M_t,$	real civilian expenditure
PC_t	the civilian expenditure deflator
MA_t	US real military expenditure
SA_t	the share of US military expenditure in income
SR_t	the share of USSR military expenditure in income
$SPILL_t$	non-UK NATO spending
$DSPILL_t = SPILL_t$	times a dummy variable = 1 after 1973.

The variables SA_t and SR_t were used as explanatory variables in DME, while $SPILL_t$ and $DSPILL_t$ were used by M&S (1984). There are familiar difficulties with measuring military expenditures. The US and UK series are on a national accounts basis (*Economic Report of the President*, National Defense series, and *National Income and Expenditure*, Current Expenditure on Goods and Services for Military Defence). The equation in DME used military expenditure deflated by its own price index and found the relative price effect very significant; M&S (1984) did not include relative prices in their equation and used military expenditure deflated by a general price index. According to the UK figures, 'military inflation' has averaged almost 2 percent per annum more than general inflation, thus the question as to how prices should be treated is important. In addition, this 'relative price effect' has featured in bureaucratic bargaining, with the Treasury opposing Ministry of Defence demands to be compensated for differential inflation.

Relatively few countries publish a price index for military expenditure, since there are substantial methodological difficulties in its calculation, particularly with respect to the treatment of productivity growth by government employees and quality change in equipment. The US has recently begun calculating a military price index that tried to allow for these problems, and this series indicates that military prices move at roughly the same rate or slightly slower than general inflation. For instance between 1982 and 1986 the US GNP deflator grew by 14.1 percent, while that for national defence grew by only 10.8 percent. Since the US and UK both face similar military technologies, and have volunteer forces, one might expect differential inflation to be similar, and it is possible that the UK pattern of higher military than civil inflation may be an artifact of the British construction procedures. When data on prices are unavailable or suspect, it is generally preferable to make the shares of expenditure, rather than the quantities consumed, the dependent variable in demand functions. Then, if prices are excluded from the equation, a price elasticity of unity rather than zero is imposed, which in economic terms is *a priori* more plausible.

UK defence policy has been geared towards a 'threat' from the Soviet Union, thus it would seem appropriate to include some measure of Soviet military expenditure. However, we have very little idea of the level or year-to-year variation in either Soviet military expenditures or output. A careful discussion of the measurement problems can be found in Ostrom and Marra (1986). In these circumstances we have to trade off the disadvantages of omitting the variable or including a very poor proxy for it. On balance, it seemed better to include the proxy, if it was significant and of the correct sign.

There is no single long series available, and a figure for Soviet military expenditure as a share of GDP was spliced together from four sources. *R1* is the Stockholm International Peace Research Institute (SIPRI) estimate of the share of military expenditure in net material product, taken from *SIPRI Yearbooks* 1974 to 1977, giving data for 1952–75; the figures for 1950 and 1951 were set at 10 percent. The 1979 *SIPRI Yearbook* gives estimates of military expenditure as a percentage of GNP, *R2*, for 1958 to 1977. Subsequently, SIPRI stopped publishing estimates. However, the US *Statistical Abstract* published a third estimate of Soviet military expenditure as a percentage of GNP, *R3*, for the years 1970–85. U.S. Arms Control and Disarmament Agency (1988) provides a fourth estimate, *R4*, for 1974–85. Both *R3* and *R4* are based on CIA (Central Intelligence Agency) calculations.

For 1975 four estimates are available. The values are *R1* = 4.8 percent, *R2* = 8.6 percent, *R3* = 14.1 percent and *R4* = 13.7 percent. The shifts in level largely reflect changes in CIA perceptions. In the mid-1970s the estimate of the share of Soviet output devoted to defense was doubled, and in the mid-1980s revised downwards somewhat. Not only do the three series differ greatly in level, but also in variance. The variances of *R3* and *R4*, the US estimates, are very small; that of *R1*, the SIPRI NMP series very large; and *R2*, the SIPRI GNP series, somewhere in between. To create a longer run of data for the Soviet share the overlapping data were used to run regressions between the different series. The measure *SR* is then given either by *R4*, when available, or the value predicted for it by the series available for that year. The figures for 1986 and 1987 were set to their 1985 values, 12.5 percent. This measure is a very crude proxy, either for what the Soviets really spent, which may be unknown even to the Soviets, and, more importantly, for what UK decision-makers at the time thought the Soviets spent, which influenced UK decisions.

Whereas measuring Soviet totals is complicated by secrecy, measuring NATO totals is complicated by exchange-rate fluctuations. M&S (1984) constructed SPILL by taking local currency military expenditure figures, converting them to 1975 prices using the consumer price index, and applying 1975 exchange rates to transform them into dollars. This would be inappropriate over the longer period used in this exercise because of the large, and often sustained, variations in real exchange rates. Instead the SIPRI constant price and exchange rate series were spliced onto a 1980 dollar base. This creates a chained series, the weights changing as SIPRI rebased their measures. When the M&S (1984) equation was reestimated over their sample, this measure gave results very close to those published by them.

It should also be recognized that total NATO expenditures relate only marginally to military forces, and even less to military capabilities, so it is not clear what the total is reflecting. Given these problems, NATO totals (which in the mid-1980s were greater than US estimates of Warsaw Pact totals) are rarely used in policy discussions. Instead, NATO uses growth rates, as in the commitment to 3 percent increases by each country adopted in the late 1970s, or shares of military expenditure in GDP. Shares have the advantage that they take account of incomes, are insensitive to the measures of inflation and exchange rates employed, and are widely used as a signal or a measure of commitment to defense. Hence their prevalence in the 'burden-sharing' debate between allies. This suggests that shares in GDP may be the appropriate variables to use in estimation.

In the UK the share of military expenditure rose from 6.1 percent in 1949 to 9.2 percent in 1952, with the Korean War rearmament, then declined; the fall slowing in 1956 with the Suez invasion, then accelerating after the Sandys defense review of 1957, which abolished conscription. Against a background of a trend decline, there were further sharp falls in 1968 and 1969 as a result of the Healey defense review. From a low of 4.6 percent in 1973, it rose to a peak of 4.9 percent in 1976, then fell in response to general government expenditure cuts to 4.5 percent in 1978. With the election of Mrs. Thatcher in 1979 it began to rise again, peaking at 5.2 percent in 1984 before starting to tend down again. Figure 6.1 shows the shares of military expenditure in output for the UK, USA, and USSR.

5 THE UK DEMAND FUNCTIONS

The theoretical derivation in Section 2 resulted in a general demand function explaining military expenditure by prices and income, together with strategic and political shift variables. To make this operational requires specification of functional form, adjustment processes, and shift measures.

Two functional forms will be considered. The first form is a standard log-linear demand function using the general price level as the numeraire. Log-linear functions have a number of advantages for expenditure data, which are non-negative by definition. Relationships are often products (price times quantities equals value) or ratios (shares of totals), which are linear in logarithms, allowing the relevant hypotheses to be tested as linear

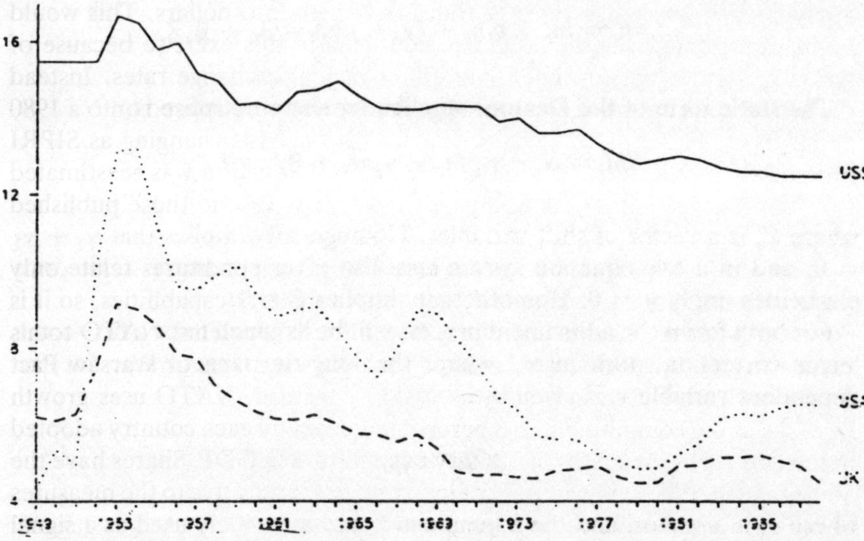

Figure 6.1 Shares of military expenditure: USSR, UK, USA

restrictions. In many cases growth rates (the differences of the logarithms) are more likely to be stationary than the differences in the levels, while if disturbances are proportional, rather than additive, the errors in logarithmic equations will be homoskedastic. Coefficients (elasticities) are independent of the units of measurement in logarithmic equations. However, log-linear demand functions do not satisfy the adding-up constraint. The second function used, the 'almost ideal demand system' suggested by Deaton and Muellbauer (1980), does satisfy adding-up, though it does not confine shares to the zero–one interval. It makes expenditure shares depend on the logarithms of prices and real incomes.

The static form of the log-linear equation is

$$m_t = \beta_0 + \beta_1 pm_t + \beta_2 py_t + \beta_3 y_t + \beta_4 Z_t,$$

where z is a vector of logarithmic shift variables. It can also be re-parameterized as an equation in the logarithm of the share of military expenditure in output for comparison with the Deaton–Muellbauer form:

$$m_t + pm_t - (y_t + py_t) = \beta_0 + (\beta_1 + 1)pm_t + (\beta_2 - 1)py_t + (\beta_3 - 1)y_t + (\beta_4 Z_t.$$

Homogeneity implies $\beta_1 + \beta_2 = 0$; homotheticity, unit income elasticity, that $\beta_3 = 1$. If in addition the price elasticity is unity ($-\beta_1 = \beta_2 = 1$), the logarithm of the share of military expenditure is given by:

$$sm_t = m_t + pm_t - (y_t + py_t) = \beta_0 + \beta_4 Z_t.$$

The static form of the Deaton–Muellbauer share equation is:

$$SM_t = \alpha + \gamma_1 pm_t + \gamma_2 pc_t + \beta y_t + \delta Z_t,$$

where Z_t is a vector of shift variables. Homogeneity implies that $\gamma_1 + \gamma_2 = 0$, and in a two-equation system this also gives symmetry. Unit price elasticities imply $\gamma_i = 0$. Homotheticity implies $\beta = 0$.

For both forms the adjustment process will be assumed to be a first-order 'error correction mechanism,' where the long-run target value for the dependent variable y_t is given by

$$y^*_t = \phi_1 \chi_t,$$

where χ_t is a vector, and the adjustment process is:

$$\Delta y_t = \phi_2 \Delta_{\chi t} - \lambda (y_{t-1} - y^*_{t-1}).$$

The vectors ϕ_1 and ϕ_2 measure the long-run and impact effects respectively, and λ is a scalar adjustment coefficient. This procedure models the change in the dependent variable terms of the changes and lagged levels of the independent variables and the lagged dependent variable.

The main strategic variables used in the share equation are the shares of military expenditure in output in the USSR and US, namely *SR* and *SA*. In the log-linear equation, in addition to *sr* and *sa*, *ma* is also included to test for a possible effect of the level of US military expenditure. The main political influences were proxied by using two dummy variables: $KD = 1$ in 1952 to allow for the Korean War rearmament; and $RD = 1$ in 1967, 1968, and 1969 to allow for the major defence reviews in which expenditure was cut. Finally a trend was added.

Beginning with the Deaton–Muellbauer share equation, the initial model explains the change in *SM*, by its lagged value and the changes and lagged values of *pm*, *pc*, *y*, *SA*, and *SR*, together with *KD*, *RD*, trend, and intercept; giving 15 parameters estimated over the 38 annual observations 1949–87. This equation provides an overparameterized framework for nested specification tests, designed to catch a wide range of effects and dynamics. The standard error of regression is 0.1643, the four diagnostic statistics do not suggest misspecification, but only six of the 15 coefficients have *t* statistics over 2.

The homogeneity restriction cannot be rejected, $F(2, 24) = 2.086$. When homogeneity was imposed the test statistic for the joint hypothesis, that income and price elasticities were unity and the coefficient of the trend was zero, was $F(5, 26) = 1.49$. The further hypothesis that the coefficients of ΔSR_t and SR_{t-1} were zero gave $F(2, 31) = 0.1$. Finally the restriction that the long-run coefficient of SR_t equaled unity was imposed, giving $F(1, 33) = 1.88$.

The process of data instigated reparameterization and restriction gives as a final equation for the period 1949–87:

$$\Delta SM_t = \underset{(0.35)}{-1.25} + \underset{(0.03)}{0.20}\, \Delta SA_t - \underset{(0.04)}{0.14}(SM_{t-1} - SR_{t-1}) - \underset{(0.11)}{0.49}\, DR + \underset{(0.20)}{1.18}\, KD$$

$$SER = 0.1749,\ \bar{R}^2 = 0.84\ F_{SC}(1, 33) = 0.02,\ F_{FF}(1, 33) = 0.07,\ \chi^2_N(2) = 0.82,\ F_H(1, 37) = 0.62.$$

The standard error of 0.1749, with five parameters, compares with a standard error of 0.1643 for the general model with 15 parameters; thus the restrictions are not rejected. The *t* statistics on the individual coefficients are all over 3. The coefficients are plausible, though the speed of adjustment, the coefficient of the error correction term might be thought rather low.[4] Excluding the dummy variables from the equation standard error increases from 0.17 to 0.28, the coefficient of ΔSA increases to 0.28, and that of the error correction term falls to 0.11, and non-normality of the errors is also indicated. The dummies should be interpreted as short-run effects, their lagged values were insignificant, $F(2, 29) = 1.64$.

The four tests reported do not show any evidence of misspecification, and in addition the LM statistic for fourth-order serial correlation was $\chi^2(4) = 0.55$, and for fourth-order autoregressive conditional heteroskedasiticy (ARCH) was $\chi^2(4) = 2.52$. The model was reestimated for 1949–74, giving very similar coefficients, with that for $(SM - SR)_{t-1}$ being slightly larger at 0.17. Between the two periods the variance ratio statistic was $F(10, 21) = 1.023$; Chow's first 'analysis of covariance' test (allowing for the two dummy variables being zero in the second period) was $F(3, 31) = 1.86$; his second 'prediction interval' test was $F(13, 21) = 1.22$. None rejects the hypothesis of structural stability. The recursive coefficients on ΔSA_t ranged from 0.205 to 0.185, and on the error correction term from −0.13 to −0.18, with the largest movement being in the 1979–85 period.

Examination of the forecasts indicated some underprediction for the period 1979–85. This may be attributable to the 1977 acceptance by Mr. Callaghan's Labour government of the commitment to NATO for a 3 percent per annum growth in real military expenditure. Although the Labour government planned this increase, it was implemented by Mrs. Thatcher's Conservative government from 1979 until the commitment was ended in 1984–5. Subsequently the growth in real military expenditure ceased. This commitment implies that if g_t is the GDP growth rate, ΔSM_t should be given by $N_t = SM_{t-1}\,(0.03 - g_t)/(1 + g_t)$ for 1979–85. When N_t was added it had a *t* statistic of 2.4; the results were otherwise similar with coefficients of 0.19 on ΔSA_t and −0.15 on the error correction term and a standard error of regression of 0.1635. The official estimate of the cost of the Falklands/Malvinas War in 1982 was £1.21 billion in a budget of £14.2 billion. Had this all been additional to what would have been spent otherwise, it would have added 0.44 to SM_t. In fact the residual for 1982 is only 0.13, within the one standard error band.

The fragility of such general to specific searches can be indicated by supposing that we had begun the same test sequence from the same general model but without the two dummies *KD* and *RD*. Then we would not even have got started. Homogeneity is rejected $F(2, 26) = 3.83$, and wrongly imposing the homogeneity restriction leads to failure on the RESET functional form test. The restricted version without the dummies is also rejected against the general model, $F(9, 26) = 4.04$.

The log-linear model allowing for the level of US military expenditure begins from:

$$m_t = \beta_0 + \beta_1 y_t + \beta_2 pm_t + \beta_3 py_t + \beta_4 sa_t + \beta_5 ma_t + \beta_6 sr_t + \beta_7 KD + \beta_8 RD + \beta_9 t,$$

which, allowing for one lag on *m*, *y*, *pm*, *py*, *ma*, *ya*, and *sr*, has 17 parameters. This gave a standard error of 0.0312, and satisfactory diagnostic statistics. The same sequence of restrictions (homogeneity, unit price and income elasticities, no trend, eliminate Δsr_t and sa_{t-1}, and impose a unit long-run coefficient on sr_t) were tested, together with the restriction that the coefficients on ma_t were zero. None of the hypotheses was rejected and the final result was:

$$\Delta sm_t = \underset{(0.04)}{-0.10} + \underset{(0.04)}{0.22}\,\Delta sa_t \underset{(0.04)}{-0.11}\,(sm_{t-1} - sr_{t-1}) + \underset{(0.03)}{0.17}\,KD_t - \underset{(0.02)}{0.08}\,RD_t$$

$$SER = 0.0342,\ \bar{R}^2 = 0.73\ F_{SC}(1, 33) = 0.19,\ F_{FF}(1, 33) = 1.41,$$
$$\chi^2_N(2) = 1.23,\ F_H(1, 37) = 0.96.$$

Testing this against the general model gives $F(12, 22) = 1.22$. The difference in fit between the linear and logarithmic forms is small. When corrected for the Jacobian of the transformation, the log likelihoods are 13.42 for the log-linear and 15.34 for the share equation, both with the same numbers of parameters, giving a marginal preference for the share version.

6 THE FRENCH DEMAND FUNCTION

One way of evaluating whether a specification is purely the product of data mining is to evaluate it on independent data. In this case an interesting test is to see whether it works for French data, particularly since M&S (1984) found that their equations determining British and French military expenditure were very similar. Fontanel (1980) also provides estimates for the demand for military expenditure in France.

For the purpose of comparison and evaluation, the share of military expenditure in GDP in France, SF_t, was explained by the change in the US share and an error correction term. If the UK model was just a chance product of sample peculiarities, produced by data mining, one would not expect it to fit to French data. The estimated equation for the sample 1951–87 was:

$$\Delta SF_t = -1.56 + 0.37\,\Delta SA_t - 0.17(SF_{t-1} - SR_{t-1})$$
$$\quad\quad (0.66)\quad (0.05) \quad\quad\quad (0.07)$$

$$SER = 0.359,\ \bar{R}^2 = 0.6224\ F_{SC}(1, 33) = 0.69\ F_{FF}(1, 33) = 4.93.$$
$$\chi^2_N(2) = 30.22\ F_H(1, 35) = 0.80.$$

Equation 16

Though the fit is worse, the results are very similar to those found for Britain; thus the UK model appears to be exportable. The long-run coefficient of the Soviet share is not significantly different from unity. When SF_{-1}, ΔSR_t, SA_{-1}, and a trend were included, the test statistic $F(4, 30) = 0.34$. There is evidence of misspecification from the functional form and normality diagnostic statistics. This seems to result from some large residuals in the early part of the period, perhaps associated with the conflicts in Indo-China, Suez, and Algeria. Thus, as for the UK, dummy variables are likely to improve the fit. The results were very similar when the sample was split into subperiods 1951–74 and 1975–87, and test statistics of $F(3, 31) = 0.21$ and $F(13, 21) = 0.6$ were obtained for Chow's first and second tests.

The covariance between the residuals of the British and French equations is very small (in both cases the *t* statistics of the residuals from one equation, when included in the other, were around 0.5); therefore joint estimation is unlikely to improve efficiency. Residual covariance represents an indirect link; direct links can be investigated by including the British share in the French equation and vice versa. The test statistic for the inclusion of ΔSM_t and SM_{t-1} in the French equation was $F(2, 32) = 1.68$ and for ΔSF_t and SF_{t-1} in the British equation was $F(2, 30) = 0.62$. Thus there is little indication of spillover between the two countries.

7 EVALUATION

The specification search has produced what appears to be broadly satisfactory demand functions for the two countries; however, there are a number of further issues that need to be examined.

The first is that the measure of the Soviet share of military expenditure used was not available until the mid-1980s. To examine the sensitivity to alternative measures, the series discussed in Section 4, and the series given in Ostrom and Marra (1986) were also tried in a variety of formulations. None of them provided any significant increase in explanation for either the UK or the French share of military expenditure. One rationalization for this is that the *ex post* constructed measure *SR* provides a better proxy for decision-makers' perceptions of Soviet military expenditure at the time than the measures then published. However, this seems a very strong presumption.

The second issue is that previous work has found a negative effect of US on UK expenditures (DME) or NATO expenditures on UK and French expenditures (M&S 1984). A negative effect is what would be expected were the countries 'free-riding' on the alliance, rather than the positive change effect obtained above. Since both previous studies used the lagged value, they could be picking up the negative coefficient on the lagged value which arises from the change. Some support was found for this interpretation. ΔSA_t was excluded from the equation, and the lagged values of other NATO expenditures $SPILL_t$, and $DSPILL_t$ ($SPILL$ times a dummy variable that takes the value 1 after 1973) included for the period 1951–86. $SPILL_{t-1}$ and $DSPILL_{t-1}$ have (scaled) coefficient of −0.45 and 0.13, with *t* statistics of −3.2 and 1.8 respectively in the UK. In France they have coefficients of −0.97 and 0.21 with *t* statistics of −3.7 and 1.7. This is exactly in accord with the M&S (1984) results. Other NATO expenditures depress military spending because of the free-rider effect, but the effect of the spillover is reduced after 1973 with the move from massive retaliation to flexible response. However, if ΔSA_t is added to the equation, the *t* statistics for $SPILL_{t-1}$ and $DSPILL_{t-1}$ are 0.54 and 0.95 for the UK, and −0.48 and 1.33 for France, and in neither case are they jointly significant. Thus the model with ΔSA_t seems preferable on statistical grounds. One economic rationalization would be that sharp changes in US military expenditure signal the need for higher military expenditure to the follower countries. The need might arise from increased perception of threat as during the 'New Cold War' after 1979, or the need to substitute for the US as in the case of the Vietnam increases. Although quite different motivations would be involved in the two cases, the adjustments might be similar.

There is also the possibility either that U.S. military expenditure is endogenous partly responding to UK spending, or that the UK responds differently to expected and unexpected changes in U.S. military expenditure. In practice it is difficult to distinguish these hypotheses. The Wu–Hausman test for endogeneity of ΔSA_t, involves checking the significance of the residual from the reduced form equation determining ΔSA_t. Lagged values of SA_t, SM_t, and SR_t were used as instruments. This residual which corresponds to the 'unexpected' part of ΔSA_t has a *t* statistic of –1.7; so we cannot reject the observationally equivalent hypotheses of exogeneity or of identical responses to expected and unexpected changes.

A third issue is the extent to which UK military expenditure has been adjusted in response to economic fluctuations. To examine this the current and lagged values of the rate of growth, the rate of unemployment, and the rate of inflation were added to the equation. Current and lagged unemployment had t statistics of 2.27 and −1.99 and lagged growth of 2.23. This appearance of significance seems to be produced by offsetting effects, since the joint test statistic $F(6,25) = 1.58$.

A fourth issue is the extent to which political administrations differ. To examine this separate dummies were included. The dummy variables for Britain were: $B2 = 1$, 1964–70; $B3 = 1$, 1971–5; $B4 = 1$, 1975–9; $B5 = 1$, 1980–7. The test statistic for their joint significance was $F(4,30) = 1.42$. This probability overstates the possible statistical influence of short-term politics, since the measure for the NATO commitment was not included in the model. With that included the test statistic is even lower. The dummy variables for France were: $F2 = 1$, 1959–69; $F3 = 1$, 1970–80; $F4 = 1$, 1981–7. The test statistic for their joint significance was $F(3,31) = 0.198$.

8 CONCLUSION

Starting from two existing models taken from the large literature explaining military expenditure, an explicit specification search produced an equation which provided a reasonable description of the process generating the change in the share of UK output devoted to military expenditure over the postwar period. The model was quite different from the equations that it was developed from, and showed features that would not be expected from prior theoretical consideration. It passed a wide variety of specification tests and explained the share of military expenditure in terms of three types of factors: sporadic national decisions such as the Korean War, defense reviews, and the implementation of the 3 percent growth commitment to NATO; a response to the change in the U.S. share; and an error correction adjustment of the British to the Soviet share. Although economic factors do not appear explicitly in the model, price and income elasticities are implicitly set to unity. A similar model also seems to work for France.

However, these conclusions are subject to the general qualifications that: the exact values of the coefficients are somewhat sensitive to the sample used; the model is essentially *ad hoc*, mined from the data rather than derived from an explicit theory; there are substantial measurement problems associated with both the Soviet figure and the specification of the dummies to take account of the sporadic factors; and other models, not revealed by the specification search, may provide a better explanation. It is probably wise to retain a degree of skepticism about the specific results until it has been shown that the model continues to work, and has wider applicability.

NOTES

1 Reproduced by permission of John Wiley and Sons Ltd. From *The Journal of Applied Econometrics*, volume 4 (1989), pp. 345–359. I am grateful to George

Alogoskoufis, Hugh Davies, Ben Lockwood, Todd Sandler, and the editor [of the *Journal*] for comments on an earlier version.

2 Chan (1987) reports a similar position with respect to the effect of military expenditure.

3 The exchange between Hartley and McLean (1978) and Smith (1978) discusses the influence of political factors in regressions explaining UK military expenditures.

4 Error correction terms are often interpreted as cointegrating vectors (Engle and Granger 1987). In this case tests for a unit root indicated that the three shares of military expenditure were all integrated of order zero, that is stationary in levels. Thus the issue of co-integration is not relevant.

REFERENCES

Baran, P. A. and P. M. Sweezy. 1966. *Monopoly Capital*. New York: Monthly Review Press.

Barro, R. J. 1981. Output effects of government purchases. *Journal of Political Economy* 89: 1086–1121.

Benoit, E. 1973. *Defence and Economic Growth in Developing Countries*. Boston: D. C. Heath.

Chan, M. W. L., C. Hsiao, and C. W. K. Keng. 1982. Defence expenditures and economic growth in developing countries: a temporal cross-sectional analysis. In O. D. Anderson and M. R. Perryman (eds.), *Applied Time Series Analysis*, pp. 53–64. Amsterdam: North Holland.

Chan, S. 1987. Military expenditures and economic performance. In *World Military Expenditures and Arms Transfers 1986*, pp. 29–38. Washington, D.C.: U.S. Arms Control and Disarmament Agency.

Cusack, T. R. and M. D. Ward. 1981. Military spending in the United States, Soviet Union and the People's Republic of China. *Journal of Conflict Resolution* 25: 429–69.

Deaton, A. and J. Muellbauer. 1980. An almost ideal demand system. *American Economic Review* 70: 312–26.

Desai, M. and D. Blake. 1981. Modelling the ultimate absurdity: a comment on a quantitative study of the strategic arms race in the missile age. *Review of Economics and Statistics* 63: 629–32.

Dunne, J. P., P. Pashardes, and R. P. Smith. 1984. Needs costs and bureaucracy: the allocation of public consumption in the UK. *Economic Journal* 94: 1–15.

Engle, R. F., and C. W. J. Granger. 1987. Co-integration and error correction: representation, estimation and testing. *Econometrica* 55: 251–76.

Fontanel, J. 1980 *Military Expenditures and Economic Growth (France and Morocco)*. United Nations and CEDSI, Grenoble.

Georgiou, G. and R. P. Smith. 1983. Assessing the effect of military expenditure on OECD countries. *Arms Control* 4: 3–15.

Granger, C. W. J. 1969. Investigating causal relations by econometric models and cross-spectral models. *Econometrica* 37: 424–38.

Granger, C. W. J. 1988. Causality, cointegration and control. *Journal of Economic Dynamics and Control* 12: 551–60.

Griffin, L. J., M. Wallace, and J. Devine. 1982. The political economy of military spending: evidence from the United States. *Cambridge Journal of Economics* 6: 1–14.

Hartley, K. and P. McClean. 1978. Military expenditure and capitalism: a comment. *Cambridge Journal of Economics* 2: 287–92.

Judge, G. G. *et al.* 1985. *The Theory and Practice of Econometrics*, 2nd edn. New York: Wiley.
Kamlet, M. S. and D. C. Mowery. 1987. Influences on executive and congressional budgetary priorities 1955–1981. *American Political Science Review* 81: 155–78.
Leamer, E. E. 1985 Sensitivity analyses would help. *American Economic Review* 75: 308–13.
McAleer, M., A. R. Pagan, and P. Volker. 1985. What will take the con out of econometrics. *American Economic Review* 75: 293–307.
McGuire, M. C. 1977. A quantitative study of the strategic arms race in the missile age. *Review of Economics and Statistics* 59: 328–39.
McGuire, M. C. 1981. A quantitative study of the strategic arms race in the missile age: a reply. *Review of Economics and Statistics* 63: 632–3.
McGuire, M. C. 1982. U.S. assistance and Israeli allocation. *Journal of Conflict Resolution* 6: 199–235.
McGuire, M. C. 1987. U.S. foreign assistance, Israeli resource allocation and the arms race in the Middle East. In Schmidt, *The Economics of Military Expenditures*, pp. 197–238. London: Macmillan.
MacKinnon J. G., H. White, and R. Davidson. 1983. Tests for model specification in the presence of alternative hypotheses: some further results. *Journal of Econometrics* 21: 53–70.
Maizels, A. and M. K. Nissanke. 1986. Determinants of military expenditures in developing countries. *World Development* 14: 1125–40.
Murdoch, J. C. and T. Sandler. 1984. Complementarity, free riding and the military expenditure of NATO allies. *Journal of Public Economics* 25: 83–101.
Murdoch, J. C. and T. Sandler. 1986. The political economy of Scandinavian neutrality. *Scandinavian Journal of Economics* 88: 583–603.
Olson, M. and R. Zeckhauser. 1966. An economic theory of alliances. *Review of Economic Statistics* 48: 266–74.
Ostrom, C. W. Jr. 1978. A reactive linkage model of the U.S. defence expenditure policy-making process. *American Political Science Review* 72: 941–57.
Ostrom, C. W. Jr. and R. F. Marra. 1986. U.S. defence spending and the Soviet estimate. *American Political Science Review* 80: 819–42.
Pesaran, M. H. and B. Pesaran. 1989. *Microfit, an Interactive Econometric Software Package*. Oxford: Oxford University Press.
Pesaran, M. H. and R. P. Smith. 1985. Evaluation of macroeconometric models. *Economic Modelling* 2: 125–34.
Rattinger, H. 1975. Armaments detente and bureaucracy: the case of the arms race in Europe. *Journal of Conflict Resolution* 19: 571–95.
Richardson, L. F. 1960. *Arms and Insecurity: A Mathematical Study of the Causes and Origins of Wars*. Pittsburgh, Penn.: Boxwood.
Schmidt, C. (ed.). 1987. *The Economics of Military Expenditures*. London: Macmillan.
Smith, R. P. 1977. Military expenditure and capitalism. *Cambridge Journal of Economics* 1: 61–76.
Smith, R. P. 1978. Military expenditure and capitalism: a reply. *Cambridge Journal of Economics* 2, 299–304.
Smith, R. P. 1980. The demand for military expenditure. *Economic Journal* 90: 811–20.
Smith, R. P. 1987. The demand for military expenditure: a correction. *Economic Journal* 97: 989–90.
Tait, A. A. and P. S. Heller. 1982. *International Comparisons of Government Expenditure*. International Monetary Fund Occasional Paper No. 10, Washington, D.C.
Trivedi, P. K. 1984. Uncertain prior information and distributed lag analysis. In D.

F. Hendry and K. F. Wallis (eds.), *Econometrics and Quantitative Economics*, pp. 173–210. Oxford: Basil Blackwell.

U.S. Arms Control and Disarmament Agency. 1988. *World Military Expenditures and Arms Transfers 1987*. Washington, D.C.: U.S. Arms Control and Disarmament Agency.

Ward, M. D. and A. Mintz. 1987. Dynamics of military spending in Israel. *Journal of Conflict Resolution* 31: 86–105.

Zuk, G. and W. R. Thompson. 1982. The post-coup military spending question. *American Political Science Review* 76: 60–74.

7 Economic growth, investment, and military spending in India, 1950–88[1]

Michael D. Ward, Amalia Cochran, David R. Davis, Mohan Penubarti, Sheen Rajmaira
University of Colorado

INTRODUCTION AND OVERVIEW

India is an important regional power and a potent economic force. It has been involved in significant regional conflicts during the course of its history, and particularly since its independence. In this research, we explore the security context of Indian defense policy. In so doing we tease out some of the putative economic implications of defense policy decisions, concentrating on the nonagricultural aspects of Indian economic development.

Three linchpins hold this research together. The first of these is national security, traditionally cast in terms of external military threats to the state. While current conceptions about what constitutes national security are broadening considerably, consideration of foreign military threat, real and imagined, continues to provide a solid cornerstone for understanding Indian defense policy. Since 1947, India has been involved in three wars with Pakistan (1948, 1965, and 1971) as well as numerous direct military conflicts with China (especially 1962). U.S. and Soviet alliances with and support for both China and Pakistan – in different times and different ways – have made a putatively neutral India especially cognizant of the potential regional threat from its larger as well as smaller neighbors. Rapidly improving Pakistani nuclear capabilities and the history of Indian–Pakistani enmity continue to give currency to India's regional threat perceptions. As Thomas (1986a, 1986b) has pointed out, India's strategic context faced enormous change in the 1970s, ranging from the breakoff of Pakistan coupled with U.S.–Chinese *rapprochement* in the early years of the decade, through joining the 'nuclear club' during the mid-1970s, on to the Soviet invasion of Afghanistan in 1979. The 1980s continued apace with regional developments of considerable import to Indian strategic thinking, and the 1990s promise continued challenges *vis-à-vis* great-power relations, and the growth of strong, vital Pacific Rim economic interests.

Military policy, the second linchpin, connects almost directly to the first. How have political enmities in South Asia and beyond been translated into military capabilities in the region? India has had uncertain regional contexts on at least three fronts in recent years. With Islamic instability to the west, Chinese enmity to the north, and wide swings in 'superpower' reliability, the foreign and military policy of India has faced strong challenges. Quite apart from the nuclear capabilities of the region, how have the Indian Army, Navy, and Air Force been (re)structured to take into account newer strategic contexts? Specifically, we focus on how the political contexts of regional competition and threat have structured weapons acquisition programs in India, and how those programs have helped to determine government spending patterns.

Finally, scholars have long studied India for insights about the putative process of economic 'development.' In particular, India has often been cast as a society in which two economies, one industrial, the other agricultural, vie for progress under the enormous weight of demographics unsupportive of 'modernization.' Indian realities have changed considerably in the last four decades, even if Western perceptions of them are slow to adjust. India in the 1990s has achieved self-sufficiency in food production, has a very high savings rate of about 20 percent, and has a sizable foreign exchange reserve. It continues, however, to be plagued by poverty, inequality, and under/unemployment.

We focus herein on India since it is one of a small number of developing societies with considerable economic growth, a sizable military establishment, and a well-developed military–industrial complex involved in both exportation and importation of armaments. This chapter is drawn from a larger manuscript (Ward *et al.* 1990) that focuses primarily on the relationship between economic growth, investment, and military and nonmilitary spending in India over the last four decades. We begin with a review of Indian development policy as articulated in agricultural and industrial arenas. We turn to a broad descriptive survey of Indian experience with these policy choices. We explore empirically what a neoclassical economic framework can tell us about economic growth and military spending in the Indian case.

INDIAN ECONOMIC DEVELOPMENT

Like many developing societies India has been faced with tremendous economic problems since independence. The sheer size of India's population coupled with the democratic political system gives enormous weight to the complexity of economic issues. We focus on the central issues of agricultural productivity and industrial capability.

Agricultural development

Agriculture has been a consistently neglected element of Indian economic development. The emphasis that was placed on rapid industrialization by Nehru in his socialist development plans was such that agriculture as a source of demand was almost entirely overlooked. In fact, the principal role of agriculture was to be a temporary means of relieving the employment strain on the Indian economy. In spite of this discouraging view of agriculture's role in Indian progress, during the immediate post-Independence period, agriculture experienced significant growth, in part due to the improved incentives from land reforms, as well as the improvement of irrigation systems. In the 1960s, improvements provided by the Green Revolution were beneficial to agricultural growth in at least some areas, and as time has passed, the benefits have become more equitably distributed throughout the nation.

The Green Revolution, and the government involvement it demanded for nationwide implementation, is probably the most prominent element of Indian agriculture since Independence. The Green Revolution in India began with the introduction of Mexican hybrid wheat into the Punjab in the late 1960s. This successfully led to improved wheat yields in this area, which was agroclimatically favorable and had excellent water management. The sticking point was the revolution needed to spread to other regions and other crops for it to truly benefit Indian agriculture. This expansion required extensive government involvement on a nationwide basis, and this assistance was something the government, in its pro-industry stance, was hesitant to provide until the mid-1970s.

Eventually the government did encourage commercial financing for the planting of high-yield varieties of crops, resulting in improved agricultural production on an almost national basis. Under the Sixth Plan, productivity targets for wheat, sugarcane, jute, and mesta were achieved in spite of area constraints and continued poor management of water resources (Alagh 1988). In the 1950s and 1960s the growth rate of agriculture was about 3 percent, but by the mid-1970s it had declined to about 2 percent. The 3 percent growth of the sector in the early 1980s is still short of the 4 percent targeted by the Seventh Five-Year Plan (M. S. Ahluwalia 1988). Estimates of growth rates in various sectors of the Indian economy vary from source to source, although the basic trends appear to be consistent across sources. See Table 7.3 below for a comparison of data from the World Bank (1978, 1983, 1987) and the International Monetary Fund.

The relationship between poverty and the agricultural sector has had a dampening effect on overall economic growth. Self-sufficient industrial growth in consumer-goods sectors was impossible until the problems of poverty and employment in the rural agricultural sector were addressed. The Green Revolution, by improving production, has provided some relief to the poverty problem, although unemployment has remained a significant problem. India has exhibited consistently low agricultural production, due in large part to government neglect of nonindustrial economic matters. Although elimination of poverty and improvement of employment were the stated goals of Nehru and his socialist approach to development, the industrial approach to development has proven to be inadequate for a society with an extensive agricultural and rural element. However, as Sen (1989) points out, India has made important gains in basic needs provision. Based on World Bank (1983) the physical quality of life indicator has risen to the mid-40s (out of 100) in recent years, an increase of 56 percent over a PQLI of about 28 in the 1960s (Morris's 1979 formula was used as the basis for calculating the PQLI).

Industrial development

India, which began low-scale consumer-goods industrialization in the late nineteenth century, has focused on industrialization as the elixir for its economic problems since the time of Independence. Nehru was impressed by Soviet industrialization, and firmly believed that allying the state with industrial development was the ideal means of progress. The importance of alleviating income inequalities, improving employment, and creating balanced economic growth promoted government intervention in the economy of the new democracy. Export pessimism encouraged India to pursue a pattern of independent growth in a relatively closed economic system. The capital-goods sector was emphasized because of the necessity of creating a national infrastructure before the secondary industrial sector could emerge. The emphasis on the capital-goods sector was intended to promote immediate expansion of Indian investment goods, which would then stimulate rapid industrialization. Nehru, then, used a mixed economy to implement objectives in the public sector and state-regulated private sector over time.

Indian industrial policy has been an integral part of the overall economic and planning policy since Independence. Because of the leading role given to industry by the Five-Year Plans, however, its importance cannot be underestimated in the context of Indian economic development. Traditionally, industrial policy has emphasized export promotion and import substitution, and has de-emphasized productive employment and equalization of regional imbalances. From the time of the Industrial Policy Resolution of 1956 until the mid-1960s, India experienced comparatively successful levels of growth. Beginning in the mid-1960s, however, heavy industry experienced a sharp downturn in its growth, for four basic reasons, according to Ahluwalia (1986). These reasons are:

(a) the slowdown of public investment and the associated impact on infrastructural investment,
(b) poor management of the infrastructure sectors,
(c) slow growth of agricultural incomes and the resulting limited demand for industrial goods, and
(d) the inclusion of both domestic industrial policy and trade policy in the industrial policy framework.

The most important implication is the resulting integration of domestic industrial policy and trade policy into a unified program. This encouraged emphasis in industrial development on the creation and expansion of heavy industry, with considerable neglect of consumer-goods industries. Consumer-goods industries exhibited consistently slower growth rates than heavy industry, leading to de-emphasis over time. Nehru's residual influence also discouraged the development of consumer-goods industries, although they tend to be the most beneficial in the long run. The upshot of this conflict over heavy industry versus consumer-goods development is that mismanagement has been prevalent. Removal of trade policy from the overall industrial policy may be sufficient to affect the changes necessary to achieve enhanced industrial development, but it is more likely that a rethinking of basic paradigms regarding the role of industry in Indian development would be beneficial.

During the 1950s and early 1960s, the growth of the Indian economy through emphasis on investment goods was substantial. The growth rate of 3.5 percent per year seemed ineluctable. In the mid-1960s, however, India's security situation *vis-à-vis* China and Pakistan became somewhat tenuous. Foreign assistance to India concurrently leveled off. Additionally, a drought in both 1966 and 1967 significantly affected agricultural production and reduced national GDP. Another important factor leading to the crisis of the 'plan holiday' in the late 1960s was the fact that all industrialization had emphasized capital-intensive development, which exacerbated the high unemployment levels. According to I. J. Ahluwalia (1988), it was the failure to create the necessary infrastructure in the Indian economy coupled with the decline in agriculture that reduced demand in the ailing consumer-goods sector.

During the late 1970s, a more logical pursuit of development, rather than concern with regulation, became the dominant theme in the promotion of Indian industry. Improvement of the infrastructure through railway refurbishment and better generation and distribution of electricity were important steps in the new development program. Trade policy, although still included in overall industrial policy, simply had become one stabilizing element in the overall economic-policy regime. Industrial growth in this period occurred at a rate of approximately 4.8 percent per year. Although an improvement, this fell short of the targeted 8 percent proposed by the Fifth and Sixth Five-Year Plans. This weak turnaround was tenuous at best, and the future of Indian industrial performance remains unclear. If *Annual Survey of Industries* data are used, it appears that industrial growth has been stagnant since the 1960s. A suggestion has been made that it will remain in that condition until controls are de-emphasized, the infrastructure is completely renovated, and significant improvement in the agricultural sector, enhancing Indian food self-sufficiency and exports, occurs (Ahluwalia 1985).

The change in political leadership from Indira Gandhi to Rajiv Gandhi signaled the putative beginning of a new *culture* in Indian economic thinking. New policies were designed to change the direction of Indian industrial development and provide greater stimulus to private industrial growth. Due to his youth and technical background, Rajiv Gandhi was immediately associated with the opening of the economy to private enterprise, introduction of modern, streamlined management systems, and the introduction of high-technology consumer goods as well as computers in India. New policies to increase exports and liberalize the economy were launched under the slogans of 'rapid economic growth,' 'efficiency,' 'modernization,' and 'export promotion.'

The private sector was allowed to invest in areas formerly reserved for the public sector, such as power, telecommunications, and electronics. The previous priority placed on the development of indigenous technology was relaxed to allow collaboration with several American, Japanese, and German firms in computer and automobile industries. While the results of the reform under Rajiv Gandhi have many supporters as well as critics, a consensus has now developed among the Indian leadership that further economic reform is imperative if India is to overcome the barriers of undevelopment and make its way into the ranks of the advanced industrial nations. The election of V. P. Singh, the chief architect of the economic reform as the finance minister under the previous administration, to the prime ministership is thought to represent continued progress toward liberalization and modernization of the economy.

Development and the military

The military–industrial complex plays a significant role in industrial development in that India has a rather large defense sector. The effects of security expenditures on growth have recently become a hotly debated issue. Military expenditures had been originally thought to have spinoff effects through the modernization they make possible, as well as the resource mobilization that may occur. It is generally agreed upon, even by those who are highly critical of the impact of defense expenditure on economic development, that the military organization may be a means of introducing new technology into a society, and can facilitate the creation of infrastructural public goods such as roads, power supplies, and communications. However, the benefits gained from these modernization effects of the military are relatively inconsequential, and are likely outweighed by the negative effects on growth that result from the decline in savings associated with the increased defense spending (Deger and Smith 1983).

In spite of speculation and writing to the contrary, strong cross-sectional evidence exists that in the context of a macroeconomic model increased defense expenditures actually serve to retard the rate of resource creation, again leading to a negative effect of defense expenditure on growth and development (Deger 1985a; Deger and Smith 1983). Biswas and Ram (1986) do, however, find cross-sectional support for the so-called modernization model in the context of neoclassical frameworks. The potential benefits of security expenditure that lie in the possibility of modernization are clear; the negative impact on savings and investment that seems to result from higher levels of defense spending, however, is such that alternative means of achieving the modernizing results could be more beneficial to the overall growth of the economy. As yet there is no strong evidence on either side of the modernization debate for the Indian case.

Beginning in the mid-1970s, a new line of reasoning was posited that claimed military expenditures actually consume resources that could be used for development, and that such expenditures force a tradeoff with other expenditures, especially those related to human resources (Russett 1970). This triggered a whole new debate over the role of military expenditures in economic development. In an examination of the effects of military expenditures on government education expenditures, Deger (1985b) acknowledged that both the military and education are means of developing human resources. However, she stated that education is the more efficient means of developing human resources, and that a relatively modest cut in defense expenditures in most developing nations can lead to a tremendous increase in the money available for educational improvements. The prevalent idea in the literature regarding military expenditures in developing nations is that some sort of tradeoff, ultimately damaging to economic development, occurs with an increased defense burden. What is not so clear is exactly where or how this tradeoff occurs.

A question exists regarding the reduced benefits to the civilian economy of the educational training provided in the circumstance of the military being a professional, as opposed to a volunteer, organization. Further, many have noted the dubious value of the training in a country where unemployment is sufficiently high that the soldier will be unable to find employment at the end of his service (Ball 1983). It has been suggested that military spending is in competition with social spending, but that military expenditure does not seem to have a direct tradeoff or substitution effect with education (Hess and Mullan 1988). Another hypothesis claims that the defense burden reduces the savings–income ratio and is, in that way, detrimental to growth, but it does not discuss the existence of a direct tradeoff in terms of human-resource capital (Deger 1986).

With specific reference to the Indian context, decentralization of public expenditures on social and developmental services has increased since the beginning of the twentieth century, and has possibly removed the need for a tradeoff. Since the individual states have acquired responsibility for social and development expenditures and defense is a national service, the concept of a tradeoff is less than compelling to some (Nagarajan 1982). However, higher education as well as most research and development remain centrally allocated and controlled. The concept of a tradeoff due to military expenditures in the case of India is obfuscated by the decentralization that does exist.

India's military expenditures are generally thought to hover around 3.5 percent of GNP over the past decade. To an extent this figure may distort the real share of the military burden on the Indian economy for two reasons. A substantial volume of economic transactions are conducted both in the black market in India and outside the monetary sectors; by and large these are not reflected in official GNP estimates. Further, many industrial resources remain untapped or idle in India; exploitation of these underutilized resources by the military sector does not directly compete with the civilian sector. On this basis, Thomas (1986) has argued that the actual share of national product devoted to the military may be somewhat lower than usually assumed.

A final area in which military expenditures are thought to affect a developing nation's economy is through the import of arms and military technology. Initially, the acquisition of arms by developing nations was based on a political dependence upon more developed nations. As time has passed and arms sources have diversified, the economic dependence of the purchasers on provider nations or international financial agencies has begun to dominate political dependency. Nevertheless, it seems that military expenditures have had a relatively insignificant impact on Third World indebtedness, and this is especially true for countries like India that are not considered to be resource-constrained. These nations are not under severe developmental limitations because available resources generally have been available to achieve an equilibrium between armed forces and total military expenditures, rather than requiring substitution of personnel for imported equipment (Looney 1989; also, see his Chapter 11 in this volume). The economic burden that many resource-constrained developing nations have imposed upon themselves has only recently become evident as nations deal with pressures to repay debt in hard currencies and suffer increased pressure of internationalization since those currencies must be acquired through trade. It seems in the Indian case that debt incurred through imports of military technologies is only a particular element, rather than the most substantial part, of the entire public debt, and so has only a limited influence on economic development.

India's recent history of military expenditure has been related to its development in several interesting ways. For many years, India's primary arms supplier was the Soviet Union because of the Soviets' acceptance of Indian rupees as an exchange currency and the existence of a barter system of payments. This situation was enhanced for the Soviets during the 1980s as India experienced inflation, leading to a decline in its balance-of-payments position. The shortage of hard currency in New Delhi meant that exchange in any medium besides the rupee would involve great difficulties, such as for any purchase package proposed by any Western European nation or the United States. Finally, in February of 1989, arms exports were increased by the Ministry of Defense in order to raise funds in hard currency for the purchase of high-technology weapons systems from the West and to upgrade the Indian military forces. These trends are widely foreseen as important for the 1990s.

Defense spending in 1988 was close to $9 billion, and the Indian military establishment wished to continue on the newly developed trajectory it had established with continued extensive spending in 1989. India makes most of its own military equipment including tanks and jet fighters, which are domestically produced under license. India has positioned itself in the world defense establishment in such a way that it produces military goods that are of a technological quality acceptable to many other newly industrializing or less developed nations and that can be exported for hard currency. In turn, the acquired hard currency may be used to import more advanced weapons and other military goods. A special agency has been created to handle inquiries regarding arms exports, as well as to identify markets where Indian military technologies are likely to be competitive. India evidently wishes to maintain or increase its status in the international defense community, and the impact of this intention on military budgeting and policy is undeniable.

One factor impacting the Indian military budget that has heretofore been neglected is the impact of threat perceptions regarding neighboring nations, especially Pakistan. Shortly after the announcement was made that the Indian defense establishment intended to boost arms exports in order to increase arms imports, Rajiv Gandhi announced that the military budget would be reduced by nearly $100 million. The magnitude of this cut is somewhat decreased due to inflation, but the important consideration is the reason provided for this reduction: an improved international climate, specifically better relationship with Pakistan, and the absence of any increase in American military assistance to Pakistan. Indication was made, however, that this decision for reduced military expenditures was subject to continued denial of Pakistani military assistance to Sikh separatists in the Punjab. Thus, as long as Pakistan did not meddle in what India considers to be its internal affairs, the reduced tensions that originated the expenditure reduction could be maintained. Although international political and economic considerations seem to play the most essential role in influencing military expenditures and policy making in India, it is evident that geopolitical considerations are not by any means neglected. A more detailed discussion of India's threat perceptions, along with new data, and a mathematical model may be found in Ward *et al.* (1990).

MODEL DEVELOPMENT

The nexus between military spending and economic growth continues to be a perplexing one. Several excellent recently published review essays will serve to guide much of the literature as it is updated and articulated in large part in relief to Benoit's seminal insights (Benoit 1972a, 1972b, 1973, 1978). These are the essays by Cappelen *et al.* (1984), Chan (1987), Gold (1990), Grobar and Porter (1989), and Lindgren (1984, 1988). From the field of economics, much of the debate will continue to be centered on the multiplier effects of military spending on growth in general, and the putative resource constraints, both couched in various specifications of a neoclassical model. Examples of this literature include, but are by no means limited to, Biswas and Ram (1986), Deger (1985b), Deger and Sen (1983), Deger and Smith (1983), Faini *et al.* (1984), and Looney (1989). Virtually every economist weighing in on the subject agrees that an evaluation of the implications that economic growth and military spending may have for each other *must* be couched in the context of a macroeconomic model of the economy itself grounded in economic theory. This should not be surprising, but does explain much of the nonoverlap between the scholarship of economists and political scientists in this area.

Further, much of the work by political scientists and by economists alike in the area has followed one of two tracks. Either it has been developed to apply to a broad cross-section of contemporary societies, a tradition that follows in the footsteps of Benoit, or it is a macroeconomic model, the implications of which are tested by cross-sectional referents. While there are a few examples of longitudinal studies (Deger and Sen 1983; Faini *et al.* 1984; Mintz and Huang 1990; Smith 1989), it is somewhat ironic that a concept such as the multiplier effect would be examined in a cross-sectional format.

In what follows, we test the Mintz and Huang (1990) two-equation defense–growth model using data on the Indian case. We then compare and contrast our results both with the findings of earlier longitudinal work, and with the implications of prior cross-sectional research on India.

A neoclassical growth model

A neoclassical formulation of economic growth has been proposed by Feder (1982), and recently applied by Mintz and Huang (1990), building on the earlier adaptation by Ram (1986). This formulation of growth is coupled with a simple investment function to examine the indirect impact of military spending on growth through its interaction with investment. We explore the salience of the Mintz-Huang formulation in the Indian context. The basic idea is quite simple. Economic growth is promoted by investment, increase in labor productivity, and government spending, both military and nonmilitary:

$$\frac{dY}{dt} = \alpha_2 + \beta_{2,1} I + \beta_{2,2} \frac{Y_{-1}}{L_{-1}} \frac{dL}{dt} + \beta_{2,3} \frac{dN}{dt} - \beta_{2,4} \frac{dM}{dt} + \varepsilon$$

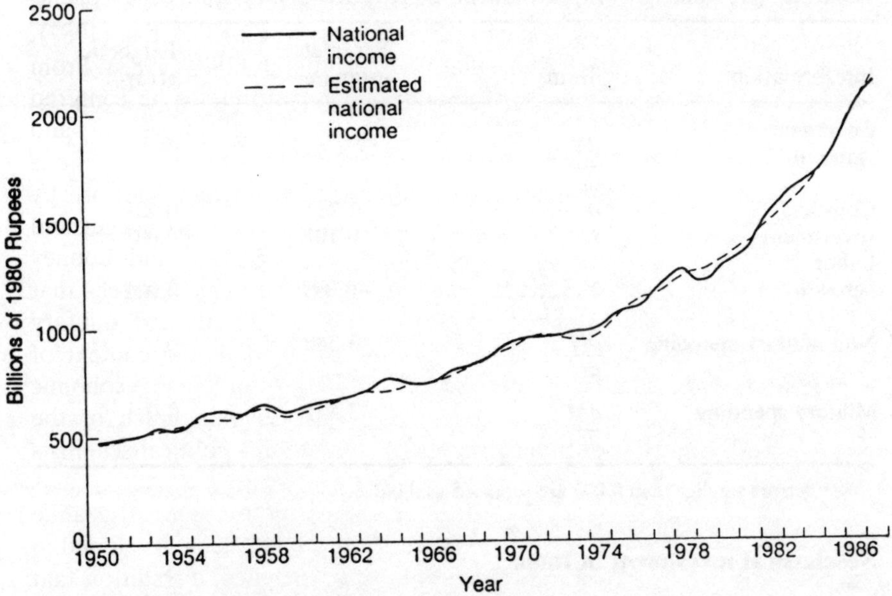

Figure 7.1 Actual and estimated economic growth
Source: Author's estimation.

where the national income is Y, investment is I, employment or labor is L, military spending is M, nonmilitary spending is N, and a subscript represents a lag, e.g., Y_{-1} represents the value of Y at time t minus 1.

This formulation can be simplified by multiplying the equation by Y_{-1} and by expressing it as a differential equation:

$$(7.1) \qquad \frac{\Delta Y}{Y_{-1}} = \alpha_2 + \beta_{2,1}\frac{I}{Y_{-1}} + \beta_{2,2}\frac{\Delta L}{L_{-1}} + \beta_{2,3}\frac{\Delta N}{Y_{-1}} - \beta_{2,4}\frac{\Delta M}{Y_{-1}} + \varepsilon$$

Results of empirical estimation of Equation 7.1 for India over the period from 1950 to 1987 are remarkable in addressing the basic question of whether and how different forms of government spending may promote economic productivity, and whether and how employment is related to productivity. These results are presented in Table 7.1 and the overall fit is portrayed in Figure 7.1. Not only is the fit between the data and the neoclassical model strong, but we also see strong evidence that greater employment levels may actually dampen economic growth in India. What this probably means is that increases in labor productivity tend to drive down employment levels. Investment and government spending both have a positive impact on growth. Separating government spending into military and nonmilitary components demonstrates that both have direct, strong, and beneficial effects on economic growth in the short run; specifically, nonmilitary spending has about a one-third greater impact than does military spending.

Table 7.1 Economic growth, investment, employment, and government spending

Interpretation	Term	Parameter estimate	Parabolic error
Economic growth	$\frac{dY}{d_t} =$		
Constant	α	3.711	0.001
Investment	I	0.101	0.001
Labor growth	$Y_{-1}\frac{dL/dt}{L_{-1}}$	−0.099	0.001
Non-military spending	$\frac{dN}{dt}$	3.340	0.001
Military spending	$\frac{dM}{dt}$	2.391	0.001

Note: Errors smaller than 0.000 are reported as 0.001.

Neoclassical investment in India

A neoclassical version of investment pins new investment to production, government spending, both military and nonmilitary, and the (depreciating) level of capital stock. Obviously, this type of formulation depends mathematically on infinite prior sums, but statistically and practically it may be usefully limited to a finite number of prior lags. This formulation allows military expenditures to influence investment in the long run which then feeds back into the growth specification. Evidence from the United States suggests the validity of this approach (Mintz and Huang 1990), although the applicability of this approach to India remains an open question to be examined in this research.

$$I = \alpha + \beta_1 \Delta P + \beta_2 \Delta N + \beta_3 \Delta M + \beta_4 K_{-1} + \epsilon \tag{7.2}$$

where I is investment, P is productivity in the private sector, N is nonmilitary government spending, M is military spending, and K represents capital stock.

Estimates of Equation 7.2 are also interesting and provide a strong fit between the data and the theory (see Figure 7.2). In particular, we note (in Table 7.2) that private consumption drives up investment, and that governmental spending, in both its military and nonmilitary components, is associated with higher levels of investment. At the same time capital stock increases investment levels. All of this is as predicted by a neoclassical model, and is consistent with Taylor's (1989) observation that the Indian economy is not supply-constrained at the aggregate level. It also gives further support to the notion that government spending is a high priority for Indian development planners, so long as revenues can be generated fast enough to keep the so-called 'debt-trap' from overtaking

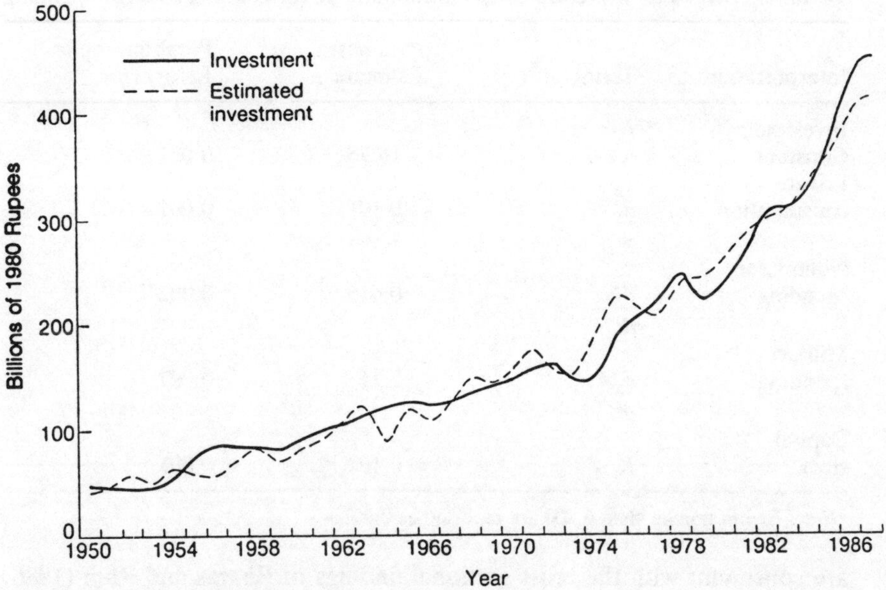

Figure 7.2 Actual and estimated investment in India
Source: Author's estimation.

macroeconomic conditions. It is especially interesting that the beneficial impact of government spending is split between military and nonmilitary spending. In particular, military spending influences investment approximately three times as much as does nonmilitary spending. Obviously, nonmilitary spending includes many transfer payments that would not be expected to increase investment. However, it is also obvious that development programs aimed at agricultural activities are not likely to see their impact felt in industrial investment; so the size of this differential impact may be overstated slightly. Equations 7.1 and 7.2 were also estimated in discrete format, using first differences to approximate derivatives. A seemingly unrelated regression was run to correct for possible error cross-correlation; none was found. Parameter estimates were of the same sign and approximately the same magnitude. While not reported in detail here, this further bolsters our confidence in the basic findings reported herein. Further, in contrast to the case of the U.S. (Mintz and Huang 1991), we did not find any overwhelming multicollinearity among the right-hand-side variables that would recommend the use of 'ridge regression' techniques in the Indian case. These results are available upon request.

SUMMING UP

The findings reported herein, while preliminary, put in relief some of the prior cross-sectional research on defense–growth tradeoffs, although they

Table 7.2 Investment, private consumption, and government spending

Interpretation	Term	Parameter Estimate	Parabolic Error
Investment	$I =$		
Constant	α	–16.78	0.071
Private consumption	$\frac{dP}{dt}$	0.101	0.001
Nonmilitary spending	$\frac{dN}{dt}$	0.615	0.002
Military spending	$\frac{dM}{dt}$	2.11	0.007
Capital stock	K_{-1}	0.104	0.001

Note: Errors smaller than 0.000 are reported as 0.001.

are consonant with the cross-sectional findings of Biswas and Ram (1986, 369). In particular, much of the literature has asserted that the impact of military spending is to depress the prospects of economic growth. Many scholars (for example, Ball 1988; Deger and Smith 1983; Faini *et al*. 1984) have suggested that while military spending may not directly depress aggregate economic output, it does depress investment and savings, which in turn will have a negative impact on medium-term economic productivity. Deger and Sen (1982, 1983) provide some results of a pooled cross-section that suggest a negative multiplier effect of the military burden on economic growth (−0.1633); a similar study by Deger and Smith (1983, 351) reports a negative multiplier for low-income nations of −0.195. The results here are not based on cross-sectional evidence, but derive from a longitudinal analysis of specific Indian experience. They suggest that the multiplier of military spending is positive in India, with the spinoff effects providing enhanced economic growth.

These results also have a certain face validity in the Indian situation for several reasons. First, India is not faced with supply-side constraints and while there have been some fits and starts of agricultural productivity over the past four decades, by and large, growth of India's agricultural productivity has lagged far behind industrial productivity. Clearly, if defense spending is to substitute for development programs that are effective in increasing agricultural productivity, its impact may well have an overall negative effect upon growth. However, much defense spending is concentrated in sectors that – especially in recent years – have been prospering in the Indian economy, namely light industry and high technology. While it is true that the heavy industries promoted by early development programs have not been effective over the long haul in establishing international competitiveness or

Table 7.3 Various growth rates for the Indian economy

	Average annual percentage change			
	1950–60	1960–70	1970–80	1980–85
GDP[a]	3.8	3.6	3.6	5.2
GDP[b]	3.6	4.0	3.3	6.9
Agriculture	3.3	1.9	1.9	2.7
Industry	n.a.	5.5	4.4	5.4
Services	n.a.	3.9	5.2	7.5
Military spending	3.7	10.2	3.7	7.8

Sources: World Development Report 1978, 1983, and 1987; Vaidyanathan 1988; International Monetary Fund, various years.
Note (a) taken from *World Development Report*; (b) taken from International Monetary Fund.

profitability, it remains the case that overall industrial output has grown considerably faster than agricultural output. Table 7.3 provides an overview of the evolution of industrial versus agrarian productivity rates in India.

Second, one can speculate about why savings, and then investment, would be depressed by higher levels of military spending. One political hypothesis is that high spending levels tend to coincide with higher levels of international tension and unpredictability. During such periods, we might expect that individuals and firms will heavily discount the future, preferring to consume rather than conserve. However, savings data for India suggest that the short-term effect of the external situation on internal savings rates is minimal. Savings rates – the ratio of savings to national product – have grown fairly steadily from about 10 percent in the early 1960s to about 20 percent by the end of the 1970s. During the 1980s they have been maintained around 20 percent. Only following the 1971 war was there a slight drop (from 13.8 to 12.5 percent), although in recent years slightly more variation (around 17 or 18 percent) may be observed. We should also remember that taxation can be considered one form of 'enforced savings.'

Finally, India's defense spending has not really grown much faster than GNP, but has fluctuated between 2 and 3.5 percent of GNP. Thus, it may well be that India has managed to remain below the constraints that would hamper economic growth. Even with the presence of potentially hostile borders and wavering international alliances and cooperation, India has managed to provide national defense at a cost that does not appear to have markedly impeded its economic progress, and may in fact have aided the development of the industrial sector.

NOTE

1 This research was supported by NSF Grant SES-8910820. The Government has certain rights in this material. Steve Chan made timely and helpful comments on this effort. Susan McMillan also substantially helped with the research

project. The support of the Institute of Behavioral Science and the Center for International Relations is also appreciated.

REFERENCES

Ahluwalia, I. J. 1985. *Industrial Growth in India: Stagnation since the Mid-Sixties*. New York: Oxford University Press.

Ahluwalia, I. J. 1986. Industrial growth in India: performance and prospects. *Journal of Development Economics* 23: 1–18.

Ahluwalia, I. J. 1988. Industrial policy and industrial performance in India. In R. Lucas and G. Papanek, (eds.), *The Indian Economy: Recent Development and Future Prospects*, pp. 151–62. Boulder, Colo.: Westview Press.

Ahluwalia, M. S. 1988. India's economic performance, policies and prospects. In R. Lucas and G. Papanek, (eds.), *The Indian Economy: Recent Development and Future Prospects*, pp. 345–60. Boulder, Colo: Westview Press.

Alagh, Y. K. 1988. Regional dimensions of Indian agriculture. In R. Lucas and G. Papanek, (eds.), *The Indian Economy: Recent Development and Future Prospects*, pp. 29–52. Boulder, Colo.: Westview Press,

Ball, N. 1983. Defense and development: a critique of the Benoit study. *Economic Development and Cultural Change* 31: 507–24.

Benoit, E. 1972a. Growth effects of defense in developing countries. *International Development Review* 14: 2–10.

Benoit, E. 1972b. A rejoinder to Professor Dorfmann's comment. *International Development Review* 14: 12–14.

Benoit, E. 1973. *Defense and Economic Growth in Developing Countries*. Lexington, Mass.: D. C. Heath.

Benoit, E. 1978. Growth and defense in developing countries. *Economic Development and Cultural Change* 26: 271–80.

Biswas, B. and R. Ram 1986. Military expenditures and economic growth in less developed countries: an augmented model and further evidence. *Economic Development and Cultural Change* 34: 361–72.

Brzoska, M. 1983. Research communication: the military related external debt of Third World countries. *Journal of Peace Research* 20: 271–7.

Cappelen, Å., N. P. Gleditsch, and O. Bjerkholt. 1984. Military spending and economic growth in the OECD countries. *Journal of Peace Research* 21: 361–73.

Central Statistics Organization. Various years. *Statistical Abstract of the Indian Union*. Delhi: Manager of Publications, Government of India.

Central Statistics Organization. Various years. *Annual Survey of Industry*. Calcutta, India: Central Statistics Organization.

Chan, S. 1987. Military expenditures and economic performance. In U.S. Arms Control and Disarmament Agency (ed.), *World Military Expenditures and Arms Transfers 1986*, pp. 29–37. Washington, D.C.: U.S. Government Printing Office.

Deger, S. 1985a. Does defence expenditure mobilise resources in LDCs? *The Journal of Economic Studies* 12: 15–29.

Deger, S. 1985b. Human resources, government education expenditure, and the military burden in less developed countries. *The Journal of Developing Areas* 20: 37–48.

Deger, S. 1986. Economic development and defense expenditure. *Economic Development and Cultural Change* 35: 179–96.

Deger, S. and S. Sen. 1983. Military expenditure, spin-off and economic development. *Journal of Development Economics* 13: 67–83.

Deger, S. and R. Smith, 1983. Military expenditure and growth in less developed countries. *Journal of Conflict Resolution* 27: 335–53.

Faini, R., P. Arnez, and L. Taylor, 1984. Defense spending, economic structure, and growth: evidence among countries and over time. *Economic Development and Cultural Change* 32: 487–98.

Feder, G. 1982. On exports and economic growth. *Journal of Development Economics* 12: 59–73.

Gold, D. 1990. The impact of defense spending on investment, productivity, and economic growth. Defense Budget Project, 236 Massachussets Avenue, N.E., Washington, D.C., 20002.

Grobar, L. M. and R. C. Porter. 1989. Benoit revisited: defense spending and economic growth in LDCs. *Journal of Conflict Resolution* 33: 318–45.

Hess, P. and B. Mullan. 1988. The military burden and public education expenditures in contemporary developing nations: is there a trade-off? *The Journal of Developing Areas* 22: 497–514.

International Labour Office. Various Years. *Yearbook of Labour Statistics*. Geneva: International Labour Office.

International Monetary Fund. Various Years. *International Financial Statistics Yearbook*. Washington D.C.: International Monetary Fund.

International Monetary Fund. Various Years. *International Financial Statistics*. Washington, D.C.: International Monetary Fund.

Lindgren, G. 1984. Armaments and economic performance in industrialized market economies. *Journal of Peace Research* 21: 375–87.

Lindgren, G. 1988. Armaments and economic performance. In P. Wallersteen (ed.), *Peace Research: Achievements and Challenges*, pp. 169–97. Boulder, Colo.: Westview Press.

Looney, R. E. 1989. The influence of arms imports on Third World debt. *The Journal of Developing Areas* 23: 56–67.

Mintz, A. and C. Huang. 1990. Defense expenditures, economic growth and the 'peace dividend'. *American Political Science Review* 84: 1283–93.

Mintz, A. and C. Huang. 1991. 'Guns' vs. 'butter': the indirect link. *American Journal of Political Science* 35: 738–57.

Morris, M. D. 1979. *Measuring the Condition of the World's Poor: The Physical Quality of Life Index*. New York: Pergamon Press.

Nagarajan, P. 1982. The time profile of public expenditure growth in India: an empirical investigation. *Economics Letters* 9: 87–93.

Ram, R. 1986. Government size and economic growth: a new framework and some evidence from cross-section and time series data. *American Economic Review* 76: 191–203.

Russett, B. 1970. *What Price Vigilance? The Burden of National Defense*. New Haven, Conn.: Yale University Press.

Sen, A. 1989. Indian development: lessons and non-lessons. *Daedalus* 118: 369–92.

Smith, R. 1989. Models of military expenditure. *Journal of Applied Econometrics* 4: 345–59.

Stockholm International Peace Research Institute. Various years. *World Armaments and Disarmament Yearbook*. London: Taylor & Francis.

Taylor, L. 1989. Macro constraints on India's economic growth. *Indian Economic Review* 23: 145–65.

Thomas, R. 1986a. India: the politics of weapons procurement. In J. E. Katz (ed.), *The Implications of Third World Military Industrialization*, pp. 151–63. Lexington, Mass.: D. C. Heath.

Thomas, R. 1986b. *Indian Security Policy*. Princeton, N.J.: Princeton University Press.

United Nations Department of Economic and Social Affairs. Various years. *Yearbook of National Accounts Statistics*. New York: United Nations.
Ward, M. D., A. Cochran, D. R. Davis, M. Penubarti, and S. Rajmaira. 1990. Indian Defense Policy. Mimeograph.
World Bank. Various years. *World Development Report*. Washington, D.C.: World Bank.

8 Muddling through security, growth, and welfare: the political economy of defense spending in South Korea[1]

Chung-in Moon
University of Kentucky

and

In-Taek Hyun
Institute of Social Sciences, Seoul, South Korea

South Korea's economy has been touted as one of the most successful cases among the developing countries. This country's economic success has produced two interesting puzzles in the field of the political economy of development. The first concerns the relationship between growth and distribution. Compared with the experience of most developing countries, rapid economic growth in South Korea has not been accompanied by severe distortions in the distribution of income and wealth, providing empirical ground to refute the thesis of incompatibility between growth and equity. The second puzzle involves the relationship between security, growth, and welfare. Acute security threats from North Korea since 1945 have caused South Korea to bear a rather heavy defense burden. For the past three decades, it has devoted about 5–6 percent of gross national product, and approximately 30 percent of the national budget to the defense sector. Despite this continued threat to national security and the resulting heavy defense burden, South Korea's performance in economic growth and social welfare has remained impressive, posing an interesting anomaly to the theories on the tradeoffs between 'guns' and 'butter.'

The compatibility between growth and distribution has been a topic of extensive research and debate, resulting in the accumulation of rich theoretical and empirical knowledge. The historical context of social formation, successful land reforms, an interventionist state, and the patterns and articulation of development strategies are often delineated as factors responsible for growth with equity (Adelman and Morris 1973; Bergsman 1979; Cumings 1984; Haggard and Moon 1983). Few have explored the second puzzle, however (Galenson and Galenson 1986; Mok 1989; Moon 1986). What are the relationships among security dilemma, defense burden, and economic performance? Can the 'Taiwanese exception' thesis be applicable to South Korea?[2] If so, to what extent? How and why?

This chapter is designed to explore these issues by looking into the dynamics of the political economy of defense spending in South Korea. The first section traces the patterns of defense spending in South Korea from 1961 to 1987, and the second explores the determinants of defense spending. In the third section, we examine the impact of defense spending on security, growth, and welfare by elucidating the actual or potential tradeoffs between defense spending and economic performance. The final section discusses the political and economic implications of defense spending in the wake of the recent democratic transition.

Our findings suggest that South Korea has borne a heavy defense burden in both absolute and relative terms over the past four decades. Heavy defense spending has been an outcome of the dynamic interplay of military interaction with North Korea, the shifting nature of alliance ties with the United States, and domestic political and economic changes. As a result of ambitious defense spending, South Korea substantially enhanced its deterrence capabilities during the period under study. Furthermore, the large defense burden does not appear to have undermined economic growth and social welfare in aggregate terms. On the contrary, positive correlations have existed over time. As Chan and Clark (1990) have asserted elsewhere, South Korea, as with Taiwan, appears to present an exceptional case which can be characterized by a 'virtuous cycle' of security, growth, and welfare.

This aggregate analysis could present a misleading picture of the political economy of defense spending in South Korea, however. A disaggregate, contextual analysis reveals that heavy defense spending has not only brought about sporadic disruptions in macroeconomic performance, but also entailed negative opportunity costs in terms of an excessive tax burden, uneven sectoral allocation of resources, and the structural distortion of the national economy. Moreover, defense spending has also severely undermined the welfare functions of the state by either ignoring or *privatizing* the social-welfare costs. Nonetheless, the South Korean government was able to increase defense spending in part owing to the continued growth in the economy and the expansion of the state's revenue, and in part owing to its national security ideology and the authoritarian mode of governance which insulated the defense sector from contending social and political pressures. Recent democratization and the changing regional and international security environment are, however, unlikely to sustain the current pattern of defense spending in South Korea.

PATTERNS OF DEFENSE SPENDING IN SOUTH KOREA

Since the national division in 1945, South Korea has faced constant military threats from the North, ranging from all-out conflict in the Korean War, to overt military provocations, to covert operations. Such threats have elevated defense security as the ultimate national goal, and the defense sector has enjoyed a privileged position in the allocation of national resources. As Table 8.1 illustrates, defense spending in South Korea has been characterized by tremendous expansion. In 1961, South Korea spent a meager $237 million on defense. This figure increased to $1.5 billion in 1976. By 1987, South Korea's defense spending had reached a record high of $5.37 billion, a 27-fold increase over the course of 26 years. Despite *constant* military threats from the North, however, defense spending in South Korea has varied. While defense spending in the 1960s reveals an erratic pattern by year, the 1970s were marked by constant annual increases. By contrast, defense spending in the 1980s shows a trend of *incremental decrease* in relative terms. In what follows, we attempt to determine the nature of variation of defense spending in South Korea not only by examining the relative weight of defense spending vis-à-vis the national economy and public expenditure, but also by analyzing the structure of defense spending in terms of the categories of appropriation.

National economy and defense spending

One way of understanding the nature and pattern of defense spending is to measure its relative weight in the national economy. The relative weight can be obtained simply by calculating the share of defense spending in the gross national product. Intuitively speaking, if the share is high, we can infer that defense burden is heavy, and that the national economy is likely to be constrained.[3]

In South Korea, defense spending as a percentage of gross national product (GNP) has varied over time (see Table 8.1). During 1961–2, nearly 6 percent of GNP was allocated to the defense sector, a high percentage compared with most countries. This share gradually declined between 1963 and 1975. In 1963, South Korea spent $227 million for defense purposes, a slight decrease from $274 million in 1962, accounting for 4.2 percent of GNP. The ratio fell to 3.6 percent in 1965. Throughout the latter part of the 1960s and the early 1970s, South Korea maintained defense spending at an average level of 4 percent. A sudden change came in 1976, when defense spending doubled from $719 million in 1975 to $1.5 billion in 1976, and its share of GNP jumped from 3.9 percent to 6.3 percent. Although there were slight variations by year, this higher level was sustained through 1981. In 1982, the share of defense spending in GNP began to decline. In 1982, defense spending accounted for 6 percent of GNP, falling to 5.8 percent in 1983, 5.2 percent in 1986, and 4.7 percent in 1987.

Overall, compared with most countries, defense spending in South Korea, measured by the share of gross national product, is quite high. This indicates that defense spending constitutes an important portion of the national economy in South Korea.

Table 8.1 Defense spending in South Korea, 1961–87

Year	GNP bn $ (current price)	Defense spending bn $ (current price)	% of GNP	% of public expenditure	Rate of increase (%)
1961	4.2	0.237	5.7	29.0	−0.5
1962	4.6	0.274	5.9	23.2	0.9
1963	5.4	0.227	4.2	28.1	3.2
1964	6.4	0.213	3.6	33.2	–
1965	6.1	0.225	3.7	32.0	22.6
1966	6.9	0.278	4.0	28.8	39.1
1967	7.2	0.297	4.1	27.4	18.4
1968	5.5	0.234	4.2	24.7	34.7
1969	7.4	0.298	4.0	22.8	29.2
1970	8.2	0.333	3.9	23.2	21.2
1971	10.0	0.411	4.1	24.6	22.4
1972	9.7	0.428	4.4	24.8	20.7
1973	12.6	0.475	3.8	28.0	5.5
1974	17.5	0.558	3.2	29.3	61.8
1975	18.4	0.719	3.9	28.8	49.0
1976	24.0	1.500	6.3	32.9	59.1
1977	31.5	1.800	5.7	34.7	34.9
1978	46.0	2.600	5.6	37.0	37.7
1979	48.3	3.181	6.6	30.8	19.0
1980	60.3	3.460	5.7	35.6	48.3
1981	63.1	3.970	6.3	33.8	15.9
1982	72.3	4.324	6.0	34.5	18.5
1983	76.6	4.407	5.8	33.0	5.9
1984	83.2	4.494	5.4	31.7	4.5
1985	83.1	4.399	5.3	30.6	8.3
1986	98.3	5.110	5.2	31.4	13.8
1987	121.3	5.730	4.7	30.4	10.9

Source: (a) Defense spending for FY1961–7 is calculated from *SIPRI Yearbook of World Armaments and Disarmament* (1968/69, 208–9). (b) The percentage of GNP for FY1961–7 is calculated from *SIPRI Yearbook* (1975, 160–1). (c) All figures for FY 1968–7 are from various years of the *Military Balance*. (d) The percentage of public expenditure and the rates of increase are from Economic Planning Board (1988, 58–9); and *Korea Statistical Yearbook* (1971, 1975).

Fiscal structure and defense spending

National security is a collective good, and defense spending is an important instrument for creating that collective good. However, defense spending is usually constrained by a country's fiscal capacity simply because national survival is not the sole objective, but only one of several. The greater the share of government expenditure allocated to defense, the higher the policy priority of national security; and vice versa. Defense spending as a share of public expenditure is also a useful indicator for measuring substitution effects between guns and butter. Since public finance involves the authoritative

Table 8.2 Public expenditures by appropriation category, 1962–88 (percentages)

Year	Defense	Social development[a]	Economic development	Others[b]	Total
1965	32.0	–	46.9	21.1	100.0
1968	24.7	–	50.2	25.1	100.0
1970	23.2	–	51.5	25.3	100.0
1972	25.9	–	36.8	37.3	100.0
1976	32.9	21.6	25.0	21.1	100.0
1979	30.8	22.7	27.8	18.7	100.0
1980	35.6	24.1	21.5	18.8	100.0
1981	33.8	24.5	18.9	22.8	100.0
1982	34.5	27.0	17.5	21.0	100.0
1983	33.0	27.6	17.2	22.2	100.0
1984	31.7	26.8	15.3	26.2	100.0
1985	30.5	26.8	16.3	26.4	100.0
1986	31.2	28.1	16.1	24.6	100.0
1987	30.4	28.0	19.4	22.2	100.0
1988	32.8	28.6	14.4	24.2	100.0

Source: Economic Planning Board (various issues). (a) Educational spending is included. (b) General administration, grants to local government, and repayments of debts and others.

allocation of scarce resources, a greater allocation to the defense budget usually entails tradeoffs in other categories of public spending.

Just as defense spending in South Korea has accounted for a large portion of GNP, it has also constituted a major portion of total government expenditures. The relative share of defense spending in total government expenditure has shown a trend similar to that in GNP. From 1962 to 1975, defense spending accounted for less than 30 percent of government expenditure. Beginning in 1976, however, defense spending began to exceed 30 percent of public expenditure (see Tables 8.1 and 8.2), increasing from 28.8 percent in 1975 to 34.7 percent in 1977, and reaching 37 percent in 1978. This figure has gradually declined since 1982, dropping to 30.4 percent by 1987, a sharp decrease from the level of the late 1970s and early 1980s.

The trend in the defense budget allocations in South Korea between 1961 and 1987 has thus been curvilinear. During the 1962–72 period, the South Korean government spent more for economic development than defense. Since 1973, however, the defense sector has been the largest recipient of government funds. This is in part due to the introduction of a new accounting system which divided the category of economic and social development. More importantly, however, it is also the result of an absolute increase in defense allocations, a trend which continues to the present. Since the early 1980s, however, the gap between defense spending and social-development spending has been narrowing, while the allocation for economic development has visibly decreased. In 1981, for example, the government allocated 33 percent of public expenditure to the defense sector, 27 percent to social development, and 18.9 percent to economic development. By contrast, in 1986, the defense budget decreased to 31.2 percent of total government expenditures, while the budget for social development increased to 28.1 percent. This variation in budget allocation reflects the shifting pattern of government policy priorities over time. In the 1960s, modernization and economic growth were the top national priorities, making it possible to allocate the largest portion of government spending to economic development. Entering the 1970s, a rapidly changing security environment such as increased military threat from the North and eroding security commitment from the United States shifted the hierarchy of national goals in favor of the defense sector. Finally, in the 1980s, distribution and welfare have become new political issues, a natural outcome of 'growth first and distribution later' policy. As a result, the government began to pay more attention to these sectors, inducing changes in budget allocations.

Structure of defense spending

In order to understand the precise impact of defense spending on the national economy, it is essential to disaggregate defense spending by appropriation categories (Chan 1985, 424). Table 8.3 presents the structure of South Korea's military expenditure by appropriation categories. A great portion of the defense budget has gone to the military's personnel costs such as wages and salaries in kind. The relative share of personnel costs has declined over time, however. In 1961, personnel costs accounted for 76.8 percent of total defense spending. This figure declined to 48.6 percent in 1974, and in 1986, the military's personnel costs represented a little more than one-third of defense spending (37.1 percent).

While the proportion of personnel costs has decreased, expenses involving the maintenance of systems and equipment, investment in equipment acquisition and base construction, and defense-related research and development have increased rapidly. In 1974, for example, while personnel costs fell to 48.6 percent, spending on maintenance and on military equipment purchases rose to 41.4 percent and 7.2 percent respectively. In the mid 1980s, the relative share of personnel costs further declined, accounting for only 37.1 percent of defense spending. By contrast, maintenance costs rose to 24.5 percent, and investment in equipment acquisition and base construction accounted for 37.1 percent. Meanwhile, investment in defense-related research and development has shown a curvilinear trend. Prior to the 1970s, research and development expenditures were nil. They remained low in the early 1970s, accounting for 0.2 percent of the defense budget in 1971; grew in the mid 1970s to reach 5.1 percent in 1976; and declined thereafter, dropping to 1.3 percent in 1986.

These appropriation trends reveal several interesting aspects of defense spending in South Korea. First, the personnel component of the defense budget has declined dramatically over time. Several factors explain this

Table 8.3 South Korean military expenditures by appropriation category, 1961–86 (current million won)

Year	Military personnel	Maintenance	R & D	Purchase of military equipment	Total
1961	12,743 (76.8)	2,948 (17.8)	–	896 (5.4)	16,587
1969	55,780 (66.1)	17,457 (20.7)	–	11,146 (13.2)	84,383
1970	69,073 (67.5)	22,968 (22.4)	–	10,295 (10.1)	102,336
1971	81,825 (60.7)	38,217 (28.4)	341 (0.2)	14,365 (10.7)	134,748
1972	96,987 (55.9)	55,500 (32.0)	2,054 (1.1)	19,097 (11.0)	173,638
1973	108,131 (58.9)	60,391 (32.9)	2,137 (1.1)	12,971 (7.1)	183,630
1974	144,107 (48.6)	123,153 (41.4)	8,234 (2.8)	21,348 (7.2)	296,842
1975	208,720 (47.2)	141,169 (31.9)	12,726 (2.9)	79,854 (18.1)	442,469
1976	298,920 (42.5)	170,975 (24.3)	36,035 (5.1)	197,818 (28.1)	703,748
1977	393,301 (41.4)	234,943 (24.7)	36,224 (3.8)	285,165 (30.0)	949,633
1978	483,557 (37.5)	336,539 (26.1)	30,878 (2.4)	438,397 (34.0)	1,289,353
1979	591,828 (38.8)	451,776 (29.6)	45,389 (3.0)	436,868 (28.6)	1,525,861
1980	792,401 (35.1)	751,607 (33.3)	70,751 (3.1)	642,624 (28.5)	2,257,383
1981	994,900 (37.2)	859,900 (32.1)	66,500 (2.5)	754,100 (28.2)	2,675,400
1982	1,198,900 (38.9)	860,500 (25.7)	64,500 (2.2)	955,300 (31.0)	3,081,000
1983	1,240,300 (38.1)	834,100 (25.7)	51,300 (1.6)	1,124,100 (34.6)	3,249,800
1984	1,305,300 (38.5)	866,300 (25.6)	64,900 (1.9)	1,153,800 (34.0)	3,390,300
1985	1,429,600 (38.4)	954,700 (25.6)	58,400 (1.6)	1,278,500 (34.4)	3,721,200
1986	1,555,900 (37.1)	1,027,200 (24.5)	56,200 (1.3)	1,554,700 (37.1)	4,194,000

Source: Korean Ministry of National Defense (1988).
Figures in parentheses represent percentages of total annual military expenditures.

trend: a gradual reduction of troop size over time; a relative increase in defense spending; a relatively stable wage structure in the military sector, which is less sensitive to the conditions of the labor market; and changing defense priorities. Second, the most visible growth has occurred in the category of investment in military equipment purchase and base construction. In the early 1970s, investment in equipment and base construction accounted for only 7 percent of defense spending. In the mid 1970s, however, that percentage increased significantly to 36 percent. The phase-out of military assistance from the United States and the conscious efforts to catch up with North Korea through ambitious force-improvement plans were largely responsible for heavy investment in this category. The increasing share of defense budget for systems maintenance and investment in equipment and base construction in turn suggests enhanced defense capabilities in terms of combat readiness, sustainability, and modernization. Third, the allocation of a noticeable share of the defense budget to investment in research and development since 1971 is the result of efforts to increase military self-reliance through defense industrialization. Finally, the relative and absolute growth in nonpersonnel expenditures (especially investment in equipment acquisition and base construction and investment in research and development) implies that defense spending in South Korea has increasingly become intertwined with the national economy through linkage effects such as cost-push inflation, bottlenecks in the supply of capital goods; and through substitution effects in the allocation of financial resources.

In sum, defense spending in South Korea has followed several interesting patterns. First, compared with most countries, South Korea's defense burden is relatively high. South Korea was the 17th largest military spender in the world in 1986 (Sivard 1989, 52) and the 5th among the 53 middle-income countries in 1987 (World Bank 1989, 184–5). Second, although South Korea has shown a constant increase in the absolute value of military spending, variations over time reveal a curvilinear pattern: slower growth in the 1960s, rapid increases in the 1970s, and a return to slow growth in the 1980s. The curvilinear pattern applies to defense spending as a share of both GNP and public expenditure. Finally, in the structure of defense spending, the personnel component of defense spending has decreased while nonpersonnel expenditures have increased substantially since the mid 1970s. This changing defense spending structure indicates increasing interconnections between defense spending and the national economy. The overall pattern of defense spending raises a number of interesting questions: What made it possible for South Korea to sustain such high levels of defense spending? What accounts for the variations in defense spending over time? Why has the structure of defense spending shifted in favor of nonpersonnel allocations?

DETERMINANTS OF DEFENSE SPENDING

Interaction effects

The most standard explanations of the determinants of defense spending rely on Richardson's arms-race model (Richardson 1960). Richardson's model is a simple mathematical formula based on the assumption that one country's defense spending is reactive to its adversary's hostile military actions, defense spending, and stockpiling of armaments. Given hostile military interactions between the two Koreas, the Richardson model would appear to have strong empirical relevance, and several scholars have applied the model to the study of South Korea's military spending (Mok 1989; Olsen 1986; Park 1986). Their findings indicate that the rate of increase in defense spending of South Korea is less sensitive to North Korea's defense spending, but is closely associated with its hostile military actions.

Actual trends of military spending in both Koreas appear to confirm their findings. In the 1960s and early 1970s, South Korea's defense spending showed virtually no sensitivity to that of North Korea. Prior to 1976, North Korea maintained a military superiority over the South in all categories, including absolute amount of military spending, actual combat force, and overall military stock (National Unification Board 1985). Furthermore, North Korea's rate of increase in military spending was much higher than that of South Korea even though the North already possessed unquestionable military superiority over the South. In 1974, for example, South Korea spent 22 percent less than North Korea on defense, while North Korea's rate of increase in defense spending in that year was higher than that of the South.

In view of its past defense-spending behavior, South Korea appears to be sensitive more to North Korea's hostile military actions than to its defense spending per se. In the mid-1970s, South Korea began to rapidly build up its military force. This military buildup, however, was more a reaction to military provocations from the North, and the eroding security environment fostered by the Nixon Doctrine, than to North Korea's defense spending. Beginning in the late 1960s, North Korea became increasingly aggressive militarily. On 21 January 1968, North Korean commandos raided the Blue House, the South Korean presidential mansion. Two days later, North Korea seized the USS *Pueblo* and its 82 crew members. A year later North Korea shot down a U.S. EC-121 reconnaissance plane and its crew of 31. These incidents led South Korean leaders to perceive a dangerous vulnerability in their country's security in the event of an all-out attack by the North. These military provocations from the North coincided with the Nixon Doctrine, which signaled potential U.S. disengagement from Asia in general and South Korea in particular (Lee and Sato 1982; Litwak 1984; Nam 1986). To cope with this eroding security environment, South

Korea initiated a series of attempts to improve its defense capabilities, including the Force Modernization Plan (1971–5), the Force Improvement Plan (1976–80) and the Second Force Improvement Plan (1982–6), and accelerated defense spending (Ha 1984; Korean Ministry of National Defense 1988; Moon 1986). Between 1974 and 1980, defense spending in South Korea increased at an annual average rate of 44.3 percent.

As a result of this big push, South Korea's defense spending in 1978 exceeded that of North Korea by more than $100 million. By 1986, South Korea exceeded North Korea in the acquisition of military weapons by $100 million. One puzzle arises here. Why has South Korea continued to increase its defense spending despite the fact that it has maintained an overall superiority over North Korea in terms of absolute defense spending and despite the fact that the rate of increase of North Korea's defense spending has declined relatively since the late 1970s? A plausible answer lies in the inertia of South Korea's catch-up mentality. South Korean military leaders continued to be obssessed with a military inferiority complex and high threat perception, and they believed that the current defense spending was *not* enough to catch up with North Korea. In this sense, military interaction effects, especially those resulting from hostile military actions, offer an important clue to the elucidation of the determinants of defense spending in South Korea. However, the action–reaction model is only one of several factors influencing the pattern of defense spending in South Korea.

Alliance effects

Inasmuch as interactions with North Korea have played an important role in shaping the parameters of defense spending in South Korea, effects resulting from alliance relations with the United States have served as a key factor. Alliance effects are here defined as a set of opportunities and constraints stemming from the management of the military alliance with the United States. Since the signing of the U.S.–Korean Mutual Defense Treaty in 1954, Washington has influenced the pattern of defense spending in South Korea in two ways.

First is the role of the United States as a provider of military assistance. During the period from 1954 to 1976, it provided a lion's share of South Korea's defense spending. South Korea's military dependence on U.S. military assistance was particularly high between 1954 and 1968 when the ratio of U.S. military aid to total defense expenditure was more than 100 percent, while South Korea contributed less than 20 percent of its own overall defense expenditures. For example, U.S. military aid as a percentage of total South Korean defense expenditures was 119.7 percent in 1966, 103.2 percent in 1967, and 128.4 percent in 1968. In this light, it becomes clear that although South Korea's defense expenditures as a percentage of GNP were relatively small during this period, when combined with the American aid, the ratio was very high. Between 1966 and 1973, the average share of defense spending in GNP was 3.9%, but when combined with U.S. aid funds spent on defense, the average rises to well over 7 percent (Galenson and Galenson 1986, 175; Lee 1982, 161). America's role as the provider of military aid explains to a large extent why South Korea spent less on the defense sector during this period despite an apparent inferiority in the arms balance with North Korea.

In 1969, however, the United States security commitment to South Korea began to decline. The haunting Vietnam syndrome, coupled with a fiscal crisis at home, produced the Nixon Doctrine and the beginnings of détente. As part of the Nixon Doctrine, the United States withdrew one combat division from South Korea, and began to decrease military assistance. Within a six-year period from 1969 to 1974, the ratio of U.S. aid to total defense spending in South Korea dropped from 56.2 percent to 14.3 percent. Beginning in 1972, military assistance was replaced by military loans, but the amount of military loans was minimal, accounting for less than 10% of total defense spending. By 1978, U.S. military assistance was completely phased out, and military loans continued to decline. It was this declining U.S. military aid that fostered South Korea's heavy defense spending in the latter part of the 1970s. In fact, South Korea has financed more than 90 percent of defense spending internally since 1975, substantially reducing its dependence on the U.S. military aid (Lee and Sato 1982). Thus, the expansion and contraction of U.S. military aid have directly influenced the pattern of defense spending in South Korea.

The second important alliance effect is U.S. pressure for defense burdens sharing. Responding to domestic fiscal crises in the mid and late 1970s, Washington began to exert pressure on its allies to take over an increasing share of the defense burden in the maintenance of military alliances. South Korea was not an exception to this new trend, not only because the United States maintains large ground forces in South Korea, but also because of South Korea's growing economic strength. Unlike other allies, Seoul was very amenable to U.S. demands. In 1979, President Park Chung-Hee of South Korea announced an expansion of defense spending significantly beyond previously planned levels, and immediately thereafter South Korea entered into an informal agreement to allocate 6 percent of GNP to the defense sector, a level comparable to the U.S. defense burden. As a result of this burden-sharing formula, South Korea spent 6.6 percent of GNP in 1980 and 6.0 percent in 1981, increasing the defense budget from $2.6 billion in 1978 to $7.2 billion in 1988. This represents a 2.8-fold increase over a ten-year period. The burden-sharing agreement with the United States has continued to serve as one of the principal determinants of South Korean defense spending ever since (Oh 1988). Alliance effects enhance our understanding of the patterns in South Korea's defense spending, but they cannot fully explain them. As Table 8.1 illustrates, despite the burden-sharing scheme, South Korea has fallen below the 6-percent-of-GNP formula since 1983. Defense spending in 1983 accounted for 5.8 percent of GNP. The ratio continued to slide over the next several years, reaching 4.7 percent in 1987. This downward trend suggests that defense burden-sharing pressure from the United States is not the sole factor shaping defense spending in South Korea. Why this noncompliance behavior? What else influences military budget allocation?

Economic effects

Broadly speaking, economic factors can influence the pattern of defense spending in two ways. One is the residual effects resulting from rapid economic growth (Benoit 1973, 275; Caputo 1975, 423–46). The other is fiscal capacity measured by the rate of increase in total government spending (Domke *et al.* 1983, 30). In the case of South Korea, the latter appears to be more significant. Our data indicate that defense budgets in South Korea have been rather sensitive to the boom and bust cycles of the national economy, with lag time effects. For example, the years of 1964, 1970, and 1974 all show the trend of slowed growth in defense spending. Common to these years is the adoption of austere macroeconomic stabilization measures to tame inflationary pressure and economic crises. Defense budgets were subjected to austere fiscal control as part of this stabilization policy. The extent to which austerity measures impacted defense spending has varied, however, becoming more pronounced during the 1982–6 period. In order to overcome economic crises, the government implemented stabilization measures, and trimmed all fiscal outlays, including the defense budget (Moon 1987; Haggard and Moon 1990). We can derive two interesting observations from the above discussion. First, it is macroeconomic stabilization policy rather than economic downturn per se that has led to the contraction or slowed the growth of defense spending. Second, contrary to the conventional wisdom in South Korea, acuteness of military threats and the political power of the military do not necessarily exempt military budgets from austere fiscal control.

Nevertheless, economic conditions do not fully explain defense spending outcomes. For example, during 1978–9, the South Korean economy was under severe economic stresses as a result of inflationary pressure, and demands for tight fiscal and monetary control were strong, yet the government continued to expand the size of defense spending. In contrast, the South Korean economy has been recovering since 1986, but the government has continued to slash defense spending. This variation cannot be meaningfully understood without taking domestic political factors into account.

Political effects

Defense spending is a policy outcome. Policy choices and the resulting fiscal outcomes are largely a function of domestic political dynamics. There is, however, no clearcut consensus on precisely how and which aspects of domestic politics shape defense spending. While some focus on political leadership or the chief executive (Cameron 1978; Kingdon 1984; Ostrom 1978; Russett 1982) and bureaucratic politics (Bobrow and Hill 1986; Davis *et al.* 1966; Halperin and Kanter 1973), others point to a military–industrial complex (Rosen 1973) and electoral cycles (Mintz 1988; Monroe 1983; Tufte 1978). None of these variables can satisfactorily explain the variations in South Korean defense spending. As Mok's (1989) recent findings indicate, electoral cycles have virtually no impact on defense spending since the electoral system in South Korea had been distorted under persistent authoritarian rule. Because South Korea has no sizable military–industrial complex, this cannot help to explain defense spending either (Moon 1986). Political leadership and bureaucratic politics, however, do shape the pattern of defense spending in South Korea.

Political leadership and bureaucratic politics cannot be separated from the overall domestic political structure. South Korea's political structure has long been characterized by a strong state with a high level of executive dominance and bureaucratic unity, resulting in the insulation of policy-making machinery from social and political pressures (Haggard and Moon 1990; Moon 1990a). This institutional character of the South Korean state, coupled with a constant military threat from the North, helped to depoliticize national-security issues, giving the political leadership a great deal of flexibility in the appropriation of funds for the defense sector.

As a result of this flexibility, the allocation of national budget has been heavily influenced by the commitment and style of political leadership. For Park Chung-Hee, national security was the foremost national goal, even if it came at the expense of growth, distribution, and welfare. This executive commitment to national security has enabled the defense budget to enjoy the privileged position in the process of budgetary planning. The level of defense budget was a 'given' around which the rest of the budget was planned. President Chun Doo-Hwan, on the other hand, was less preoccupied with the defense budget. Chun had justified his seizure of political power on the need to stabilize social and economic situations, which became choatic with the abrupt end of Park's regime in 1979. In order to manage the economic crises, Chun pursued aggressive neoconservative economic reforms composed of austere macroeconomic stabilization measures and structural adjustment (Moon 1987), and subjected the defense budgets to the political economy of Chun's legitimacy building. This variation in executive commitment to national-security goals and political leadership style explains why defense spending under the Chun regime has declined, despite economic recovery and defense burden-sharing pressure from the United States, while the Park regime continued to expand defense spending despite impending economic crisis.

The degree of executive commitment to a goal shapes the dynamics of bureaucratic politics in that issue area. Under Park, decision-making power was highly concentrated in the hands of the presidential office, and there was virtually no room for bureaucratic politics. Once Park and his close associates decided the scope of defense spending, the proposed budget did not encounter any opposition from other branches of the government. With Park's backing, the Ministry of National Defense prevailed over other bureaucratic agencies. By contrast, defense spending under the Chun regime became increasingly politicized within the executive branch. As Chun was more concerned with economic stability, the Economic Planning Board wielded more power in the allocation of national budgets, and the Ministry of National Defense had to lobby hard to get its own share. Likewise, the chief executive's preferences and the resulting realignment of decision-making power among bureaucratic agencies influenced the budgetary outcomes, including the defense budget.

In sum, defense spending in South Korea has been determined by the dynamic interplay of multiple factors. While military interactions with North Korea and the changing nature of alliance relations with the United States have shaped the overall scope and composition of military budget, the boom and bust cycles and related fiscal capacity, and domestic political dynamics have determined where defense spending decisions are made, and the criteria for judging their contents. Given the economic stagnation of North Korea and recent domestic and international political developments of South Korea, fiscal capacity and domestic political considerations are likely to become increasingly crucial in mapping out the nature and direction of defense spending in South Korea.

MUDDLING THROUGH SECURITY, GROWTH, AND WELFARE: IMPACT ASSESSMENT

So far, we have discussed the patterns, structure, and determinants of defense spending in South Korea. This section assesses the contribution of defense spending to South Korea's overall national well-being. The political-economic outcomes of defense spending can be approached from three angles. The first concerns the relationship between defense spending and security performance. Defense spending is an instrument of enhancing national security, but increased defense spending does not guarantee an enhanced security position. Some countries such as Libya and Saudi Arabia continue to be vulnerable to external military threats, despite high levels of defense spending. The second approach to evaluating defense spending involves the relationship between defense spending and economic growth. Here it is necessary to examine two sets of factors. First is the extent to which the defense budget is tied to the national economy. Second is the impact of defense expenditures on the national economy and its performance. Finally, defense spending can be evaluated in light of the tradeoff between defense spending and welfare. Defense spending involves an authoritative allocation of *scarce* resources (that is, public expenditure).

Therefore, the expansion and contraction of defense expenditures can profoundly influence performance in social welfare. In the next section, we will examine the impact of defense spending on security, growth, and welfare.

Defense spending and security performance

South Korea faces constant and real threats to its national security. Under these circumstances, South Korea's cardinal strategic objective is attaining credible deterrence, and the contribution of defense spending to national security can be measured against this objective. During the pursuit of defense buildup, military provocations from the North declined relative to the late 1960s, while military tension remained intact.[4] To what extent and how was this decline in North Korean military hostilities related to increases in South Korea's defense expenditures? There are two components to credible deterrence: demonstrating the intent to use force if necessary, and presenting a force structure capable of defending the country from offensive attacks by the enemy (Jervis 1976). South Korea's massive defense buildup definitely signaled the intent and will to use military force if necessary, to put an end to the North's hostilities and in this sense, the high levels of defense spending can be said to have deterred North Korean aggression.

Actual military capabilities, however, are more important than will and intention in providing for credible deterrence. To what extent then has increased defense spending strengthened South Korea's force structure? Assessment varies (Ha 1988). According to the official government position, South Korea has failed to maintain strategic parity with the North. Despite extensive defense spending, South Korea's defense capability has reached only 65 percent of the North Korean force level (KMND 1988; Oh 1989). Conservatives, mostly from the military camp, share this rather pessimistic view, focusing on quantitative dimensions (for example, personnel size and number of weapons). On the other hand, progressive intellectuals and radical students argue that South Korea's defense capability has already exceeded that of North Korea and that any further defense buildup in the presence of U.S. troops could undermine the military balance of power and strategic stability in the Korean peninsula (Lee 1988, 140–166).[5] They cite as empirical evidence South Korea's overall economic strength, qualitative improvement, and combat experience. By contrast, Ha Young-Sun (1988) suggests a middle view, arguing that an overall military balance has been achieved between North and South Korea when measured by physical force, strategic orientation, and psychological factors.

The current debates on the comparison of military forces between the two Koreas are more normative and ideological than factual. The defense establishment emphasizes the relative weakness of South Korea's military capability in order to secure more defense budgets. The opposition bloc argues that government figures are largely fabricated and that it is time for the government to give more emphasis on the welfare sector by seeking a peaceful coexistence with the North and national unification. Two problems confront efforts to resolve these debates. The first is the lack of data. Most of the national-security data in South Korea are classified, and analysts rely heavily on unverified foreign data. The second is methodological differences in force estimates. While the government emphasizes quantitative elements, the opposition bloc focuses on the qualitative dimensions of force structure.[6]

Nonetheless, we can conclude that South Korea has achieved strategic parity with the North as a result of the rapid military buildup during the past two decades. The Japanese Self-Defense Agency (1988) recently concluded that South Korea has obtained considerable deterrence capabilities, if not superiority to the North. The Rand Corporation has also projected that South Korea will be able to surpass North Korea by 1992 (Wolf *et al.* 1985). These assessments are based on two common observations. First, quantitatively (for example, in the size of military personnel and number of weapons), North Korea leads South Korea. But qualitatively (for example, modernization, sustainability, combat readiness), South Korea is superior. Second, modern warfare involves both military and nonmilitary capabilities, especially economic strength, where South Korea is far superior to North Korea. In addition, the conventional, tactical nuclear, and command, control, communication, and intelligence capabilities of U.S. forces in South Korea serve as a considerable deterrent to North Korea's military forces (Moon 1990b).

An important aspect of South Korea's improved defense capability is the increasing level of military self-sufficiency. In the 1960s and early 1970s, South Korea depended solely on the United States for military weapons. Increased defense budgets and the promotion of defense industrialization have greatly reduced Seoul's military dependence on Washington. Furthermore, domestic production of defense articles has drastically improved the South Korean defense force's combat capabilities by expanding its access to topline equipment. For example, until the mid 1970s, the majority of South Korean soldiers used M-1 or Calvin rifles manufactured during World War II or the Korean War. Today all soldiers and even reserve forces use the M-16 because it is produced domestically. Similar improvements have been achieved in the armored, artillery, and infantry units. In addition to improving the quality of equipment used by South Korea's defense forces, the existence of the relatively diversified domestic defense industry has enhanced South Korea's peacetime industrial readiness in logistics supply (Moon 1986, 1989).

Finally, the rapid increases in defense spending have enhanced the confidence of South Koreans in their security. Immediately following North Korea's military provocations in the late 1960s, psychological defeatism was relatively high among South Koreans, resulting in economic uncertainties. The trend has reversed, and South Koreans are now much more confident.

This is an important security dividend brought by heavy defense spending in the 1970s.

Defense spending and economic growth

The impact of defense spending on economic growth remains a controversial subject. While Benoit (1973) and several others have argued that defense spending has positive effects on economic growth, Deger and Smith (1983) and Rothschild (1973) have counterargued that defense spending adversely impacts on economic growth not only because of its role in increasing the tax burden and deficit financing, but also because it contributes to the deterioration of trade balance, weakening of the currency, and fostering structural unemployment. How does the South Korean case fit in this debate?

As Table 8.4 indicates, defense spending does not appear to have undermined economic growth in aggregate terms. With the exception of 1980, when South Korea's economy declined by −6.6 percent, growth rates in defense spending have been positively related to aggregate economic growth rates. Similarly, growth rates in defense spending have consistently been positively related to the rates of growth in exports. The current account balance is the only economic indicator that is inversely related to the rate of increase in defense spending, and the deficits in that account during the 1960s and 1970s were more a function of the structural distortions of the Korean economy than of defense spending. Furthermore, since the mid 1980s, South Korea has enjoyed a surplus in the current account despite the fact that defense spending continued to increase during that time in absolute terms, thus weakening the statistical relationship between defense spending and the current account balance.

In view of the above, it would be difficult to make a case supporting the argument that defense expenditures in South Korea have 'crowded out' economic growth. On the contrary, a study by the Korea Institute for Defense Analysis found that 58 percent of defense spending during the 1970s contributed to the formation of gross domestic products in terms of value-added effects (KMND 1988). Galenson and Galenson (1986) also point out that the dynamic cost of defense spending has been low. In other words, the cost of defense spending in relation to the growth rate of total output is rather small, and, therefore, defense spending in South Korea does not divert a significant amount of resources away from the current private consumption and savings. Besides, military expenditures in South Korea have impacted the national economy in two additional ways. First is technological spinoff through the promotion of defense industrialization. Defense industrialization served as a major catalyst in the transformation of the South Korean economy from labor-intensive to capital- and technology-intensive industries, and it is highly unlikely that South Korea could have attained its current level of international

Table 8.4 Defense spending and economic growth: major indicators, 1968–88

Year	Defense expenditure (rate of increase)	GNP growth (rate of increase)	Export increase (rate of increase)	Balance of payments (current US$ in million)
1968	30.4	11.3	45.2	−440.3
1969	30.6	13.8	35.4	−548.6
1970	21.1	17.6	34.0	−622.5
1971	39.0	8.8	28.3	−847.5
1972	27.6	5.7	48.1	−371.2
1973	1.1	14.1	95.1	−308.8
1974	61.8	7.7	38.0	−2,022.7
1975	49.0	6.9	10.8	−1,886.9
1976	59.1	14.1	56.2	−313.6
1977	34.9	12.7	28.6	12.3
1978	37.7	9.7	26.5	1,085.2
1979	19.0	6.5	18.4	−4,151.1
1980	48.3	−6.6	16.3	−5,320.7
1981	15.9	6.6	21.4	−4,646.0
1982	18.5	5.4	2.8	−2,649.9
1983	5.9	11.9	11.9	−1,606.0
1984	4.5	8.4	19.6	−1,372.6
1985	9.3	5.4	3.6	−887.4
1986	13.8	12.3	14.6	4,617.0
1987	10.9	12.0	36.2	9,853.9
1988	19.3	12.2		14,160.0

Source: Economic Planning Board (various years)

competitivess in heavy industrial goods had it not been for the backing of growing defense expenditures in the mid-1970s (Moon 1986, 1989). Second is the positive impact on employment. As of 1988, the South Korean military employed 140,000 professional soldiers and 27,000 civilians. An additional 50,000 workers were employed by the defense industrial sector, and roughly 500,000 workers were employed in defense-related sectors (KMND 1988, 128).

Despite the positive contributions that defense expenditures *can* make to economic growth, when they exceed the boundaries of economic rationality, they disrupt the national economy and constrain growth. This was the case in South Korea during the defense buildup of the 1970s. First, a sharp increase in defense spending and a heavy emphasis on the defense industry resulted in massive investment in the heavy-chemical industry during 1976–79, which exceeded the levels dictated by market size, financing capacity, and even technical and engineering capability. This investment pattern contributed to waste and inefficiencies, and more importantly to the artificially overheated economy and the record inflation rate (over 30 percent) in 1979 and 1980. Although other factors such as the second oil crisis, a large influx of foreign exchange, supply bottleneck, and real-estate speculation contributed to the economic crisis of the late 1970s, rapid increases in defense spending during the 1970s also played an important role by creating inflationary pressures in the factor-input markets (Haggard and Moon 1990; Moon 1986, 1989).

Second, defense industrialization and improvement of defense force in terms of the acquisition of advanced foreign weapons systems during the 1970s were partially financed by borrowing abroad at a time of high international interest rates. The result was a rapid increase in foreign debt from $3.3 billion in 1975 to over $43 billion in the early 1980s. This burgeoning debt burden contributed to the economic crisis of the late 1970s and has increased South Korea's sensitivity to movements in the international capital markets. Although 'three lows' – low interest rates, low oil prices, and low value of the South Korean currency since 1986 – have given Seoul a temporary reprieve, efforts to upgrade defense capabilities through the acquisition of most advanced weapons will continue to strain its foreign exchange position and economic growth.

Third, the promotion of defense and heavy-chemical industrialization has resulted in dangerous levels of concentration in South Korea's business structure. South Korea has long been characterized by the existence of large business conglomerates – the *chaebols*. In promoting heavy-chemical industrialization, however, the Park regime strategically allocated credit for this purpose to the already large *chaebols*. As a result, these business conglomerates have come to dominate the South Korean economy. In 1973, the top fifty *chaebols* accounted for 32 percent of GDP. By 1980, the *chaebols* dominated the economy, accounting for 49 percent of GDP, 24 percent of total sales, 18 percent of manufacturing employment, and over half of Korea's total exports (Haggard and Moon 1990; the newspaper, *Hankuk Ilbo*, 29 September 1981). This concentration has distorted South Korea's industrial structure, undermined small and medium-sized firms, and widened disparities in the distribution of income and wealth.

Finally, the increase in defense spending in the 1970s was accompanied by increases in the tax burden, thus compressing private consumption and savings. Prior to 1975, defense expenditures were allocated from general revenue sources. Beginning in 1975, however, the Park regime introduced the National Defense Tax specifically to finance defense spending. As Table 8.5 illustrates, defense surtaxes constituted only 3.8 percent of total revenues and 14 percent of defense spending in 1975. But their share of total revenue increased to more than 11 percent between 1976 and 1979 and 14 percent in 1988. Their share in defense spending had also increased to over 40 percent since 1983, culminating in 48 percent in 1987. As a result, the overall tax burden has deepened. Prior to 1975, an average ratio of tax burden to GNP was less than 10 percent. The ratio, however, increased from 15.4 percent to 19.0 percent in 1988. Apart from the National Defense Tax, the government's enforcement of voluntary contributions to a defense fund, albeit a tiny

Table 8.5 Defense taxes and tax burden

Year	% of total taxes	% of defense spending	Tax burden/GNP
1975	3.8	14	15.4
1976	11.3	38	16.7
1977	11.4	36	16.7
1978	11.7	36	17.1
1979	11.5	40	17.4
1980	12.9	37	17.9
1981	13.4	40	18.1
1982	12.3	37	18.8
1983	12.1	40	19.4
1984	12.5	42	18.7
1985	12.8	44	18.6
1986	12.5	43	18.4
1987	13.0	48	19.0
1988	14.0	43	

Source: Economic Planning Board (1988, 56)

fraction of defense budget, further aggravated the private sector's financial burden.[7]

In sum, when measured simply in terms of aggregate correlations between military spending and economic growth, there does not appear to be a tradeoff between security and growth. However, aggregate measures hide the negative impacts of increased defense expenditures on the national economy because the South Korean economy was growing rapidly throughout the period under discussion, and government revenues expanded without interruption. When disaggregated, it becomes clear that high levels of defense spending do have a significant detrimental impact on economic growth, stability, and distribution.

Defense spending and welfare

What is the impact of defense spending on social welfare? As with tradeoffs between security and growth, there are divergent views on the substitution effects between defense spending and social welfare. While most analysts believe there is a tradeoff between military spending and welfare spending (Benoit 1973; Mosley 1985; Peroff 1977; Russett 1970; Smith 1977), some have shown reservation on the explicit tradeoff between the two (Caputo 1975; Chan 1988; Domke *et al.* 1983). Are there any tradeoffs between defense and welfare in South Korea? A recent empirical study by Mok (1989) concludes that there has been no significant tradeoff between defense and social spending categories (such as justice/police, transportation, development spending), and that there is a positive and statistically significant relationship between defense spending and educational spending. Descriptive statistics in Table 8.2 appear to support this finding; despite rapid increases in defense expenditures, spendings on social welfare and education have either remained constant or increased incrementally. Therefore, it can be said that there is no explicit tradeoff between defense spending and social-welfare spending. In fact, assessed according to overall social and economic indicators, South Korea has shown rather strong performance relative to most countries. Regarding the physical-quality-of-life index, South Korea outperforms most developing countries. Infant mortality is very low, and literacy rates and life expectancy are comparable to those in most developed countries (Sivard 1989; World Bank 1989).

There is, however, an interesting disparity between the structure of public spending and overall welfare performance. As Table 8.6 illustrates, in the categories of government spending on defense, education, and economic services, South Korea ranks high relative to other comparable (that is, middle-income) countries. For example, in 1987, South Korea ranked third in terms of defense spending and eleventh in terms of education spending among the 18 upper-middle-income countries. In contrast, South Korea spent far less than other countries on health, housing, and welfare. The South Korean government allocated only 2.3 percent of total public expenditure to health, which ranks it the third lowest among the upper-middle-income countries in 1987. The figure is far below the average spending (5.1 percent) of the 53 middle-income countries. In the case of housing, amenities, social security and welfare, South Korea spent 5.9 percent in 1972 and 7.2 percent in 1987, ranking it the second lowest of the upper-middle-income countries and the eleventh lowest among the 53 middle-income countries.

Why is there this mismatch between public spending and overall performance? How could South Korea show strong performance in the provision of basic needs and social welfare despite the meager allocation of government resources? This is to a large extent explained by the *private* assumption of welfare costs. In South Korea, there is virtually no subsidized housing, despite a chronic housing shortage and rampant real-estate speculation which have increased the private burden in finding and paying for housing. There is no compensation for unemployment, loss of income due to sickness, or being temporarily disabled, nor payments to the elderly, nor family, maternity, or child support. Simply put, welfare benefits in the Western sense do not exist. Public health services are also poor, and private citizens bear most medical costs. Expenditure on medical care as a share of total household consumption accounted for 5 percent during 1980–5, which is quite high by the stantard of developing countries. Even in the category of education spending, private costs are very high. Despite relatively high government spending on education, private educational spending as a share of total household expenditure during 1980–5 was 9 percent, the second highest among all the middle-income countries, only lower than Egypt's (World Bank 1989).

Table 8.6 Composition of government expenditure: rankings

	1972			1983			1987		
	a	b	c	a	b	c	a	b	c
Defense	11.6	25.8	3 (5)	11.4	31.9	1 (2)	11.8	29.2	3 (5)
Education	12.0	15.9	12 (45)	12.1	20.5	11 (34)	11.6	18.3	11 (31)
Health	6.3	1.2	20 (60)	4.5	1.6	18 (57)	5.1	2.3	15 (48)
Housing; Amenities; Social security and welfare	20.7	5.8	18 (49)	17.0	5.9	18 (47)	18.9	7.2	17 (42)
Economic services	27.4	25.6	10 (40)	21.9	13.6	16 (52)	21.0	16.6	14 (42)
Other	22.6	25.7	11 (41)	33.1	26.5	16 (50)		28.2	12 (39)
Total expenditure (% of GNP)	21.4	18.0	16 (41)	26.2	18.3	20 (53)	24.7	17.4	17 (45)

Notes:
(a) the average of middle-income countries
(b) South Korea
(c) rankings. The first figures indicate South Korea's ranking among upper-middle-income countries. Figures in parentheses indicate South Korea's ranking among middle-income countries. Ranking may vary by appropriation category due to missing values for some countries.
Source: World Bank (1985, 1989).

Aware of this problem, since the early 1980s the South Korean government has repeatedly emphasized the realignment of policy priorities from growth and security to social welfare. This move was essential to appease and co-opt the large segment of national population whose tolerance has increasingly waned amid growing inequality and worsening living conditions. Yet, no significant improvement has been made in this area. South Korea still resembles a minimalist 'night watch' state where social welfare belongs to the exclusive domain of private responsibility. Why this privatization of social-welfare costs? This has been an unavoidable outcome of fiscal rigidity caused by a heavy defense burden.

In sum, heavy defense spending has significantly enhanced South Korea's security position in terms of credible deterrence and improved defense capabilities. Our findings suggest that there is no explicit tradeoff between defense spending and economic growth. It is also hard to find empirical evidence to support the thesis of substitution effects between defense spending and social-welfare spending in aggregate terms. When the impact of defense spending is disaggregated and analyzed in its own context, however, some crucial negative effects become visible. Heavy defense spending has not only entailed negative implications for growth, distribution, and economic stability, but has also severely constrained government spending on social welfare, fostering the privatization of social-welfare costs. In view of this, South Korea *cannot* be characterized as an exceptional case where security, growth, and welfare form a virtuous cycle. The pursuit of security through excessive military spending has impeded growth and undermined government performance in delivering social-welfare services. Nevertheless, the South Korean government was able to muddle through these tradeoffs and the resulting political tensions in part owing to the growing economy and expanding revenue sources, and in part through the ideological hegemony of security and growth and an authoritarian political structure, both of which have been instrumental in blocking the rise of distributional coalitions and their political activism.

CONCLUSION

Can South Korea sustain the current pattern of defense spending? Both domestic and international changes are likely to hinder the continuation of current defense spending. Recent democratic transition has altered parameters underlying the political economy of public spending in South Korea. The liberalization of politics has fostered the proliferation of interest groups, and they have begun to exert formidable political influence through various channels ranging from the vote to street protests. The government is losing political leverages to insulate the defense sector from these new competing social pressures. The government can no longer sacrifice distribution and welfare in the name of national security and growth. People's expectation is high, and a failure to deliver social-welfare services can significantly undermine the regime's legitimacy and political stability. The regime faces the exhaustion of national security ideology. National security is no longer accepted as *deus ex machina*.

The regional and international security environments have been also rapidly changing in favor of reduced military spending. The coming of the end of the Cold War is as visible on the Korean peninsula as anywhere else, and is pushing for the peaceful resolution of the Korean conflict. Arms control, arms reduction, and peaceful national unification have become new political catchphrases. In this circumstance, it is hardly feasible to justify the continued expansion of defense spending.

NOTES

1 We thank Steve Chan and Alex Mintz for their comments, and Leigh Harris and Seok-Soo Lee for research assistance.
2 The 'Taiwanese exception' thesis is borrowed from Chan (1988) and Chan and Clark (1990).
3 The impact of defense spending on economic growth has remained controversial. See Chan (1985) for an excellent and balanced review of the issue.
4 There were two significant provocations. One is North Korea's military attacks on five western islands in 1973, and the other is an attack on American soldiers at Panmunjum in 1977. The former was undertaken before the South's military buildup, while the latter was accidental.
5 North Korea's official position is similar to this view.
6 On this issue, see Ha (1988).

7 During 1973–88, the amount of voluntary contribution to the defense fund has reached 609 million won, about 0.1 percent of total defense expenditures during this period.

REFERENCES

Adelman, Irma and Cynthia Morris. 1973. *Economic Growth and Social Equity in Developing Countries*. Stanford, Calif.: Stanford University Press.

Benoit, Emile 1973. *Defense and Economic Growth in Developing Countries*. Lexington, Mass.: D. C. Heath.

Benoit, Emile. 1978. Growth and defense in developing countries. *Economic Development and Cultural Change* 26: 271–80.

Bergsman, J. 1979. *Growth and Equity in Semi-industrialized Countries*. World Bank staff working paper no. 351, Washington, D.C.: World Bank.

Bobrow, Davis B. and Steven Hill. 1986. Managing your protector: Japan's use of military budgets. Paper presented at the annual meeting of the International Studies Association, Washington, D.C.

Cameron, David. 1978. The expansion of the political economy: a comparative analysis. *American Political Science Review* 72: 1243–61.

Caputo, David, A. 1975. New perspectives on the public policy implications of defense and welfare expenditures. *Policy Science* 6: 423–46.

Chan, Steve. 1985. The impact of defense spending on economic performance: a survey of evidence and problems. *ORBIS* 29: 403–34.

Chan, Steve. 1988. Defense burden and economic growth: unraveling the Taiwanese enigma. *American Political Science Review* 82: 913–20.

Chan, Steve and Cal Clark. 1990. Can good things go together?: A virtuous cycle in East Asia. *International Studies Notes* 15: 4–9.

Cumings, Bruce. 1984. The origins and development of the Northeast Asian political economy. *International Organization* 38: 1–40.

Davis, O., M. Dempster, and A. Wildavsky. 1966. A theory of the budgetary process. *American Political Science Review* 60: 529–49.

Deger, Saadet and Ron Smith. 1983. Military expenditure and growth in less developed countries. *Journal of Conflict Resolution* 27: 335–53.

Domke, William, Richard Eichenberg, and Catherine Kelleher. 1983. The illusion of choice: defense and welfare in advanced industrial democracies, 1948–1978. *American Political Science Review* 77: 19–34.

Economic Planning Board. 1975. *Korea Statistical Yearbook*. Seoul: Economic Planning Board.

Economic Planning Board. Various years. *Korean Economic Indicators*. Seoul: Economic Planning Board.

Faini, Riccardo, Patricia Arnez, and Lance Taylor. 1984. Defense spending, economic structure and growth: evidence among countries and over time. *Economic Development and Cultural Change* 32: 487–98.

Frederiksen, Peter and Robert Looney. 1982. Defense expenditures and economic growth in developing countries. *The Journal of Economic Development* 7(1).

Frederiksen, Peter and Robert Looney. 1986. Defense expenditures, external public debt and growth in developing countries. *Journal of Peace Research* 23: 329–38.

Galenson, Walter and David W. Galenson. 1986. Japan and South Korea. In David B. Denoon (ed.), *Constraints on Strategy: The Economics of Western Security*. pp. 152–94. New York: Pergamon-Brassey's.

Ha, Young Sun. 1984. South Korea. In James Katz (ed.), *Arms Production in Developing Countries*, pp. 225–33. Lexington Mass.: Lexington Books.

Ha, Young Sun. 1988. The Korean military balance: myth and reality. Seoul: Korean Institute of Defense Analysis.

Haggard, Stephan and Chung-in Moon. 1983. The Korean state in the international economy: liberal, dependent, or mercantile. In John Ruggie (ed.), *Antinomies of Interdependence*, pp. 131–89. New York: Columbia University Press.

Haggard, Stephan and Chung-in Moon. 1990. Institutions and economic growth: theory and a Korean case study. *World Politics* 42: 210–37.

Halperin, Morton H. and Arnold Kanter (eds.). 1973. *Readings in American Foreign Policy: A Bureaucratic Perspective*. Boston: Little, Brown.

Japan Self-Defense Agency (JSDA). 1988. *Whitebook on Defense*. Tokyo: Japan Self-Defense Agency.

Jervis, Robert. 1976. *Perception and Misperception in International Politics*. Princeton, N.J.: Princeton University Press.

Kingdon, J. 1984. *Agendas, Alternatives, and Public Policies*. Boston: Little, Brown.

Korean Ministry of National Defense (KMND). 1988. *Whitebook on National Defense*. Seoul: Korean Ministry of National Defense (in Korean).

Lee, Chae-jin and Hideo Sato. 1982. *U.S. Policy Toward Japan and Korea*. New York: Praeger.

Lee, Kyung-Heon. 1982. National defense and national budget. In Chong-kee Park and Kyuoek Lee (eds.), *National Budget and Policy Objectives*. Seoul: Korea Development Institute (in Korean).

Lee, Young Hee. 1988. Comparative study of war capabilities between North and South Korea. *Sahoi wa Sasang* 1: 140–66 (in Korean).

Litwak, Robert S. 1984. *Detente and the Nixon Doctrine: American Foreign Policy and the Pursuit of Stability, 1969–1976*. New York: Cambridge University Press.

Mintz, Alex. 1988. Electoral cycles and military spending: a comparison of Israel and the U.S. *Comparative Political Studies* 21: 368–81.

Mok, J. 1989. Defense enigma: the South Korean tradeoff over guns or butter. In *The Proceedings of the World Conference of Korean Political Studies*. Seoul: Korean Political Science Association.

Monroe, K. 1983. Political manipulation of the economy: a closer look at political business cycle. *Presidential Studies Quarterly* 13: 37–49.

Moon, Chung-in. 1986. South Korea: between security and vulnerability. In James Katz (ed.), *The Implications of Third World Military Industrialization*, pp. 241–66. Lexington, Mass.: D. C. Heath.

Moon, Chung-in. 1987. The demise of a developmentalist state?: Political consequences of neoconservative reforms in South Korea. *Journal of Developing Societies* 6(2).

Moon, Chung-in 1989. Arms production in a newly industrializing country: economic, political, and technological implications. In Chandran Jeshurun (ed.), *Arms and Defense in Southeast Asia*. Singapore: Institute of Southeast Asian Studies.

Moon, Chung-in. 1990a. Beyond statism: the political economy of growth in South Korea. *International Studies Notes* 15: 24–7.

Moon, Chung-in. 1990b. The structure of the Korean conflict and U.S. troops in South Korea. Seoul: Daehan Institute of Policy Development (in Korean).

Mosley, H. 1985. *The Arms Race: Economic and Social Consequences*. Lexington, Mass.: D. C. Heath.

Nam, Joo-hong. 1986. *America's Commitment to South Korea: The First Decade of the Nixon Doctrine*. New York: Cambridge University Press.

National Unification Board. 1985. *Assessment of Military Capability in North and South Korea*. Seoul: National Unification Board.

Nincic, Miroslav and Thomas Cusack. 1979. The political economy of U.S. military spending. *Journal of Peace Research* 16: 105–15.

Oh, Kwan-chi. 1988. Some thoughts on ROK–US alliance and burden-sharing. Seoul: Korean Institute of Defense Analysis.

Oh, Kwan-chi. 1989. Assessment of North and South Korean military power. *Wolgan Gunsa Vison* 6: 32–40 (in Korean).

Olsen, Edward. 1986. The arms race on the Korean Peninsula. *Asian Survey* 26: 851–67.

Ostrom, Charles. 1978. A reactive linkage model of the U.S. defense expenditure policy making process. *American Political Science Review* 72: 941–57.

Park, Tong Whan. 1986. Political economy of the arms race in Korea: queries, evidence, and insights. *Asian Survey* 26: 839–50.

Peroff, Kathleen 1977. The warfare–welfare tradeoffs: health, public aids and housing. *Journal of Sociology and Social Welfare* 4: 366–81.

Richardson, Lewis F. 1960. *Arms and Insecurity*. Chicago: Quadrangle Books.

Rosen, Steven (ed.). 1973. *Testing the Theory of the Military–Industrial Complex*. Lexington, Mass.: D.C. Heath.

Rothschild, Kurt W. 1973. Military expenditure, exports and growth. *Kyklos* 26: 804–14.

Russett, Bruce 1970. *What Price Vigilance? The Burdens of National Defense*. New Haven, Conn.: Yale University Press.

Russett, Bruce M. 1982. Defense expenditure and national well-being. *American Political Science Review* 71: 767–77.

Sivard, Ruth Leger. 1989. *World Military and Social Expenditure 1989*. Washington, D.C.: World Priorities.

Szymanski, Albert. 1973. Military spending and economic stagnation. *American Journal of Sociology* 79: 1–14.

Tufte, Edward. 1978. *Political Control of Economy*. Princeton, N.J.: Princeton University Press.

Waynes, D. 1979. *The Economics of Third World Military Expenditure*. London: Macmillan.

Wolf, Charles, D. Henry, K.C. Yeh, J. Hayes, J. Schunk, and R. Sneider. 1985. *The Changing Balance: South and North Korean Capabilities for Long-Term Military Competition*. Santa Monica, Calif.: Rand.

World Bank. Various years. *World Development Report 1989*. Washington, D.C.: World Bank.

9 Military burden, economic growth, and income inequality: the Taiwan exception

Steve Chan
University of Colorado

Most existing research suggests that high military spending tends to have a deleterious effect on a country's economic growth, export competitiveness, and capital formation, whereas a large military establishment tends to promote social welfare and income equality. At the same time, rapid economic growth has been found to undermine political stability and exacerbate social frustration. Taiwan presents an interesting deviant case to these cross-national generalizations about the relationships among defense burden, economic performance, and social welfare. It has historically borne a heavy defense burden in both dollars and manpower. Yet its economy has achieved one of the world's fastest and most sustained growths in the past four decades, and its successful export drive has made it the world's second largest holder of foreign reserves. Moreover, the island's rapid economic growth has taken place in a context of general political stability and, until the 1980s, increasing income equality. It has also brought about major improvements in physical quality of life, so that Taiwan has now reached the standards of advanced Western countries in this respect.

This chapter undertakes a time-series analysis of the Taiwan case with its focus on the direct and indirect impact of military burden on income distribution. It is organized in five sections: (1) summary of the pertinent literature, (2) historical overview of Taiwan's political economy, (3) specification of analytic model, (4) discussion of the regression results, and (5) interpretation of the Taiwan case in light of its historical experiences.

LITERATURE REVIEW

Military burden takes two distinct forms: (a) dollar expenditures relative to a country's gross national product (GNP), and (b) armed-forces personnel relative to a country's population size (sometimes called the military-participation ratio). They represent respectively the capital-intensive and the manpower-intensive approaches to national defense. The existing research reports quite different empirical effects of these two types of military burden on the size distribution of income.

Several cross-national studies (such as Andreski 1968; Chan 1989; Dixon and Moon 1986; Garnier and Hazelrigg 1977; Weede 1986; Weede and Tiefenbach 1981a) have found that a high military-participation ratio contributes to income equalization or physical quality of life. After controlling for the effects of per capita income, countries with larger armed forces tend to generally have more equitable income distribution or more adequate satisfaction of basic human needs than their counterparts with smaller military establishments. These outcomes have been explained as a consequence of the sociopolitical mobilization due to severe foreign threats. These threats are hypothesized to produce various concessions by the incumbent elite to the masses, including a more equitable income system and higher government spending for social welfare.

Several analysts (for example, Benoit 1973, 1978; Weede 1983, 1986 as well as his Chapter 12 in this volume) have suggested that military service contributes to human capital formation, which in turn increases the growth potential of a country. In this light, the armed forces of the developing nations serve as an important 'modernizing agent' that equips their citizens with the sort of attitudes and skills necessary for economic development. The military establishment also offers an important institutional setting, where social integration and mobility for the less privileged members of society can take place. Thus, Weede (1986, 310) concludes that 'high military-participation ratios tend to improve the growth prospects of nations and to equalize income shares somewhat.'

Much more empirical work has been done on the economic effects of defense expenditures as an operational indicator of the military burden. One argument suggests that defense contracts encourage fuller utilization of the existing production facilities, thereby inducing faster economic growth (Benoit 1973). A second argument posits that defense expenditures are especially likely to divert human and physical resources from the most dynamic civilian sectors, which tend to be export-oriented. Consequently high defense spending is expected to dampen export competitiveness, which in turn slows down domestic economic growth (Rothschild 1973). In the absence of a global war, this spending seems also to stimulate imports (Russett 1970), thereby creating an unfavorable balance of trade. Yet a third argument indicates that defense spending has a negative effect on the savings and investment rates, which in turn are the chief determinants of economic growth (Deger and Smith 1983; Smith 1980). The aggregate evidence from recent research tends to be more supportive of the second and third arguments; it suggests that, on balance, defense spending is likely to hamper rather than improve economic growth (Cappelen *et al*. 1984; Deger and Smith 1983; Frederiksen and Looney 1983; Leontief and Duchin 1983; Lim 1983; Rasler and Thompson 1988; Russett 1970).

The effects of economic growth on the size distribution of income have also been a long-standing topic of empirical research by economists, sociologists, and political scientists. It has been argued that a high rate of economic growth tends to increase rather than decrease income inequality (Olson

1963). Rapid economic growth and its likely companion of high inflation tend to lower the median income, even though the average income may be rising. Cross-national research has produced some evidence of this inverse relationship between the speed of economic expansion and the equality of income distribution (such as Chan 1989; Jackman 1975).

More commonly, the level of economic development (as indexed by per capita income) has been used as an explanation of income inequality. The relationship between these two variables has been characterized as an inverted U-curve (Kuznets 1955). According to this view, income distribution is relatively equal among the low-income countries, but this equality deteriorates among the middle-income countries. However, this deterioration is arrested and reversed among the high-income countries, which generally have a low degree of distributive inequality. This pattern has been confirmed by several studies (such as Adelman and Morris 1973; Ahluwalia 1974, 1976a, 1976b; Chenery and Syrquin 1975; Kuznets 1963, 1976; Weede and Tiefenbach 1981a).

In addition to its effects on economic growth, defense spending can indirectly affect the size distribution of income through its impact on the government's welfare expenditures. To the extent that there is a tradeoff between 'guns and butter,' high defense spending reduces public support for social welfare. Cutbacks or removal of the 'safety net' provided by social-welfare programs will in turn adversely affect the income of poor people, thereby widening the gap between them and the rich.

The evidence in support of a tradeoff relationship between defense spending and welfare spending is, however, neither strong nor consistent. The most recent studies on this subject suggest that these two kinds of expenditures may not consistently pose a zero-sum budgetary choice, at least among the advanced Western countries (see, for example, Clayton 1976; Domke *et al.* 1983; Mintz 1989; Peroff and Podolak-Warren 1979; Russett 1982). This tradeoff may be more salient for the less developed countries, perhaps especially for those countries faced with severe financial constraints (Dabelko and McCormick 1977; Frederiksen and Looney 1983; and Looney's Chapter 11 in this volume).

Finally, defense spending can affect the size distribution of income through its indirect effects on employment and inflation. To the extent that poor people are the last ones to be hired and the first ones to be fired as a reflection of changing economic conditions, to the extent that high levels of military expenditures result in chronic economic stagnation and structural unemployment, and to the extent that defense procurement programs are capital- and technology-intensive (thereby increasing the income of those who have money or expertise), income distribution is apt to become more unequal. Similarly, to the extent that wages (especially for unskilled workers) are 'stickier' than general prices, poor people will suffer more from the inflationary effects of defense spending. These inflationary effects can result from a government's fiscal deficits. They can also be due to cost-push factors, if defense procurement crowds out civilian production. As a third possibility, defense payroll can induce inflation because it increases consumer demand without expanding supply.

However, the available evidence regarding the impact of defense spending on unemployment and inflation is neither conclusive nor entirely supportive of the expectations outlined in the preceding paragraph. Defense spending does not bear a simple linear relationship with unemployment levels among the small number of advanced Western countries (Szymanski 1973). At the same time, the hypothesized inflationary impact of defense spending varies according to different countries and time periods. Little evidence of such an impact could be found for the U.S. and the U.K. during 1956–79 (Starr *et al* 1984). On the other hand, a reciprocal relationship between defense spending and inflation seems to have existed for France and West Germany.

THE TAIWAN CASE

In 1950, Taiwan was on the verge of political and economic collapse. The Kuomintang had lost the Chinese mainland to the Communists, and was struggling to maintain control in its last territorial remnant. Taiwan's economy had been severed from its traditional markets in both China and Japan, and was suffering hyperinflation as a consequence of government mismanagement and a loss of popular confidence. The economic and social dislocation created by World War II (when the island was a Japanese colony) was compounded in short order by the massive influx of refugees from the mainland. Had it not been for the outbreak of the Korean War and the subsequent U.S. intervention (which led to the 'neutralization' of the Taiwan Strait and the Chinese counterintervention in the Korean conflict), Taiwan would probably have succumbed to the Communist invasion force being assembled across the channel. The massive U.S. assistance programs resulting from Washington's containment policy helped to stabilize and, later, reinvigorate the Kuomintang government on the island.

Despite its heavy foreign economic, military, and political dependence, Taiwan's developmental history since 1950 belies the expectations of orthodox dependency theory. From its beginning as an agricultural backwater with a GNP per capita of about US$100, this island has undergone a fundamental economic transformation to become a highly industrialized and affluent society. In 1989, its GNP per capita reached an estimated US$7,600, and its physical-quality-of-life index (PQLI) stood at about 95 points. Thus, Taiwan's per capita income is comparable to those of Ireland and Spain, thereby qualifying it as a member of the so-called industrial market economies. In terms of PQLI, it has reached levels prevailing in some advanced Western countries, including the United States. Yet this PQLI achievement has been made with much less public-welfare expenditure than in the advanced Western democracies.

These impressive accomplishments were achieved despite the island's heavy military burden. The percentage of Taiwan's GNP devoted to defense spending averaged 8.30 during 1961–87, and the percentage of its population serving in the armed forces averaged 3.3 during the same period. Both of these two forms of military burden have declined significantly since their peak years in the 1960s (see Table 9.1). During those years close to 12% of GNP went to defense spending, and over 5% of the population were serving in the armed forces (we do not have figures for the pre-1961 years, but surmise that they would indicate an even heavier military burden). Compared to all the other countries with available information, Taiwan ranked in the 94th percentile in defense spending, and 100th percentile in military participation ratio in the mid 1960s. Few other countries had higher or even comparable degrees of military burden.

Yet the dire consequences of a heavy military burden did not come to pass. In the years since 1950, Taiwan has achieved one of the fastest and most sustained economic expansions in the world. After adjustment for inflation, its average rate of GNP increase has been over 9 percent annually (see Table 9.1). Few other countries in the developed or developing world can match this record of rapid economic growth, which has been fueled by very high rates of export expansion and capital formation.

Despite the suggestion that high defense spending impairs competitiveness in international trade, Taiwan's exports have been increasing at an average annual rate of over 23 percent since 1961. In 1989, this island has compiled a foreign reserve of US$75 billion, which is the highest in the world in per capita terms and second highest (after Japan) in absolute amount. Taiwan's high savings rate has also contradicted the cross-national tendency for defense spending to dampen capital formation. Since 1959, this rate has always been above 10 percent of GNP; and since 1976, it has always been above 30 percent of GNP. Indeed, during the 1980s there had been an excess of capital in relationship to domestic investment opportunities. The island has begun to make large foreign investments so that, for example, it is now the leading foreign investor in the Philippines.

With regard to the dependent variable of this analysis – the size distribution of income – Taiwan presents again an exceptional case. Despite the expectation that rapid economic growth should undermine income equality, this island has maintained one of the most egalitarian income systems in the capitalist world. In 1987, the richest 20 percent of the island's population received 38.04 percent of the national income whereas the poorest 40 percent received 21.61 percent. The ratio between the income shares of these two groups is therefore 1.76. By comparison, the most recent World Bank (1988, 273) figures indicate that this ratio was 2.32 for the United States (in 1980), 2.21 for Denmark (1981), 2.18 for the United Kingdom (1979), 2.04 for Sweden (1981), and 2.02 for Norway (1982). Thus, by this calculation Taiwan has a more egalitarian income system than these advanced Western democracies.

Table 9.1 Taiwan's time-series data

Year	Armed forces as % of population	Military expenditure as % of GNP	GNP % change	Export % change	Capital% change	GNP per capita	Inequality ratio
1961	50.40	9.50	6.80	30.90	7.50	142.0	3.66
1962	47.90	9.40	7.90	11.80	1.20	148.7	3.12
1963	44.30	9.60	9.40	52.10	18.20	157.9	2.57
1964	47.60	9.50	12.30	30.70	12.60	172.2	2.03
1965	40.30	7.70	11.00	3.60	30.10	185.9	2.03
1966	40.70	11.20	9.00	19.30	4.30	197.2	2.04
1967	39.90	11.70	10.60	19.50	32.70	212.7	2.05
1968	37.70	10.50	9.10	23.20	16.70	226.7	2.06
1969	38.80	10.40	9.10	33.00	8.80	241.7	1.92
1970	35.80	10.60	11.30	41.20	21.30	263.5	1.78
1971	36.20	10.00	13.00	39.10	17.90	291.8	1.77
1972	36.20	8.80	13.40	45.00	11.90	324.7	1.77
1973	32.50	8.10	12.80	42.80	20.50	359.5	1.75
1974	31.20	6.80	1.20	25.20	33.90	357.1	1.73
1975	31.30	7.30	4.40	–5.70	–14.50	366.1	1.69
1976	28.90	6.80	13.70	53.80	16.10	407.8	1.65
1977	27.40	7.40	10.30	14.60	3.60	440.7	1.65
1978	27.50	7.50	14.00	31.90	13.10	493.2	1.64
1979	26.80	6.70	8.50	23.60	22.80	524.7	1.68
1980	26.10	6.60	7.10	22.90	8.30	551.3	1.62
1981	25.40	6.50	5.70	16.50	0.20	572.3	1.64
1982	24.80	7.80	3.40	4.20	–11.10	581.1	1.66
1983	24.20	8.00	8.00	16.30	0.20	617.3	1.69
1984	24.70	6.60	10.60	19.80	3.10	672.4	1.68
1985	22.80	7.60	5.10	1.50	–12.70	697.2	1.71
1986	20.00	7.00	11.70	23.20	2.30	769.6	1.75
1987	18.50	4.60	11.90	13.20	39.90	851.7	1.76
1988	n.a.	n.a.	7.30	1.40	30.00	904.5	n.a.

Sources: U.S. ACDA (various years), and Council for Economic Planning and Development (1989).
n.a. = not available

The temporal pattern of the island's income data also is unusual. As mentioned earlier, cross-national research suggests an inverted U-curve pattern – income inequality is initially low before the onset of economic development; it increases with the onset of rapid growth; and it declines again after the achievement of mass affluence and industrial maturity. Taiwan's pattern shows instead a straight U-curve pattern. Table 9.1 reports the over-time changes in the ratio of income inequality obtained by dividing the income share of the richest 20% of population by that of the poorest 40%. This ratio of income inequality declined dramatically and consistently from 1961 till 1980 – a period of economic takeoff and rapid growth. During the 1980s, however, there has been a gradual but persistent increase in income inequality, so that the inequality ratio has increased from 1.62 to 1.76. Thus, just as Taiwan is about to enter the ranks of the industrialized countries, its income distribution has become more and not less unequal. Nevertheless, as seen in the last paragraph, a ratio of 1.76 still puts Taiwan substantially ahead of the Scandinavian social democracies in income equality. Among the advanced market economies, only the Netherlands (1.62 in 1981), Belgium (1.67 in 1978–9), and Japan (1.71 in 1979) can boast of a lower inequality ratio.

In short, Taiwan's political economy presents a number of contradictions to expectations derived from cross-national research in the West. Somehow this island has managed to cope with several seemingly incompatible policy goals suggested by this research. It has combined a heavy military burden with fast and sustained economic growth, a very competitive export sector, and unusually high levels of capital formation. It has also achieved rapid economic growth while maintaining relative political stability and income equality. Finally, it has accomplished rapid improvements in PQLI even though it has eschewed massive welfare programs.

MODEL SPECIFICATION

The dependent variable for this study is income inequality as measured by the ratio between the income share of the top quintile (20%) of population and that of the bottom two quintiles (40%). A high value for this ratio means greater distributive inequality, whereas a low value means less inequality.

Previous research has shown that the size distribution of income is related to both the level and the rate of economic development. A number of cross-sectional analyses (such as Ahluwalia 1976b; Bollen and Jackman 1985; Chenery and Syrquin 1975; Muller 1988; Weede 1980, 1986) have used a quadratic polynomial regression of income inequality on economic development, after indicators of the latter concept (for example, GNP per capita or energy consumption per capita) have been logarithmically transformed. Income inequality is therefore expected to increase with initial economic development, and then to decrease with further economic progress. Based on alternative measures, several other cross-sectional studies (for instance, Chan 1989; Jackman 1975; Ward 1978) have also shown that the rate of economic growth is positively related to income inequality. That is, the faster-growing economies tend to have more unequal income distribution than the slower-growing economies.

Recent cross-national studies have also shown a tendency for population density to be negatively related to income inequality, and foreign capital penetration to be positively related to it (Bornschier and Chase-Dunn 1985; Chan 1989). In this analysis, two slightly different measures are used to examine the over-time changes in Taiwan's income-distribution pattern. These measures are the island's annual population growth rate, and its net foreign investment or lending as a percentage of gross capital formation. Taiwan experienced a role reversal with regard to the latter variable during the time period being analyzed in this paper. It changed from a net importer of foreign capital (including investment, loans, and U.S. aid) in the 1950s and 1960s to a net exporter in the 1980s. This status reversal extends an opportunity to ascertain any concomitant change in the island's income-distribution pattern, a topic that has been a source of some controversy in prior cross-national research (Bornschier 1981; Weede and Tiefenbach 1981b).

As a central concern of this analysis, the military-participation ratio is included as a potential predictor of income inequality. As mentioned earlier, previous cross-national research has indicated that a high military-participation ratio tends to be associated with greater income equality (such as Chan 1989; Garnier and Hazelrigg 1977; Weede and Tiefenbach 1981a). It is not clear, however, whether the causal inference suggested by this association can be verified by time-series analysis.

The existing research on the size distribution of income has also attended to the effects of state strength, regime ideology, and political democracy (for example, Bollen and Jackman 1985; Chan 1989; Muller 1988). But because variations along these dimensions have been relatively small or recent in Taiwan, I have not included them in this analysis. The government's welfare expenditures have also not been included, because a previous longitudinal study of Taiwan's time series has failed to uncover any significant evidence of a tradeoff between defense spending and welfare spending (Davis and Chan 1990).

Another earlier time-series analysis was unable to establish any causal influence of defense spending on unemployment or inflation, or vice versa, in Taiwan's case (Chan and Davis 1991). Still a third longitudinal study found that although this spending has adversely affected capital formation on the island, there is little statistical evidence of its having a similar negative impact on Taiwan's export competitiveness (Chan 1988). This latter study did, however, find export expansion to be the main cause of Taiwan's economic growth. On the other hand, capital formation (defined as gross domestic capital formation as a percentage of GNP) failed to be statistically associated with the rate of change in the island's GNP in the same year. Consequently, these studies concluded that the expectations discussed in the first section of this paper received only partial support from the Taiwan data.

In this study, I use an alternative measure of capital formation (the annual rate of change in gross capital formation), and provide for a lag of one year in the search of its contribution to GNP growth. This variable, the annual rate of change in the island's export value, Taiwan's defense expenditures as a percentage of its GNP, and the extent of foreign capital penetration are used as predictors of the rate of its GNP growth. In turn, the rate of GNP growth is hypothesized to be positively related to income inequality as discussed above.

The previously mentioned considerations lead to the following equations to be analyzed by two-stage least-squares regression.

$$(9.1)\quad INCRATIO_t = a - b_1 MPR_t + b_2 GNPRATE_t + b_3 \ln GNPPC_t - b_4 (\ln GNPPC_t)^2 - b_5 POPRATE_t + b_6 FORPEN_t$$

$$(9.2)\quad GNPRATE_t = a - b_1 MEGNP_t + b_2 CAPRATE_{t-1} + b_3 EXPRATE_t - b_4 FORPEN_t$$

INCRATIO = ratio of income inequality (income share of top 20% divided by income share of bottom 40%)
MPR = military participation ratio (armed forces personnel as a percentage of population)
GNPRATE = annual rate of real change in GNP
ln*GNPPC* = natural logarithm of GNP per capita after adjustment for inflation
POPRATE = annual rate of population growth
FORPEN = foreign capital (investment, loans, and aid) penetration as a percentage of gross capital formation
MEGNP = military expenditures as a percentage of GNP
CAPRATE = annual rate of real change in gross capital formation
EXPRATE = annual rate of real change in export value

The data on military expenditures and manpower used in this analysis are from the U.S. Arms Control and Disarmament Agency (various years). All other data on Taiwan's political economy are from the Council for Economic Planning and Development (1989). All dollar figures have been adjusted for inflation. We interpolate the data on income inequality in order to estimate several missing observations in this time series. The analysis covers the years 1961–88. Thus, the decade of the 1950s – a period of economic and political uncertainty – is not included in the analysis.

REGRESSION RESULTS

The results of the two-stage regression analysis are reported in Table 9.2. They offer support for some of the expectations raised earlier, but contradict many others. In general, they indicate that military burden – whether defined in dollar or manpower terms – has played an insignificant role in Taiwan's economic growth and income distribution.

Equation 9.1 indicates that GNP per capita is the most important determinant of the size distribution of income. In conformity with previous cross-sectional research, it shows that GNP per capita has a curvilinear relationship with income inequality. However, in contradiction to this same research, this relationship is characterized by a U-curve rather than an inverted U-curve. That is, during the earlier years of Taiwan's economic takeoff, rising GNP per capita (in its log form) reduces income inequality. On the other hand, with further increases in affluence GNP per capita

Table 9.2 Two-stage least-squares regression

Equation 9.1			
$Y = INCRATIO_t$	Adjusted $R^2 = 0.784$		Significance $F = 0.0000$
X	B estimate	Standard error	T significance
constant	39.618	11.496	0.003
MPR_t	0.043	0.031	0.181
$GNPRATE_t$	0.005	0.026	0.852
$\ln GNPPC_t$	−13.669	3.649	0.001
$(\ln GNPPC_t)^2$	1.188	0.306	0.001
$POPRATE_t$	−0.051	0.088	0.566
$FORPEN_t$	0.004	0.003	0.241
Equation 9.2			
$Y = GNPRATE_t$	Adjusted $R^2 = 0.488$		Significance $F = 0.0007$
X	*B* estimate	Standard error	*T* significance
constant	6.211	2.848	0.040
$MEGNP_t$	−0.136	0.345	0.697
$CAPRATE_{t-1}$	0.106	0.040	0.014
$EXPRATE_t$	0.113	0.032	0.002
$FORPEN_t$	−0.011	0.016	0.486

(as measured by the square of its log value) becomes positively related to income inequality during the later years of the time series. Thus, the changes in Taiwan's income distribution over the past 30 or so years present a trend that is exactly the opposite of cross-national pattern (according to which income inequality should first rise and then decline with economic development).

The Taiwan time series also contradicts the expectation that a high military-participation ratio should reduce income inequality. In Equation 9.1, the former variable is not significant at the 0.05 level and, in fact, carries a 'wrong' coefficient sign. Indeed, without controling for the effects of GNP per capita, the military-participation ratio is significantly and positively associated with income inequality (see Equations 9.3 and 9.4 in Table 9.3). A brief review of Table 9.1 helps to clarify this association. The former variable has undergone a persistent decline during the time period of this analysis (1961–88) and, during much of this same period (1961–80), the latter variable has also gone down. Thus, the temporal patterns of these variables are not congruent with the view that large armed forces facilitate greater income equality.

The results of Equation 9.1 also fail to support several other expectations derived from earlier cross-national studies. The speed of GNP growth, the extent of foreign capital penetration, and the rate of population growth all fall quite a bit short of conventional levels of statistical significance. Therefore, the hypothesized influences of these variables on income inequality cannot be verified by the longitudinal data from Tawain.

Turning to Equation 9.2, we see that military spending has not been a direct determinant of Taiwan's economic growth. Instead, the island's GNP growth has been significantly influenced by its export performance and by the previous year's investment rate. Both of the latter variables have had a positive influence on economic expansion. They therefore support the view that Taiwan's economy has been heavily dependent on exports, and that capital formation has facilitated its economic growth. However, foreign capital has apparently played a minor role in this growth, at least during the period under analysis (during the 1950s, U.S. aid was quite important for the island's economy; this aid stopped in 1965).

Can defense spending affect the GNP rate indirectly through its effects on capital formation and export competitiveness? In Table 9.3 Taiwan's defense spending has been used to explain the over-time changes in its capital formation (without any lag in Equation 9.5 and with a one-year lag in Equation 9.6). The results in Equation 9.5 are insignificant, while the *t*-value for defense spending is significant at the 0.1 level in Equation 9.6. Note, however, that the positive regression sign in the latter case indicates that defense spending has tended to stimulate rather than impair capital formation. We encounter the same phenomenon in Equation 9.7, which tries to assess the influence of defense spending on export expansion without any annual lag. Although the regression results in this case again fall short of conventional standards of statistical significance, the positive coefficient featured by *MEGNP* contradicts the expectation that defense spending should undermine export competitiveness. The results in Equation 9.8, with the provision of a one-year lag, are totally insignificant.

SOME HISTORICAL REFLECTIONS

Clearly, the Taiwan case deviates from cross-national patterns in a number of significant ways. Its military-participation ratio has not had an ameliorating effect on income inequality as hypothesized, nor has its defense spending had a dampening impact (directly or indirectly) on its economic growth. Furthermore, this island has managed to achieve one of the most egalitarian income systems in the capitalist world despite its rapid economic growth, heavy external dependence (in defense as well as trade), and limited government support for social welfare. How can we account for this Taiwan exception?

First, at least during the 1950s and 1960s, Taiwan's high military-participation ratio was due to the Kuomintang's huge army withdrawn to the island after losing the civil war on the Chinese mainland. In other words, this transplanted military establishment probably did not initially have the hypothesized positive effects on human capital formation as its continental size would imply. Second, the massive U.S. aid (especially in the 1950s) helped to lessen the burden of defense expenditures, and allowed the Kuomintang regime to divert resources to urgent civilian projects. In the absence of this infusion of foreign funds, the tradeoffs between military and civilian programs would have been much more severe. Third, in view of its disastrous setback on the mainland (in part brought about by a loss of

Table 9.3 Regression with adjustment for autocorrelated error

Equation 9.3
$Y = INCRATIO_t$ Adjusted $R^2 = 0.349$

X	B estimate	Standard error	T significance
constant	0.656	0.358	0.079
MPR_t	0.041	0.010	0.001

Equation 9.4
$Y = INCRATIO_{t-1}$ Adjusted $R^2 = 0.398$

X	B estimate	Standard error	T significance
constant	0.490	0.382	0.212
MPR_t	0.048	0.011	0.000

Equation 9.5
$Y = CAPRATE_t$ Adjusted $R^2 = -0.081$

X	B estimate	Standard error	T significance
constant	8.463	13.658	0.541
$MEGNP_t$	0.357	1.611	0.826

Equation 9.6
$Y = CAPRATE_{t-1}$ Adjusted $R^2 = 0.036$

X	B estimate	Standard error	T significance
constant	–9.465	11.822	0.432
$MEGNP_t$	2.400	1.401	0.100

Equation 9.7
$Y = EXPRATE_t$ Adjusted $R^2 = 0.007$

X	B estimate	Standard error	T significance
constant	4.063	13.930	0.773
$MEGNP_t$	2.424	1.643	0.153

Equation 9.8
$Y = EXPRATE_{t-1}$ Adjusted $R^2 = -0.084$

X	B estimate	Standard error	T significance
constant	21.141	15.290	0.180
$MEGNP_t$	0.421	1.813	0.819

popular confidence due to rampant inflation), the Kuomintang government practiced very conservative fiscal policies on the island in order to tame and control inflation. Low social overhead expenditures helped to offset somewhat the high defense spending. In this respect, Taiwan and South Korea are quite different from the U.S. and the U.K., which have historically refused to make the hard choices between 'guns' and 'butter.' The attempt by the latter liberal democracies to get 'a quart out of a pint pot' (that is, to have both guns and butter and to refuse increasing taxes) has had perhaps a more deleterious socioeconomic impact than the prodefense and antilabor policies pursued by the former authoritarian regimes.

Like its other capitalist East Asian counterparts, the Kuomintang government has, in view of its anti-Communist outlook and authoritarian attitudes, traditionally imposed stringent controls on labor organization. Indeed, industrial peace and low wages have been a hallmark of the East Asian NICs (newly industrializing countries) in their attempt to entice foreign investment in manufacturing. Yet, despite their traditional labor-suppressing policies and despite their relatively low levels of public spending for social welfare, these countries have achieved a more egalitarian income system than either Western liberal democracies or Latin American corporatist regimes in which organized labor has played a prominent and long-standing role as a member of the 'ruling pact.'

In the case of Taiwan, the economy has been dominated by many medium and small manufactures, a large number of which are owned and operated by relatives as family enterprises. In other words, the island has not thus far had a unionized industrial workforce, which often constitutes a labor aristocracy in other developing and developed countries (and thus indirectly increasing the income inequality within the ranks of workers). The decentralized nature of Taiwan's economy also means that the costs of economic slowdowns are spread more evenly across different firms and sectors, another feature that tends to diminish the impact that economic downturns can have in exacerbating income differentials. Additionally, many urban workers (especially during the 1960s and 1970s) have maintained ties with their ancestral villages, where they tend to return when economic conditions in the cities deteriorate. In other words, farm earnings and rural employment help to check widening income inequality during economic downturns. Finally, the benevolent paternalism characteristic of industrial relations in the capitalist East Asian countries – such as lifetime employment, profit-sharing in the form of year-end bonuses, living arrangements organized and subsidized by companies – offers a safety net in lieu of the welfare programs typically undertaken by the government in the Western advanced countries.

The chief source of income disparity in many countries is the income differential between the rural and urban sectors. Taiwan had a very successful land reform in the early 1950s. One of the main reasons that the Kuomintang lost the civil war was its failure to carry out any meaningful land reform on the mainland, because the landlord class was its main base of political support. However, when it moved to Taiwan (a former Japanese colony), it was no longer beholden to the same rural conservative interests, and was thus able to translate the slogan of 'land to the tillers' into a social reality. The improving income equality shown by the data series during 1961–80 can be primarily attributed to the land reform undertaken in the early 1950s. Indeed, the farmers of Taiwan have in some ways fared considerably better economically in recent years than have urban dwellers. Urban and industrial development has brought about a shortage of commercial land on the island, and many farmers have become very wealthy because of their land holdings. In contrast, ordinary urban dwellers have been increasingly hurt by the escalating cost of housing.

Foreign capital penetration has been yet another common source of income inequality in many developing countries. However, multinational corporations have never assumed an important position in Taiwan's political economy. Moreover, the inflow of foreign capital, at least during the 1950s and 1960s, was much more motivated by Washington's political and military desire to contain Communism in Asia than an attempt to seek commercial gains or economic domination on the island. In contrast to most developing countries, Taiwan has also had very high rates of savings and investment. Therefore, it has not had to cope with the problem of capital shortage to the same extent as other Third World countries. In fact, in recent years, the island has had to manage an embarrassing surplus of liquid capital. This massive amount of idle cash, accumulated as a result of persistent trade surpluses, has fueled a speculative binge in the stock market and real estate. Ironically, it has been this development – rather than military burden – that has increased income inequality in recent years. Thus, the Taiwan exception suggests that there is this downside to having too much of a good thing (in terms of rapid growth, capital surplus, trade expansion, and mass affluence).

REFERENCES

Adelman, Irma and Cynthia T. Morris. 1973. *Economic Growth and Social Equity in Developing Countries*. Stanford, Calif.: Stanford University Press.

Ahluwalia, Montek S. 1974. Income inequality: some dimensions of the problem. In Hollis Chenery, Montek S. Ahluwalia, C.L.G. Bell, John H. Duloy, and Richard Jolly (eds.), *Redistribution with Growth* pp. 3–37. London: Oxford University Press.

Ahluwalia, Montek S. 1976a. Inequality, poverty and development. *Journal of Development Economics* 3: 307–42.

Ahluwalia, Montek S. 1976b. Income distribution and development: some stylized facts. *American Economic Review* 66: 128–35.

Andreski, Stanislav. 1968. *Military Organization and Society*. Stanford, Calif.: Stanford University Press.

Benoit, Emile. 1973. *Defense and Economic Growth in Developing Countries*. Lexington, Mass.: Heath.

Benoit, Emile. 1978. Growth and defense in developing countries. *Economic Development and Cultural Change* 26: 271–80.

Bollen, Kenneth A. and Robert W. Jackman. 1985. Political democracy and the size distribution of income. *American Sociological Review* 50: 438–57.

Bornschier, Volker. 1981. Comment. *International Studies Quarterly* 25: 283–8.

Bornschier, Volker and Christopher Chase-Dunn. 1985. *Transnational Corporations and Underdevelopment*. New York: Praeger.

Cappelen, Ådne, Nils P. Gleditsch, and Olav Bjerkholt. 1984. Military spending and economic growth in the OECD countries. *Journal of Peace Research* 21: 361–73.

Chan, Steve. 1988. Defense burden and economic growth: unravelling the Taiwanese enigma. *American Political Science Review* 82: 913–20.

Chan, Steve. 1989. Income inequality among LDCs: a comparative analysis of alternative perspectives. *International Studies Quarterly* 33: 45–65.

Chan, Steve and David R. Davis. 1991. Defense allocation, inflation, and unemployment in South Korea and Taiwan: a Granger analysis. *Korean Journal of Defense Analysis* 3: Forthcoming.

Chenery, Hollis and Moise Syrquin. 1975. *Patterns of Development 1950–1970*. London: Oxford University Press.

Council for Economic Planning and Development. 1989. *Taiwan Statistical Data Book: 1989*. Taipei: Council for Economic Planning and Development.

Dabelko, David and James M. McCormick. 1977. Opportunity costs of defense: some cross-national evidence. *Journal of Peace Research* 14: 145–54.

Davis, David R. and Steve Chan. 1990. The security–welfare relationship: longitudinal evidence from Taiwan. *Journal of Peace Research* 27: 87–100.

Deger, Saadet and Ron Smith. 1983. Military expenditure and growth in less developed countries. *Journal of Conflict Resolution* 27: 335–53.

Dixon, William J. and Bruce E. Moon. 1986. The military burden and basic human needs. *Journal of Conflict Resolution* 30: 660–84.

Domke, William K., Richard C. Eichenberg, and Catherine M. Kelleher. 1983. The illusion of choice: defense and welfare in advanced industrial democracies, 1948–1978. *American Political Science Review* 77: 19–35.

Frederiksen, Peter C. and Robert E. Looney. 1983. Defense expenditures and economic growth in developing countries. *Armed Forces and Society* 9: 633–45.

Garnier, Maurice A. and Lawrende E. Hazelrigg. 1977. Military organization and distributional inequality. *Journal of Political and Military Sociology* 5: 17–33.

Jackman, Robert W. 1975. *Politics and Social Equality: A Comparative Analysis*. New York: Wiley.

Kuznets, Simon. 1955. Economic growth and income inequality. *American Economic Review* 45: 1–28.

Kuznets, Simon. 1963. Quantitative aspects of the economic growth of nations VIII: The distribution of income by size. *Economic Development and Cultural Change* 11: 1–80.

Kuznets, Simon. 1976. *Modern Economic Growth: Rate, Structure and Spread*. New Haven, Conn.: Yale University Press.

Leontief, Wassily and Faye Duchin. 1983. *Military Spending: Facts and Figures. Worldwide Implications and Future Outlook*. Oxford: Oxford University Press.

Lim, David. 1983. Another look at growth and defense in less developed countries. *Economic Development and Cultural Change* 31: 377–84.

Mintz, Alex. 1989. 'Guns vs. butter': a disaggregated analysis. *American Political Science Review* 83: 1285–93.

Muller, Edward N. 1988. Democracy, economic development, and income inequality. *American Sociological Review* 53: 50–68.

Olson, Mancur Jr. 1963. Rapid growth as a destabilizing force. *Journal of Economic History* 23: 529–52.

Peroff, Katheleen and Margaret Podolak-Warren. 1979. Does spending on defense cut spending on health? A time series analysis of the U.S. economy since 1929–1974. *British Journal of Political Science* 9: 21–40.

Rasler, Karen A. and William R. Thompson. 1988. Defense burdens, capital formation, and economic growth: the systemic leader case. *Journal of Conflict Resolution* 32: 61–86.

Rothschild, Kurt W. 1973. Military expenditure, exports and growth. *Kyklos* 26: 804–14.

Russett, Bruce M. 1970. *What Price Vigilance? The Burdens of National Defense*. New Haven, Conn.: Yale University Press.

Russett, Bruce M. 1982. Defense expenditures and national well-being. *American Political Science Review* 76: 767–77.

Smith, Ron P. 1980. Military expenditure and investment in OECD countries, 1954–1973. *Journal of Comparative Economics* 4: 19–32.

Starr, Harvey, Francis W. Hoole, Jeffrey A. Hart, and John R. Freeman. 1984. The relationship between defense spending and inflation. *Journal of Conflict Resolution* 28: 103–22.

Szymanski, Albert. 1973. Military spending and economic stagnation. *American Journal of Sociology* 79: 1–14.

U.S. Arms Control and Disarmament Agency. Various years. *World Military Expenditures and Arms Transfers*. Washington, D.C.

Ward, Michael D. 1978. *The Political Economy of Distribution: Equality Versus Inequality*. New York: Elsevier.

Weede, Erich. 1980. Beyond misspecification in sociological analyses of income inequality. *American Sociological Review* 45: 497–501.

Weede, Erich. 1983. Military participation, human capital formation, and economic growth. *Journal of Political and Military Sociology* 11: 11–19.

Weede, Erich. 1986. Rent seeking, military participation, and economic performance in LDCs. *Journal of Conflict Resolution* 30: 291–314.

Weede, Erich and Horst Tiefenbach. 1981a. Some recent explanations of income inequality. *International Studies Quarterly* 25: 255–82.

Weede, Erich and Horst Tiefenbach. 1981b. Rejoinder. *International Studies Quarterly* 25: 289–93.

World Bank. 1988. *World Development Report 1988*. New York: Oxford University Press.

10 The dual economy and Arab–Israeli use of force: a transnational system?

Alex Mintz
Texas A & M University

and

Bruce Russett
Yale University

War and peace decisions are rooted in domestic politics as well as international politics. Of course international politics matter. It matters what the international balance of power is, how that balance is changing, and what the fears and ambitions of allies and adversaries are. But every political leader also must worry about her/his base of domestic political support: what coalitions may form against the leadership, how elections or coups may operate to replace the leaders, popular satisfaction with recent performance of the domestic economic and political system, and the level and distribution of political support for the policies the leader intends to pursue. Action or inaction in the international arena can strengthen or shatter a leader's domestic power base.

Indeed, action in the international arena may be taken predominantly as a means to strengthen domestic political authority, and only incidentally for its effect on international power balances. A leader may seek to defuse a long-standing international dispute in order to use the army to crush domestic opposition, or in order to channel military resources to internal civilian purposes; Mikhail Gorbachev seems to have been motivated importantly by the latter. Or a leader may try to rally internal opponents by invoking a common external threat or opportunity; the Argentine generals attempted this with their invasion of the Falklands/Malvinas in 1982 (Levy and Vakili, 1991). Military action against foreign adversaries may be used to divert attention from domestic economic adversity, or to rally the voters at election time. Adversaries may also take these conditions into account: they may be tempted to attack a state beset by economic or political difficulties or, conceivably, may refrain from provoking a state which is undergoing difficulties.

In the field of the political economy of national security, most attention has gone to the effects of military activity on the national economy, in such forms as a 'guns–butter' tradeoff or stimulation of the economy by military spending. Much less attention has been paid to the effects of changes in the economy – in turn thereby affecting domestic politics – on decisions to use military force. In this chapter we 'bring politics back in' by showing that the domestic political economy has a powerful impact on decisions to use force, and that adversary states may take some of those impacts into account in reaching their own decisions about using military force. We investigate the influence of Israeli elections and economic conditions on decisions by both Israeli and Arab governments to take military action against each other. In doing so we look not only at the effects of conditions throughout the Israeli economy, but especially at those within the 'core' sector of the dual economy.[1]

ECONOMIC INCENTIVES TO INTERNATIONAL CONFLICT

Our theoretical orientation begins from the large corpus of social–psychological theories which assert that leaders of groups may often, and often successfully, try to divert hostility derived from frustrations into aggressive words or acts toward outsiders (LeVine and Campbell 1972, ch. 8; Levy 1989; Shaw and Wong 1988). One version of such theories as applied to international relations suggests that political conflict within a country will be causally related to manifestations of external conflict. But whereas examples abound, systematic empirical research has uncovered little basis for confident generalization (Stohl 1980; Zinnes 1980). The reason, however, may lie less in the absence of any systematic relation than in a failure to specify a rather complex relationship of circumstances and domestic conditions that apply. When such a specification is carried out, evidence for a causal connection begins to emerge.

In modern democracies we know that governments' popularity is closely connected with the state of the national economy, and that votes for the party in power depend heavily upon the improvement or deterioration of general economic conditions in the year or so immediately before those elections. There is also substantial evidence that government leaders are well aware of this association and, to the degree they can do so, often try to manipulate the short-term state of the economy so as to increase their popularity at election time.[2] Nonetheless, some politically relevant goals may be mutually incompatible (for example, increase employment and reduce inflation), and the available fiscal or monetary instruments for manipulating the economy are crude, uncertain in effect, and not always available to the policy-maker. Hence a democratic leader who wishes to raise her or his level of electoral support by stimulating the economy may be unable to do so.

From the perspective of a 'rational, self-interest-maximizing' democratic national leader, an alternative to manipulating the economy may be one of diverting dissatisfaction or antagonism toward peoples outside the national political system. The plausibility of this alternative is strengthened by the abundant evidence that leaders' popularity is significantly increased – often by 5 to 10 percentage points in the 'job performance' polls – by many kinds of international events. The effect, well known as the 'rally 'round the flag' effect (Brody 1984; Kernell 1978; Mueller 1973), varies somewhat for different actions and according to how the leader is perceived by the voters. But assertive speeches and relatively short, low-cost uses or threats of use of military force almost always invoke this short-term popularity increase. Support for Prime Minister Menachem Begin and Defense Minister Ariel Sharon rose more than 10 points after they invaded Lebanon in 1982 – though it dropped almost as fast when it became clear that the war would be neither short nor low-cost (Arian 1985; Yaniv 1987, 127–8).[3] Speeches and military actions are important because they represent relatively manipulable actions available to a leader (Marra *et al.* 1990).

The rally effect apparently applies not only to popularity ratings among the general public, but in the United States is translatable into votes for the president's party in congressional elections and to legislative approval of other key executive international initiatives (Marra and Ostrom 1989; Stoll 1990, 64–8). Thus not only does a theory of self-interested diversion of dissatisfaction predict that international military actions would sometimes occur, there is increasing evidence that democratic leaders often initiate such actions so as to strengthen their position in domestic politics. In the post-1945 era, U.S. presidents have been more likely to use force when the economy was experiencing inflation or high unemployment, and the percentage of the population considering the economy to be the 'most important problem' was high (Ostrom and Job 1986). Over a century-long period, the United States was more likely to use force two years following negative or very slight economic growth. The same was true for Britain and some other democracies, but not for authoritarian states (Russett 1990a, ch. 2, 1990b).

Military–industrial-complex theories, in liberal as well as neo-Marxist variants, frequently assert that capitalist interests – and especially the interests of the military or internationally oriented industry – will incite or approve of acts of military force against foreign adversaries. They specify both that particular actions may benefit those industries (by using up armaments and munitions which must then be replaced, or by protecting foreign markets, supplies, and investments), and that these interests may benefit from the high level of international tension that accompanies the frequent threat or use of military force, especially by increasing popular willingness to sustain a large military establishment. The empirical evidence for such propositions is on the whole mixed, and at most mildly supportive. For example, 'Fortune 500' vice-presidents in the United States were only moderately more in favor of military preparedness or foreign intervention than other comparable civilian-leadership groups, and less so than high-level military officers. Also, they turned sharply against the Vietnam War when it became extended and expensive, endangering domestic economic and political stability.[4] Several scholars, however, have shown that the military–industrial complex is influential in shaping Israel's national security policies (Lissak 1983; Mintz, in press; Peri and Neubach 1984).

In the case of Israel it is appropriate, in addition to the military–industrial complex, to introduce the concept of a dual economy; that is, the distinction between the modern ('core') and the traditional ('periphery') sectors in the national economy (Gilpin 1987). Oster (1978, 33) described the U.S. economy as composed of 'a core of powerful, concentrated, unionized, capital-intensive, technologically progressive industries, and a periphery marked by the absence of these features.' Core firms differ from periphery firms 'in terms of economic size, organizational structure, industrial location, time perspective, and market concentration' (Averitt 1968, 1). Core firms 'employ different technologies and operate on quite a different scale while shaping the market for their products rather than responding to the market.'[5] They are multi-million-dollar corporations with thousands of employees, a complex organizational structure and a diversified set of products. The periphery, in contrast, consists of thousands of small firms run by a single individual or family and producing a limited range of products for limited markets (Averitt 1968; Bowring 1986). The size and market position of core firms give them far more control over inputs and the demand for their products than is available to small firms.

Rowley *et al.* (1988) identified the Israeli economy as consisting of two essentially distinct sectors: the large holding groups in core industry and thousands of small firms in the periphery.[6] The 'big economy' consists of such conglomerates as Koor Industries, Clal Israel, and Discount Investment. It grew rapidly until the late 1970s (mainly via mergers and acquisitions), and while the business sector as a whole appropriated a decreasing share of the GNP in the form of net profit, an increasing part of these profits went to the large holding groups in core industry. Core firms show marked differences from the rest of the economy in market profit performance. Koor, Clal Israel, and Discount Investment leaped forward in their profits after 1975, while the rest of the economy started to stagnate.[7]

Key industries in Israel have been dominated by core firms. In turn, the major industrial concerns of the core sector have substantial influence on government policy. Core firms are the major employers in the country (Koor alone employs almost 20 percent of the industrial labor force) and they enjoy most of the capital resources allocated by the government. Rowley *et al.* (1988, 15) observed, 'the complex ownership/control ties among these groups, the financing relations among the groups, . . . property rights enjoyed exclusively by [these groups] . . . and the family ties and informal relations among the people who own and control these groups.' As in many other countries, military–industrial activity in Israel concentrates in the core sector. Koor, for example, controls Tadiran and Soltam, Koor Metals, and other defense companies. More important, however, is the close alliance of Koor and other conglomerates with the major political parties in Israel (see below).

It is well documented that Israeli security policy is influenced by Arab military actions and threats, though some (Inbar 1990) have noted a strong 'expressionist' (noninstrumental) tendency as well. Here we hypothesize that declining profits in core industry in Israel would also contribute to an increase in Israeli use of force because:

1. Israeli leaders, in view of the national history including the failure to conduct a preemptive strike in 1973, may adopt a position of 'better safe than sorry.' In security matters they fear a worst-case scenario. During periods of economic crisis Israeli decision-makers, concerned about the possibility that Arab leaders will exploit Israel's economic vulnerability, will be tempted to '*preempt*.'
2. Periods of declining profits in key industries are typically followed by greater military spending. Increased Israeli spending in turn may lead to *increases in Arab military spending* (Mintz and Ward 1989) which may, in a further turn, be interpreted as threatening Israel.
3. Israeli leaders may want to *divert attention* from the economic crisis in the most powerful and visible sectors and firms in the economy. Koor is the industrial arm of the Histadrut (the General Federation of Labor) and closely associated with the Labor Party. Therefore, the economic well-being of Koor and other concerns serves as a 'barometer' by which Labor's effectiveness in managing the economy is judged. The government has often assisted the expansion of core companies, and bailed them out during periods of severe crisis. Because of the relatively equal size of the Likud and Labor blocs, Israeli elections are highly competitive. The economic well-being of giant concerns such as Koor has been an important political issue in all elections since 1973. Likud has frequently attacked Labor for mishandling Koor, implying that a Labor-led government will bring an economic collapse upon Israel. Labor in turn has attacked Likud for mishandling the national economy.
4. The government may be under pressure particularly by the military–industrial sector to '*do something*.' Koor of course controls some of the major defense industries. The government depends on core firms for economic and political stability and may use force more frequently when they suffer. In a crisis there will be more pressure to be active, not reactive; in addition, the use of military force may provide an immediate boost to those industries' sales, for munitions, supplies, and replacement of equipment.

We also hypothesize that Israel's domestic conditions may invite Arab military challenge. Some of the reasons are:

1 In the case of a power like Israel whose adversarial relations are with states or coalitions of roughly equivalent power, its adversaries will see it at times as *vulnerable*, and hence it may be the object rather than the initiator of attack. An adversary may try to take advantage of political weakness if the government, for example, is thought to be absorbed with economic problems and their political ramifications, perhaps as manifested in strikes and demonstrations. Arguably, Iraq's Saddam Hussein chose the time of Iran's economic and political disorganization after the revolution as a chance to settle old scores against a weakened opponent.[8] An adversary may expect that an Israeli government suffering reduced popularity will be unable to mobilize resources and rally the population against external aggression. Arab leaders know that any large-scale military action by Israel will require calling up reserves and paralyzing much of the civilian economy; an Israel already suffering from economic adversity might be less willing to make further economic sacrifices.

Economic difficulties in Israel's core economy may make Arab countries especially likely to use force. Because core firms are the most profitable and powerful corporations in the entire economy, declining profits of key firms in key industries mean more than just an economic slowdown of traditional, labor-intensive firms and may indicate a severe general economic crisis. Weakness of the core economy reflects weakness of the military–industrial sector, and export-oriented, technologically progressive companies.

2 Arab leaders may also initiate what they consider to be '*preemptive*' strikes when they see Israeli economic difficulties. Military spending in Israel has increased in response to declining profits of major industrial concerns. Arab leaders may interpret such increases as offensive and as a threat to their own security. Or they may anticipate that Israel will use military force (for the variety of political–psychological and economic reasons suggested) against them in times of crisis in the core economy. The dual economy may therefore play a key role in influencing both Arab and Israeli actions.

ELECTORAL INCENTIVES TO INTERNATIONAL CONFLICT

Characteristics of particular *political* systems interact with and often magnify economic incentives to use force. Deterrence may fail – states use military force internationally – due to changes in domestic conditions of the 'deterree' rather than changes in the policy or capability of the deterrer. General deterrence (Morgan 1983, 42–4) pertains to long periods of enduring rivalry between nation-states, during which decision-makers' intentions, and the persona of decision-makers themselves, may change frequently and dramatically. Such changes may vastly increase the influence of domestic politics on foreign-policy decisions as compared with their influence in the course of a short-term immediate deterrence crisis. Moreover, in crises initiated largely from domestic motivations decision-makers may be more risk-acceptant and thus less amenable to efforts at crisis management.[9]

During a crisis of immediate deterrence decision-makers must focus intently on the threats or concessions being put forth by their international adversaries; an inadequate response to either can bring immediate disaster. But in deciding whether to *initiate* an international crisis, leaders can try to choose a time when the crisis will be most useful in rallying domestic political support or in diverting domestic antagonism toward the external adversary. Similarly, decision-makers may try to choose a time when the leaders of the adversarial power will be under greatest domestic pressure to make concessions, or be under least domestic pressure to demonstrate toughness and resolve. To investigate the circumstances under which states may use military force requires a research design that looks for changes in political conditions and in national behavior over long periods of sustained international rivalry.

Governments of democratic countries are likely to use force when their performance ratings in the public-opinion polls are problematic (perhaps because the economy has been doing badly), and also when elections are near. The evidence includes:

Presidents more often use military force when their performance rating is in the 'critical' 40–60 percent range (when a boost is most useful), and when recent erosion in that rating is greater among their supporters than in the opposition (whom they may discount anyway) (Morgan and Bickers 1992; Ostrom and Job 1986; Ostrom and Simon 1985). Post–World War II U.S. presidents were more likely to use military force if they were seeking reelection during a developing or ongoing war; that is, when they knew voters would be more concerned than usual with foreign affairs (Stoll 1984). Presidents' rhetoric toward the Soviet Union becomes less cognitively complex in the latter half of election years, and a decline in leaders' cognitive complexity in turn is associated with a greater likelihood of undertaking military interventions and a lesser likelihood of reaching international agreements (Tetlock 1985; Tetlock and McGuire 1985).

Over the past century, U.S. presidents have been more likely to use military force during election years, and more during presidential than congressional election years (Russett 1990a, ch. 2). Among democracies in general, *wars* are more common in the year immediately after an election, consistent with the view that wars themselves may be unpopular – but the militarized disputes that often ultimately produce them may be relatively popular and more common during election years (Gaubatz 1991). U.S. strategic-weapons spending has been higher in election years and – from carryovers – in the subsequent year than during the middle years of the presidents' terms; arms-control agreements evidence just the opposite timing (Nincic 1990). Domestic political or economic vulnerability will not always cause leaders to challenge a major international rival or its allies; they may prefer a safer and easier target, or they may have other very different options.[10]

In many but not all of the studies reviewed above, some effort has been made to distinguish between disputes or military acts initiated by the government in question, and those directed against it by adversaries. For the U.K. and the United States, governments facing elections or deteriorating economies are more likely to be initiators, consistent with the ability of great powers to exercise substantial choice as to when they will use military force, including whether and when to respond to challenges from weaker states.

Conditions of perceived weakness in domestic politics may lead to 'vulnerability' as well as 'opportunity' motivations (Lebow 1981). A combination of diversionary and defensive motivations suggests less the overt, deliberate diversion of domestic unrest toward foreign powers than feelings of weakness and insecurity of leaders' personal power that lead them to misinterpret or exaggerate the actions of foreign powers. Such feelings are likely to be greatest during political unrest, or before elections when leaders may be insecure in their tenure in office. Economic or domestic political weakness may attract moderate challenges, and once the crisis erupts the weakened state is then in turn more likely to respond militarily or to escalate. This interpretation leads to the idea of 'motivated misperception' as serving less-than-conscious purposes (Jervis 1976).

Note also that the international actions under review are comprised of uses or threats of military force in general, not necessarily the initiation of large-scale wars. Full-scale wars often are not popular, and typically less so as they build in duration, casualties, and economic cost. Thus our perspective suggests less that domestic political considerations would impel a leader to go to *war* in the course of a major international crisis than that s/he might be more inclined to *initiate or moderately escalate* such a crisis in the first place.

ANALYZING ARAB–ISRAELI REALITIES

Some systematic quantitative research on Arab–Israeli actions found that the Israeli government has used military force across de facto international borders more often preceding elections than at other times. This is true both for election years as compared with others, and in the months before an election compared with those afterwards. It is also true even when controls are introduced for Arab military actions (Barzilai and Russett 1990; Russett and Barzilai 1991). A case in point was the Israeli air strike against the Iraqi nuclear reactor at Osirak, an attack conducted less than a month before the 1981 election. While few Israelis overtly questioned the desirability of striking Osirak, many considered the timing of the strike to be politically motivated (Sacher 1987, 129–31).[11]

On the matter of economic incentives, simple correlations showed an unexpected positive simultaneous correlation between per capita GDP growth and both Arab and Israeli military actions, and the expected negative correlation only when the actions were lagged behind economic growth. None of these correlations was very high, and multivariate analysis including both sides' military actions and an election variable washed out the apparent effect of economic conditions (Barzilai and Russett 1990). A more complex pattern of causation needs to be posited:

Military action may be produced by an economic downturn, but only after a period of military preparation which might itself stimulate economic recovery. Furthermore, a government may use both economic stimulation and military actions to strengthen its electoral appeal (military actions, current economic growth, and election years are all moderately correlated; see Barzilai and Russett 1990), with the result that military action in an election year would be stimulated by economic distress in the year prior to the election, and correlated with government-induced economic recovery in the election year itself. It may also be that the government acts militarily less in response to conditions in the economy in general than to a decline in the income or profitability of particular sectors such as 'core' military or export-oriented industry. In this chapter we examine the impact of Israeli political and economic conditions on Arab and Israeli use of force.

We will be focusing primarily on 'sublimited' conflict and not on 'strategic' or 'limited' war.[12] Whereas the analysis of strategic deterrence primarily concerns the deterrence of nuclear war and the analysis of 'limited' deterrence primarily focuses on conventional war, the deterrence of sublimited, low-intensity conflict centers on conflict below the level of 'limited' conventional interstate war and primarily refers to border disputes, retaliatory actions, insurgency, infiltration, and so on. Although the analysis of strategic and limited deterrence has received considerable scholarly attention, there has been virtually no quantitative research on the deterrence of sublimited conflict, which is by 'denial' or by 'punishment.'

In the Arab–Israeli case we have chosen to exclude periods of large-scale interstate wars (the Six-Day War of June 1967, the War of Attrition of March 1969–August 1970, the Yom Kippur War of October 1973, and the Invasion of Lebanon of June 1982–May 1983). We did that because decisions to go to war or how to conduct the war – rather than decisions to mount or respond to lower-level incidents like raids, shootings, and bombings – were so important for national security that they were less likely to be heavily influenced by domestic economic and political conditions.

Our data set on the frequency of Arab and Israeli military actions, Israeli elections, and change in Israel's per capita GDP is that used by Barzilai and Russett (1990). The economic and election data in turn came from standard Israeli government sources. In accord with the interest in the effect of elections, in election years only the months preceding the election were included. Thus the dependent variable is the monthly average of military actions for each year, excluding wartime and postelection months. The military action data were compiled by Barzilai from many Israeli newspaper and archival sources.

Data on core-industry profits for the period 1960–86 were originally compiled by Rowley *et al.* (1988)[13] and were converted to constant 1980 prices using the GDP price deflator taken from the International Monetary Fund, *International Financial Statistics*. Similar data were used by Mintz and Ward (1989) in their analysis of military spending in Israel. The measure refers to the profits of the leading industrial concerns in Israel: Koor Industries, Clal Israel, and Discount Investment. Thirty-nine of Israel's hundred largest industrial firms are owned or controlled by these conglomerates: 23 by Koor, 8 by Clal, and 8 by Discount Investment. Fourteen of the top twenty largest industrial firms in Israel are controlled by these concerns and the Israeli government. The net profits of these (and two other holding groups) as a percentage of the Israeli GNP was higher than the comparable figure for all the largest 500 corporations in the United States. Koor, Clal, and Discount Investment are leading firms in key industries such as defense, electrical products and electronics, metal products, and building products. More importantly, these firms have received a growing share of Israeli Defense Force orders which, since the mid-1970s, have become the most profitable activity of Israeli industry (Bichler 1986; Rowley *et al.* 1988).

We begin with an analysis of the influences on *Arab* military actions. Our analysis consists of ordinary least squares estimates of Arab military actions as the dependent variable, and various measures of Israeli economic activity as independent variables. These include growth in total GDP per capita, 'core'-industry profits, and profits merely for Koor industries (which nonetheless constitute 20 percent of all Israeli manufacturing capacity). Other independent variables include Israeli military actions lagged one year, Arab military actions lagged one year, and elections. We have also experimented with various lag structures, different measures, and different control variables (such as elections and political parties). This will enable us to assess the reaction of Arab countries (Egypt, Jordan, Syria) not only to the economic situation in Israel, but also to Israeli and Arab actions in previous years.[14] The results are reported in Table 10.1.

Column 1 shows the effect of changes in the *overall* Israeli economic situation (GDP per capita) in the context of other variables. First, note that the impact of *Israeli actions* in the previous year ($t-1$) on Arab actions is, in contrast to our expectation, negative, indicating that the more Israel retaliates or initiates attacks against Arab targets, the *less* the likelihood that Arab leaders will initiate attacks in the short term.[15] The deterrent effect may operate in the Arab–Israeli context only with a time lag, since the impact of Israeli actions on Arab actions in the same year is significant and in the predicted (positive) direction.[16] *Lagged Arab actions* show the positive relationship that would

Table 10.1 The dual economy and the use of force by Arab states, 1961–86: regression estimates

Independent variable	Dependent variable Arab actions (1)	Arab actions (2)	Arab actions (3)
Constant	2.32***	3.20*	3.39*
% Δ GDP per capita *t*-1	−0.01		
% Δ core profits *t*		−0.83**	
% Δ Koor profits *t*-1			−0.34**
Israeli actions *t*	2.24*	1.39**	1.84*
Israeli actions *t*-1	−1.22**	−1.03**	−1.24 **
Arab actions *t*-1	0.31	0.31	0.29
Election	−0.73***	−0.78**	−0.95 **
Adjusted R^2	0.56	0.68	0.65
Durbin's (1970) test for autocorrelation	−0.31	0.01	−0.15

Note:
* significant at the 0.01 level
** significant at the 0.05 level
*** significant at the 0.10 level

be expected from essentially autocorrelated phenomena in a protracted conflict.[17]

Secondly, *Israeli elections* do influence Arab actions, though in a complex and perhaps counterintuitive way. In general, Arab use of force before an Israeli election is *less* frequent than in other periods. Since Labor held the prime minister's post for most of the period, Arab restraint probably was intended to help Labor.[18] By contrast, the Arab attack on an Israeli bus in the West Bank just days before the 1988 election occurred when a Likud prime minister was in charge. Arab leaders may have tried to hinder Likud's reelection prospects by increasing hostilities. If so, however, this would mean that the Arab leaders did not understand the 'rally 'round the flag' effect, and were impervious to the fact that by taking military actions against a Likud government they actually improved its electoral prospects.

Another interpretation, of course, is that Arab leaders well understood what they were doing, and that some have tried to scuttle the prospects of those who advocated a departure from the adversarial status quo. Given the rivalry among Arab states and Palestinian groups, both explanations may be right – different reasons for different groups. For example, whereas Egyptian leaders condemned the 1990 attack on an Israeli bus in the Sinai desert, several radical Palestinian groups praised the attackers; much the same occurred with the 1988 bus attack and many other incidents. Presumably the Arabs understand that their military actions strengthen the hardliners in Israeli politics. *Israeli* military actions produce a rally 'round the *incumbents*; military actions by Israel's *adversaries* help the *hardliners*, regardless of who are the incumbents.

Turning to the assessment of the impact of the *economic* variables on the use of force, the coefficient in the first column shows that the Arab countries are slightly more likely to use military force against Israel following a decline in Israel's per capita GDP growth; that is, when Israel is economically weak and vulnerable – as was the case prior to the Six-Day War. But this term is not significant, nor, in another specification, was that for Arab action and change in Israeli per capita GDP in the same year.

Column 2 shows much the same pattern for all variables, except that the impact of economic decline in the powerful *core sector* of the Israeli economy on Arab actions is stronger than was the effect of changes in the entire economy (GDP). It also is more consistent across other specifications (not shown here) than was GDP growth. This core-sector variable is not significant at time $t-1$ but is significant at time t. We therefore consider this result somewhat problematic, since some of the Arab actions may precede the decline in the economy. It is unlikely that Arab actions would directly or immediately cause the economy to decline – these are, after all, small-scale military actions, not wars. They may cause delayed and indirect damage to the Israeli economy through the costs Israel accrues by military mobilization and action. If these actions persist and eventually lead to a larger-scale conflict – as was the case before the 1956 Sinai campaign – the effects may be severe. Since the lag effect for core profits is insignificant, we cannot be sure whether the declining economy is a product of Arab actions, or whether the Arab actions come in response to the declining economy.

We now turn to column 3, showing that Arab reaction to the economic well-being of *Koor* industries, the largest concern, is, as hypothesized, negative and significant at $t-1$. Among the core-industry groups, Koor is not only the largest, but is also highly visible and the one most clearly linked to a political party – Labor. Again we have a suggestion of rather sophisticated Arab action, responding not just to the state of the Israeli economy as a whole, but especially to the most politically powerful segments.

A comparison of these results with those obtained in the analysis of series which include GDP data on the 1950s (profits data are available only for the 1960–86 period) reveals some interesting differences (not shown here). Arab reaction to Israeli actions in the previous year is either positive or insignificant, but not negative (as in the 1961–86 period), indicating that over time the cumulative impact of Israeli actions may have discouraged even more actions by the Arab countries. There is also some statistical evidence (though not conclusive) that Arab reaction to the weakness of the Israeli economy was stronger in the entire 1950–86 period than in the 1961–86 period alone.

The Arab calculus of action and reaction thus has seemed to change over the years, and there is evidence that it has become more sophisticated. In recent years, it may have been more influenced by Israeli military actions, and by Arab understanding of Israeli domestic politics. Over the years, Arab leaders may have realized that economic decline does not necessarily weaken Israel in the battlefield, whereas Israeli retaliations and counterattacks raise the costs of initiating an attack.

Table 10.2 The dual economy and Israeli use of force, 1961–86: regression estimates

Independent variable	Dependent variable Israeli actions (1)	Israeli actions (2)	Israeli actions (3)
Constant	0.81*	0.66*	0.72*
% Δ GDP per capita *t*–1	−0.11**		
% Δ core profits *t*		−0.37*	
% Δ Koor profits *t*–1			−0.13**
Israeli actions *t*–1	0.14	0.13	0.04
Arab actions *t*–1	0.23**	0.13***	0.17***
Adjusted R^2	0.42	0.58	0.43
Durbin's (1970) test for autocorrelation	−1.28	−0.84	−0.64

Note:
* significant at the 0.01 level
** significant at the 0.05 level
*** significant at the 0.10 level

All in all we find considerable support for the hypothesis that Arab leaders are more likely to initiate military actions when the core industrial sector in Israel is weak economically, and less likely to attack before an Israeli election (if Labor is in charge) and following earlier Israeli attacks or retaliatory acts.[19] Arab actions are directly related to economic weakness or indirectly motivated by the increase in military spending by Israel in response to economic crises.

We also examined the impact of various influences, including core profits, on *Israeli* actions. Those results (reported in Table 10.2) show that the lag value of per capita GDP growth is negative and significant at the 0.05 level. Earlier work (Barzilai and Russett 1990; Russett and Barzilai 1991) did not find this relationship, because it is sensitive to different lag structures and different specifications; that is, it is not robust. But when we look at the effect of core profits on Israeli actions the result is similar to that of core profits on Arab actions: the impact of core profits on Israeli actions at *t* is strong and consistent. The impact of Koor profits at *t*–1 is also, as with Arab actions, strong and consistent across different models. The impact of Arab actions is, as expected, positive and significant. The lag effect of Israeli actions in the previous year is not significant.

We suggested four reasons why deteriorating economic conditions might lead the Israeli government to take military actions. The second, proposing a 'preemption' merely in response to greater Arab military spending, which in turn is influenced by Israeli actions, is the least persuasive. It implies a relatively long time lag, and our evidence is of a rise in Israeli military action within a year of the economic downturn. The first reason, suggesting 'preemption' of anticipated Arab actions, is plausible given the evidence, from Table 10.1, that the Arabs are more likely to use force when profits in the Israeli core economy decline. The explanations which spotlight conditions in the core and Koor industries rather than in the economy as a whole are also consistent with this evidence. The third reason proposed military action as an attention-diverting mechanism, and the fourth emphasized the importance of being proactive in the military sphere. Together, we have government reaction direct to Israeli economic weakness in combination with anticipation of Arab reaction to that weakness. The anticipatory reaction may be excessive but has roots in deep Israeli concerns in the realm of security.

A TRANSNATIONAL POLITICAL–ECONOMIC CONFLICT SYSTEM

Both Israeli and Arab leaders react to each other's military actions. Their patterns differ, however. Whereas Israel responds positively to the use of force by the Arab states, Israeli actions tend, after a lag, to *discourage* actions by the Arab states. (The spontaneous reaction of the Arab states is positive, but after a lag, perhaps for reflection to consider the costs, the Arab reaction is to reduce military activities against Israel.) While previous studies of conflictual interactions (Schrodt and Mintz 1988; Ward 1982) virtually always reported symmetrical behavior for rival countries, our findings showed asymmetrical interactions. The two 'partners' indeed are not in a symmetrical situation. Once Israel had achieved strategic depth after the 1967 war, it relied less on an offense-oriented military doctrine and concentrated more on the deterrence of low-intensity Arab attacks.

This investigation also showed the importance of the concept of the 'dual economy' to the study of interstate conflict. Conflict at the 'sublimited' level is strongly influenced by declining core-industry profits. Governments may try to divert attention from economic crises in core sectors of the economy by using force against their enemies. The statistical analysis showed that both the Arab states and Israel used force more frequently during and following crises in Israel's core industry and especially in the politically affiliated Koor sector of core industry. This convergence of Arab and Israeli reaction to core-industry weakness is a strong and surprising result.

We also found that the electoral competition in Israel has a significant influence on the use of force by the Arab states. Russett and Barzilai (1991) showed that Israel uses force against its Arab neighbors *more* frequently before elections than in other periods, despite the fact that Arab use of force against Israel is *less* frequent before elections than in other periods. Surprisingly, the effect of elections on stimulating Israeli actions is somewhat less robust than that of elections in reducing Arab actions. (It holds for the entire 1950–88 period, but not for the shorter 1961–86 period which we used here with the new data on profits, so the election variable is excluded from Table 10.2.)

For several years now, researchers have been uncovering systematic evidence that economic conditions within a country influence its government's readiness to use or threaten to use military force. And ever since Tufte (1978), research on the political control of the economy has centered on the impact of elections on the economy in the country where the elections were being held. Here, however, we show that elections and economic conditions may induce military action by *other* countries toward the country evincing economic weakness or holding elections. A transnational political–economic conflict system results. The theoretical perspective and the empirical support for it come together in a new way. They deserve further investigation as additional evidence becomes available.

All in all, we find strong evidence to support our basic theoretical argument that military decisions are rooted not only in international politics, but also in considerations of domestic politics. While the calculus of action and reaction may change over time, domestic political and economic conditions are almost always involved. Both parties respond to similar economic and political stimuli, but not always in the same direction.

The process is complex and only partially explained here, but parts of the solution emerge. We find a combination of domestic political economy and exaggerated action–reaction sequence. One plausible scenario is that Arab leaders will act when the Israeli core economy is weak; the Israelis will react and even overreact before elections and when the economy is weak, and in anticipation of Arab military actions. In short, the makings of a vicious spiral are present. The dual economy – neglected in previous studies – emerges as a key element in this spiral. Israeli economic prosperity could play a role in breaking the spiral; all parties have a stake in that. Alternatively, should Israel's economy stagnate – Arab and Israeli military actions across borders may increase.

NOTES

1 This research was supported by Grants No. SES-8911030 and SES-8810836 from the National Science Foundation. We are grateful to Gad Barzilai for sharing his data, to Samuel E. Hudson for his help in data analysis, and to Donald Green and David Kinsella for comments. Of course, only we are responsible for the results.

2 Russett (1990a, ch. 2) discusses in some detail the literature on political–business cycles and their control. For evidence that the state of the economy affects the outcome of Israeli elections, see Ben Hanan and Temkin (1986) and on the

use of Israeli military spending to manipulate the cycle for electoral purposes, see Mintz (1988) and Mintz and Ward (1989).

3 Israelis also say yes (88 percent) to the question, 'Do you believe it is essential, or not, to support a government during a security crisis, like war, even when one does not agree with what it is doing?' Reported in Arian (1988, 104); also see Stone (1982, 217).

4 For reviews of military–industrial-complex theories and evidence, see Mintz (in press), Mintz (1991), and Russett and Hanson (1975) who report the beliefs of business executives.

5 Galbraith (1973) refers to these as the 'planning system' and the 'market system,' respectively. Many analysts agree that dualism is characteristic of many developing countries and that it has a significant impact on the process of growth.

6 The distinction between 'core' and 'periphery' can be based either on the firm or on the industry as the unit of analysis. In the Israeli case, 'core' firms also dominate 'core' industries.

7 The correlation between change in core profits and GDP is not significant during the period under study.

8 Alternatively, Iranian fervor to export the revolution, a fervor reinforced by the disorganization of the Iranian economy and polity, so threatened Iraq as to induce the attack. See Karsh (1987).

9 Clearly international actions may increase a leader's utility because of what they may do to increase domestic support. A leader in the realm of losses due to a threat to her/his domestic power position will also be more risk-acceptant (Huth and Russett 1990; Kahneman and Tversky 1984).

10 States may take the same action for one of several purposes, or one of several acts for similar purposes (Most and Starr 1984).

11 Aronson and Horowitz (1971) originally suggested a connection between election times and greater use of force.

12 See George and Smoke (1974) and Dougherty and Pfaltzgraff (1990) for a discussion of the three levels of deterrence.

13 Data for 1985 and 1986 were supplied by Bichler.

14 See Ward (1982) on the importance of reaction and memory in models of conflictual interactions.

15 Brams and Kilgour (1988) discuss the conditions under which this result may occur.

16 Full understanding of the matter of timing and causation in action–reaction processes is difficult, and requires a finer-grain analysis than with annual data and a complex structure of distributed lags and simultaneous equations. We shall subsequently specify and estimate such a model; here we only present single-equation estimates.

17 Durbin's (1970) test for autocorrelation (when the lagged dependent variable appears in the right-hand side of the equation) is nonsignificant in all the equations; that is, the null hypothesis of no serial correlation is accepted. The correlation matrix of independent variables and the variance inflation factors indicate that multicollinearity also is not a serious problem.

18 There are only two elections (1981 and 1984) with a Likud government in power, so it was not appropriate to include a dummy variable for party. Note, however, that the lowest score for Arab actions was recorded for 1977, the first time in which Labor was really challenged by Likud.

19 In other specifications we used an interactive term for elections times economic change. The result was a negative coefficient as would be predicted, usually

stronger than the (also significant) election term alone, and usually making the economic terms alone not significant.

REFERENCES

Aharoni, Yair. 1976. *Structure and Performance in the Israeli Economy*. Tel Aviv: Tel Aviv University, Institute for Business Research.

Arian, Asher. 1985. *Israeli Opinion and the War in Lebanon*. Tel Aviv: Tel Aviv University, Jaffee Center for Strategic Studies.

Arian, Asher. 1988. *National Security and Public Opinion in Israel*. Tel Aviv: Tel Aviv University, Jaffee Center for Strategic Studies.

Aronson, Shlomo and Dan Horowitz. 1971. A strategy of limited retaliation. *State and Government* 1: 77–99 (in Hebrew).

Averitt, Robert T. 1968. *The Dual Economy*. New York: W. W. Norton.

Barzilai, Gad and Bruce Russett. 1990. The political economy of Israeli military action. In Asher Arian and Michal Shamir (eds.), *The Elections in Israel – 1988*, pp. 13–35. Boulder, Colo.: Westview.

Ben Hanan, Uriel and Benny Temkin. 1986. The overloaded juggler: the electoral economic cycle in Israel. In Asher Arian and Michal Shamir (eds.), *The Elections in Israel, 1984*, pp. 15–35. New Brunswick, N.J.: Transaction.

Bichler, Shimshon. 1986. *The Political Economy of Defense*. M.A. Thesis, Department of Political Science, The Hebrew University of Jerusalem (in Hebrew).

Bowring, Joseph. 1986. *Competition in the Dual Economy*. Princeton: N.J.: Princeton University Press.

Brams, Steven J. and D. Marc Kilgour. 1988. Threat escalation and crisis stability: a game-theoretic analysis. *American Political Science Review* 81: 833–50.

Brody, Richard. 1984. International crises: a rallying point for the president? *Public Opinion* 6: 41–3.

Cotton, Timothy Y. C. 1986. War and American democracy: voting trends in the last five American wars. *Journal of Conflict Resolution* 30: 616–35.

Dougherty, James E. and Robert L. Pfaltzgraff, Jr. 1990. *Contending Theories of International Relations*. New York: Harper & Row.

Durbin, J.M. 1970. Testing for serial correlation in least squares regression when some of the regressors are lagged dependent variables. *Econometrica* 38: 410–21.

Galbraith, John Kenneth. 1973. *Economics and the Public Purpose*. Boston: Houghton Mifflin.

Gaubatz, Kurt Taylor. 1991. Election cycles and war. *Journal of Conflict Resolution* 35: 212–44.

George, Alexander L. and Richard Smoke. 1974. *Deterrence in American Foreign Policy: Theory and Practice*. New York: Columbia University Press.

Gilpin, Robert. 1987. *The Political Economy of International Relations*. Princeton, N.J.: Princeton University Press.

Huth, Paul and Bruce Russett. 1990. General deterrence between enduring rivals: testing three competing models. Paper presented at the annual meeting of the American Political Science Association, San Francisco, August.

Inbar, Efraim. 1990. Attitudes toward war in the Israeli political elite. *Middle East Journal* 44: 431–45.

Jervis, Robert. 1976. *Perception and Misperception in International Politics*. Princeton, N.J.: Princeton University Press.

Kahneman, Daniel and Amos Tversky. 1984. Choices, values, and frames. *American Psychologist* 39: 341–50.

Karsh, Ephraim. 1987. The Iran–Iraq War: a military analysis. *Adelphi Papers* no. 220.

Kernell, Samuel. 1978. Explaining presidential popularity. *American Political Science Review* 72: 506–22.

Lebow, Richard Ned. 1981. *Between Peace and War*. Baltimore: Johns Hopkins University Press.

LeVine, Robert A. and Donald T. Campbell. 1972. *Ethnocentrism: Theories of Conflict, Ethnic Attitudes, and Group Behavior*. New York: Wiley.

Levy, Jack. 1989. The diversionary theory of war: a critique. In Manus Midlarsky (ed.), *Handbook of War Studies*, pp. 259–88. London: Unwin Hyman.

Levy, Jack S. and Lily Vakili. 1991. External scapegoating by authoritarian regimes: Argentina in the Falklands/Malvinas Case. Offprint, Political Science Department, Rutgers University.

Lissak, Moshe. 1983. The Israel Defense Forces and Israeli society. *Maarachot* 287: June (in Hebrew).

Marra, Robin and Charles W. Ostrom. 1989. Explaining seat change in the U.S. House of Representatives, 1950–1986. *American Journal of Political Science* 31: 541–69.

Marra, Robin, Charles W. Ostrom, and Dennis Simon. 1990. Foreign policy and presidential popularity: creating windows of opportunity in the perpetual election. *Journal of Conflict Resolution* 34: 611–51.

Mintz, Alex. 1988. Electoral cycles and defense spending: a comparison of Israel and the United States. *Comparative Political Studies* 21: 368–82.

Mintz, Alex (ed.). 1991. *The Political Economy of Military Spending in the United States*. London: Routledge.

Mintz, Alex. In press. *Israel's Military–Industrial Complex*.

Mintz, Alex and Michael D. Ward. 1989. The political economy of military spending in Israel. *American Political Science Review* 83: 521–33.

Morgan, Patrick. 1983. *Deterrence: A Conceptual Analysis*. Beverly Hills, Calif.: Sage.

Morgan, T. Clifton and Kenneth Bickers. 1992. Domestic politics and aggressive foreign policy: a causal link? *Journal of Conflict Resolution* 35.

Most, Benjamin and Harvey Starr. 1984. International relations theory, foreign policy substitutability, and 'nice' laws. *World Politics* 36: 383–406.

Mueller, John E. 1973. *War, Presidents, and Public Opinion*. New York: Wiley.

Nincic, Miroslav. 1990. U.S. Soviet policy and the electoral connection. *World Politics* 42: 370–96.

Oster, Gerry. 1978. A factor analytic test of the theory of the dual economy. *Review of Economics and Statistics* 61: 33–9.

Ostrom, Charles W. and Brian Job. 1986. The president and the political use of force. *American Political Science Review* 80: 541–66.

Ostrom, Charles W. and Dennis Simon. 1985. Promise and performance: a dynamic model of presidential popularity. *American Political Science Review* 79: 334–58.

Peri, Yoram and Amnon Neubach. 1984. *The Military–Industrial System in Israel: Interim Report*. The International Center for Peace in the Middle East (in Hebrew).

Rowley, Robin, Shimshon Bichler, and Jonathan Nitzan. 1988. *Some Aspects of Aggregate Concentration in the Israeli Economy 1964–1986*. Montreal: McGill University, Department of Political Science.

Russett, Bruce. 1990a. *Controlling the Sword: The Democratic Governance of National Security*. Cambridge, Mass.: Harvard University Press.

Russett, Bruce. 1990b. Economic decline, electoral pressure, and the initiation of interstate conflict. In Charles Gochman and Alan Ned Sabrosky (eds.),

Prisoners of War? Nation-States in the Modern Era, pp. 123–40. Lexington, Mass.: D.C. Heath.

Russett, Bruce and Gad Barzilai. 1991. The political economy of military actions: Israel and the United States. In Alex Mintz (ed.), *The Political Economy of Military Spending in the United States*. London: Routledge.

Russett, Bruce and Elizabeth C. Hanson. 1975. *Interest and Ideology: The Foreign Policy Beliefs of American Businessmen*. New York: W. H. Freeman.

Sacher, Howard M. 1987. *A History of Israel, Vol. II: From the Aftermath of the Yom Kippur War*. New York: Oxford University Press.

Schrodt, Philip A. and Alex Mintz. 1988. The conditional probability analysis of international events data. *American Journal of Political Science* 32: 217–30.

Shaw, Paul R. and Yuwa Wong. 1988. *Genetic Seeds of Warfare: Evolution, Nationalism, and Patriotism*. Boston: Unwin Hyman.

Stohl, Michael. 1980. The nexus of civil and international conflict. In Ted R. Gurr (ed.), *Handbook of Political Conflict: Theory and Research*, pp. 297–330. New York: Free Press.

Stoll, Richard J. 1984. The guns of November: presidential reelections and the use of force. *Journal of Conflict Resolution* 28: 231–46.

Stoll, Richard J. 1990. *U.S. National Security Policy and the Soviet Union*. Columbia, S.C.: University of South Carolina Press.

Stone, Russell A. 1982. *Social Change in Israel: Attitudes and Events, 1967–79*. New York: Praeger.

Tetlock, Philip. 1985. Integrative complexity of American and Soviet foreign policy rhetoric. *Journal of Personality and Social Psychology* 49: 1565–85.

Tetlock, Philip and C. McGuire. 1985. Integrative complexity as a predictor of Soviet foreign policy behavior. *International Journal of Group Tensions* 14: 113–28.

Tufte, Edward. 1978. *Political Control of the Economy*. Princeton, N.J.: Princeton University Press.

Ward, Michael. 1982. Dynamics of cooperation and conflict in foreign policy behavior: reaction and memory. *International Studies Quarterly* 26: 87–126.

Yaniv, Avner. 1987. *Dilemmas of Security: Politics, Strategy, and the Israeli Experience in Lebanon*. New York: Oxford University Press.

Zinnes, Dina. 1980. Why war? Evidence on the outbreak of international conflict. In Ted R. Gurr (ed.), *Handbook of Political Conflict: Theory and Research*, pp. 331–60. New York: Free Press.

11 The impact of military expenditures on human-capital development in the Arab Gulf States

Robert E. Looney
Naval Postgraduate School

INTRODUCTION

It is often argued (Cummings, *et al.* 1980, 38–49) that the post-1973/4 expansion in military expenditures undertaken by the Persian Gulf States has led to competition between the military and civilian sectors for skilled labor. Furthermore, military expenditures are said to have preempted funds that might have otherwise been allocated to education and the improvement of human capital. As a result, it is argued, military expenditures in the region tended to frustrate the oil exporters' ambitious economic-development programs, especially those of the less-populated oil-exporting countries.

Another view originally presented by Stephanie Neuman (1978) in her analysis of the pre-Revolutionary Iranian situation is that some of the skills taught by the military can benefit the civilian sector. As she (Neuman 1978, 589) points out, however, a question still remains as to:

> how one would distinguish between the military and the civilian costs and benefits. What is the net balance over the long and short term? Furthermore, how are the skill levels related to the kinds of military technology imported? Does more technology demand higher skills and, therefore, indirectly upgrade the educational level of the country? Instead, does it draw away needed skilled manpower from the civilian sector?

Clearly, the ability of these countries to adapt to changing and, in most cases, more austere economic environments will depend in large part on how effectively they take advantage of the years of abundant revenue to increase the education and skills of their domestic workforces.

The purpose of this chapter is to address whether military expenditures in the Arab world in general, and the Gulf States in particular have come at the expense of national human-resource development. Based on this analysis several implications are drawn as to the development of human capital in the Gulf States.

MANPOWER SHORTAGES AND GOVERNMENT EXPENDITURES

Human-capital accumulation can be stimulated in developing countries through public education expenditure, as well as government spending on health and other social services. Clearly, governments are by far the most important agencies in this area and can do much more than private enterprises could ever hope to achieve.

Government initiative in this area has expanded in recent years, with Arab countries as a whole increasing their educational expenditures as a percentage of GNP from 3.87 (1974) to 5.08 (1984, see Table 11.1). The corresponding figures for non-Arab countries were 3.33 percent and 4.01 percent. Health expenditures have not shown such a dramatic increase, however, rising from 1.39 percent of GNP (1974) for the Arab countries to 1.59 (1984). A similar pattern was observed in the non-Arab countries. Here, health expenditure increased from 1.32 to 1.62 percent of GNP during the same period.

On the other hand, the governments of developing countries also have made extremely strong commitments to military expenditure in order to bolster security and counter threats. Aggregate defense expenditure is almost always state-induced, and the consumption of scarce resources to support the military as well as reallocation of valuable inputs into arms production must generally be provided for in national budget. In terms of general magnitudes, Arab countries expanded their military expenditures as a share of GNP from 7.87 percent (1974) to 12.39 percent (1984). Militarization in the non-Arab countries was not nearly as dramatic, with defense expenditures increasing from 3.01 to 3.72 percent of GNP over the corresponding time period.

In short, concurrent with rapid economic growth in the Arab world, there has been an acceleration in military spending. For the region as a whole, military purchases have been partially financed by oil revenues and by military aid and grants from the major arms suppliers. Lebovic and Ishaq (1987, 107) have noted that while the absolute regional military spending has been phenomenal, the military has also controlled a greater percentage of the central government budget in the Middle East and twice as much of the national output as in other developing countries or in the world as a whole:

> Middle Eastern defense accounted for one-third of the military spending of developing countries and almost one-half of world arms imports. During the 1973–1982 period, the average annual economic growth rate for individual Middle Eastern states was about 6.0%, while military expenditures grew by approximately 13.0% per year. Although military expenditure levels vary greatly across countries, in a great majority of

Table 11.1 Contrasts in human-resource and military expenditures: Arab and non-Arab countries, 1974–84 (means)

Variable	Arab countries	Sample size	Non-Arab countries	Sample size
Military expenditures				
(percentage of GNP)				
1974	7.87	20	3.01	74
1979	10.54	19	3.37	80
1984	12.39	20	3.72	84
($ per capita)				
1974	139.82	20	32.50	74
1979	559.74	20	58.21	80
1984	539.31	20	75.64	84
Educational expenditures				
(percentage of GNP)				
1974	3.87	20	3.33	80
1979	4.81	19	4.01	84
1984	5.08	20	4.01	85
($ per capita)				
1974	83.98	20	20.54	80
1979	270.81	18	52.96	84
1984	221.37	18	64.37	85
Health Expenditures				
(percentage of GNP)				
1974	1.39	20	1.32	80
1979	1.35	18	1.64	82
1984	1.59	18	1.62	85
($ per capita)				
1974	33.06	20	9.07	80
1979	64.65	18	23.14	82
1984	96.13	18	27.05	85

Source: Ruth Leger Sivard (various years).

the countries the growth rate of military spending outpaced economic growth. This indicates a striking trend in the region toward higher military burdens.

As Lebovic and Ishaq (1987, 107) point out, besides the simple guns-versus-butter tradeoff, economic theory does not unambiguously indicate whether a higher military burden retards or promotes economic growth. Empirical evidence on the subject has become the focus of considerable controversy.

Again, as Charles Wolf (1981, 89) has noted:

> Military and paramilitary forces can contribute to economic development by their contributions to internal and external stability. Moreover, the real economic costs imposed by the military on developing countries can be reduced to the extent these forces provide training, construction, technological and industrial spill-overs that contribute to economic

growth. Evidence in support of both of these propositions is provided by the experience of several of the successfully modernizing countries during the past decade.

In a more recent study, Weede (1983, 17) finds considerable empirical support for the proposition that increased military-participation rates increase overall economic growth:

> In my view, the positive effect of military service on economic performance should be explained as follows: the military teaches discipline and creates a useful habit of obeying orders. Where the military participation ratios are high, the military is more likely to be disciplined and effective than elsewhere, since there is a perceived need to be on the alert against foreign enemies. Moreover, the higher the military participation ratio, the more young men acquire discipline and obedience. That is why I regard the military participation ratio as a discipline related indicator of human capital formation, why I suggest to broaden the notion of human capital formation so as to include abilities and discipline.

Clearly, the Arab World, given its relatively low levels of human-capital formation, should be one of the areas most receptive to this link between military expenditure, military participation, human-capital formation, and economic growth. However, in their study of the relationship between defense burdens and growth in the Middle East, Lebovic and Ishaq (1987) find in general the relationship was negative for the non-oil-exporting countries, but that no statistically significant pattern existed for the total sample (seventeen countries). The negative finding is consistent with those obtained by Frederiksen and Looney (1983) who make a distinction between resource-constrained and resource-abundant countries.

Given the small sample sizes of oil producers in the Middle East, Lebovic and Ishaq were not able to test for any potential positive relationships between defense expenditures and economic growth, a relationship identified by Frederiksen and Looney for larger samples of developing countries. These positive relationships have, however, been identified through time-series analysis for certain individual countries and periods of time.

For example, in the case of Saudi Arabia it was found that (Looney 1987, 225–6):

1. In general, military expenditures have had a net positive impact on the country's overall gross capital formation. That is after controlling for government expenditures and oil revenues, increases in military expenditures have had a net stimulating effect on investment in the Kingdom. The same also applies to non-oil investment. Here, however, the strength of defense expenditures was low compared with that of government investment.
2. Military expenditures do not appear to stimulate either total private-sector expenditures or consumption. Again government investment

appears particularly productive in contributing to increased levels of private-sector consumption.

3 Military expenditures do not appear to increase levels of imports nearly as much as do the overall levels of government expenditures or oil revenues.

4 Interestingly enough, military expenditures appear to induce private-sector investment whereas government investment seems to crowd out or preempt resources that might otherwise flow toward this sector.

5 In the net, military expenditures appear to contribute more to overall demand than does government consumption. The stimulating effect of military expenditures on other types of government expenditures tended to reinforce this effect.

In short, military expenditures in the Saudi Arabian context appear to have (in addition to their security value) a number of significant impacts on the private sector, not all of which are negative. In particular, several of the major areas of private-sector activity appear to derive more of a stimulus from government expenditures than from other forms of government allocations. The same also appears to apply to the overall level of gross capital formation and non-oil investment.

In addition, these results suggest that a careful shifting of government allocations from public-sector consumption to capital formation (providing that profitable areas for investment have not been exhausted) rather than across-the-board reductions in military expenditures is the most productive policy open to the authorities for contributing to private-sector expansion.

In a slightly different context, it has been suggested that excessive defense expenditures led to the economic instability preceding the Iranian Revolution. While this argument sounds quite plausible, recent cross-sectional research has reached the counterintuitive conclusion that Iran may have actually derived a number of beneficial economic impacts from allocations to the military. However, cross-sectional analysis only looks at one point in time, and hence its results are always sensitive to the dates chosen for examination.

To determine if longitudinal analysis provides a different perspective on the impact of the country's military expenditures, another time-series study (Looney, 1988) attempted to quantify the impacts of military expenditures on the Iranian economy over the 1959–77 period, and in particular the consequences associated with the rapid military buildup undertaken by the Shah in the mid-1970s.

In general, the main findings of this study indicated that while a case could be made that the Iranian economy received positive net benefits from defense expenditures in the 1960s, this relationship broke down in the 1970s, with added military expenditures, perhaps through the bottlenecks they created, having a negative impact on a number of sectors and types of capital formation. Interestingly enough, these negative effects were not systematically associated with other types of government expenditures, indicating that defense expenditures were unique in their marginal negative impact on private-sector output after the 1973–4 revenue boom.

Again these findings are consistent with cross-sectional analysis which indicates that resource-constrained countries generally experience negative impacts from military expenditures while those not constrained by foreign exchange and/or domestic savings are capable of experiencing positive impacts from increased allocations to defense.

Looking at the impact of military expenditures from a different perspective, that of labor scarcity, Cummings *et al.* (1980) note that the labor shortages in the Gulf States created by expanded military expenditures may be a far greater long-term impediment to growth in the region than any effects associated with the diversion of capital or foreign exchange to military activities. In a somewhat similar manner, Mousad (1984) found that a 10 percent reduction in the military-spending ratio (percentage of GNP) or a decrease of around $12.9 billion would increase education expenditure by around $8.1 billion per year.

Along these lines, Deger (1984, 42–3) estimated that a 15 percent reduction in the military-spending ratio, that is from 6.3 percent of GDP to 5.4 percent (approximately $13 billion in absolute terms), would increase the education-expenditure ratio to 2.93 percent of national output. In absolute terms this would amount to about $4.5 billion a year. These estimates were made for developing countries as a whole, with no distinction made between countries as being resource-abundant or resource-constrained, labor-abundant or labor-scarce, and so on.

The purpose of this chapter is to extend several strands of the analysis surveyed above. Specifically, we are primarily interested in examining the Arab states, a set of countries characterized as generally having by Third World standards very high military burdens (military expenditures as a percentage of GNP) together with lower-than-average levels of human capital. In addition, we are interested in determining whether and to what extent military expenditures act independently of total government expenditures in affecting human-capital development in the region. Finally, are the linkages between military expenditures and human-capital development fundamentally different in the Arab states from those experienced in other parts of the world? If so, why?

FRAMEWORK FOR ANALYSIS

The main measurable variables pertain to allocations to defense, government expenditures, and public education that may generate human capital. The latter is proxied by the ratio of public education expenditure as a proportion of GDP. Following Deger (1985, 42–3), we assume that public-education spending as a proportion of the national product is a crucial determinant of human-capital formation (*HC*). In other words, if this ratio falls, the rate of growth of human capital will, in all probability, also fall.

As Lebovic and Ishaq (1987, 110) have noted, one of the main difficulties with previous studies was their lack of clarity as to whether the military burden acted in some way as a statistical proxy for government expenditures. To avoid this problem, total government expenditures were included in the analysis in addition to military expenditures, with each defined in terms of a different ratio. Specifically, government expenditures (*GEY*) were treated in terms of their share of GNP.

To avoid spurious correlations with government expenditures, allocations to defense were defined in ways other than the traditional military burden (military expenditures as a share of GNP). Since the literature is unclear as to the most appropriate manner to define the defense burden, three alternative measures were used: (a) military expenditures per soldier (*MEAF*), (b) the defense share of the central-government budget (*MEGE*), and (c) the military-participation rate, the number of soldiers per 1000 population (*AFP*).

Increases in human-capital formation over any time period are likely to be affected by the initial level of human-capital resources. That is, countries beginning with a relatively low level of human-capital development are more likely to experience rapid increases. To control for this factor, the rate of human-capital development at the beginning of the period (that is, *HC74* for the 1974–84 interval) was introduced into the regression equation.

Finally, increases in per capita income may expand the demand for education. This is the so-called Wagner's Law, (Whynes 1979, ch. 2) which also implies an increase in defense share of the government budget at higher levels of per capita income. To control for this factor, the increase in per capita income (*YP*) was also introduced into the regression equations.

In sum, the model with expected signs used for examining the impact of military expenditures on human-resource development was of the form:

$$HC = [\underset{(+)}{GEY},\ \underset{(?)}{MEAF},\ \underset{(?)}{MEGE},\ \underset{(?)}{AFP},\ \underset{(+)}{YP},\ \underset{(-)}{HC0},\ \underset{(+)}{GEY74}]$$

where:

HC	=	educational expenditures/GNP
GEY	=	total government expenditures/GNP
MEAF	=	military expenditures per soldier
MEGE	=	the share of defense in the central-government budget
AFP	=	the number of soldiers per 1000 population
YP	=	per capita income (GNP/population)
HC0	=	educational expenditures/GNP in the base year
GEY74	=	total government expenditures/GNP in the base year

Data were taken from Sivard (various years). The original sample of developing countries consisted of 109 nations. Because of missing observations on several countries, the usual sample size was around ninety countries. The Arab countries are defined as those nations where the majority of the population is Arab. The presumption here is that these countries share a common set of social institutions and cultural values. These, in turn, influence the manner in which resources are allocated to the military and socioeconomic programs.

The Arab countries are all members of the Arab Monetary Fund, and consist of: Jordan, the United Arab Emirates (UAE), Bahrain, Tunisia, Algeria, Saudi Arabia, Sudan, Syria, Somalia, Iraq, Oman, Qatar, Kuwait, Lebanon, Libya, Egypt, Morocco, Mauritania, Yemen Arab Republic, and the People's Democratic Republic of Yemen. Again because of missing observations, Lebanon, Qatar, and Mauritania were absent from most of the regressions.

All variables except *HCO* and *GEY74* were defined in terms of their rate of growth over the period under consideration. To get an idea of the robustness of the results, stepwise regressions were undertaken for the entire time interval 1974–84, together with its two five-year subperiods, 1974–9 and 1979–84.

RESULTS

The results for the period as a whole (1974–84) produced several interesting findings (Table 11.2):

(a) For developing countries, in general, the estimated model (Equation 1 in Table 11.2) explained approximately 70 percent of the changes in human-capital formation. The coefficient for the government-expenditure term (*GEY*) was very stable, not changing appreciably with varying model specification.

(b) While increased military expenditures per soldier (*MEAF*) did not detract from human-capital development, other measures of military expenditures did. In particular, increases in the defense share of the public-sector budget (*MEGE*) tended to reduce human-capital development during this period. The same was also the case for increase in the military-participation rate (*AFP*).

(c) In terms of individual Gulf States, it appears that several countries (Iraq and Saudi Arabia) had increases in human-capital formation considerably below that predicted by the model (Equation 2 in Table 11.2), while Iran and Oman had rates of human-capital formation considerably above that anticipated by the model.

Looking at countries in terms of Arab/non-Arab classifications (Equations 2 and 3 in Table 11.2), however, produces a considerably different picture of the factors at work affecting human-capital formation:

Table 11.2 Factors affecting human-capital formation in the Third World, 1974–84 (standardized regression coefficients)

Third World countries – total sample

(1) $HC = 0.84GEY - 0.11MEAF - 0.17MEGE - 0.13GEY74$
(10.36) (−1.16) (−2.31) (−1.890)

$+ 0.10YP - 0.20AFP$
(1.37) (−2.62) r2 = 0.697; F = 31.12; df = 87

Country	Residual	Standard error	Student residual	Cooks' *D*
Bahrain	−0.08	0.68	0.33	0.001
Iraq	−3.12	0.62	−5.05	0.883
Kuwait	−0.27	0.68	−0.41	0.001
Oman	1.39	0.67	2.08	0.037
Qatar	n.a.	n.a.	n.a.	n.a.
Saudi Arabia	−1.14	0.66	−1.73	0.033
UAE	0.00	0.67	0.01	0.000

Arab countries

(2) $HC = -0.26GEY + 1.74MEAF - 0.49MEGE - 0.26GEY74$
(0.02) (5.03) (−3.19) (−2.76)

$- 0.90\ YP + 0.42\ AFP$
(−3.13) (2.15) r2 = 0.942; F = 30.21; df = 17

Country	Residual	Standard error	Student residual	Cooks' *D*
Bahrain	0.49	0.55	0.89	0.068
Iraq	−0.45	0.35	−1.28	0.716
Kuwait	−0.35	0.60	−0.59	0.017
Oman	0.41	0.53	0.77	0.061
Qatar	n.a.	n.a.	n.a.	n.a.
Saudi Arabia	−1.26	0.63	−2.03	0.139
UAE	−0.07	0.56	−0.13	0.001

Non-Arab countries

(3) $HC = 0.87\ GEY - 0.34\ MEAF - 0.21\ MEGE - 0.16\ GEY74$
(8.89) (−3.27) (−2.41) (−2.00)

$+ 0.06\ YP - 0.23\ AFP$
(0.69) (−2.52) $R^2 = 0.942$; F = 30.21; df= 70

Note: R^2 = the coefficient of determination; F = the F statistic; df = the degrees of freedom; ( ) = the t statistic.

(a) While by itself the share of government expenditures in GNP accounts for well over 65 percent of the observed fluctuations in human-capital formation in the Arab World, this relationship breaks down with more complete model specification. In the completely specified model (Equation 2, Table 11.2) increases in the government-expenditure share of GNP are no longer significant in affecting the pace of human-capital formation.

(b) Perhaps more important, several of the military-expenditure terms are now statistically significant. Both expanded rates, military expenditures per soldier (*MEAF*) and the military-participation rate (*AFP*), tended to increase human-capital development during this time period.

Table 11.3 Factors affecting human-capital formation in the Third World, 1974–9 (standardized regression coefficients)

Third World countries – total sample

$$(1)\ HC = 0.58\,GEY + 0.50\,MEAF - 0.53\,MEGE - 0.20\,GEY74$$
$$(7.39)\quad (2.56)\quad (-6.12)\quad (-2.91)$$
$$-0.51\,YP + 0.10\,AFP$$
$$(-2.82)\quad (1.37)\ R^2 = 0.679;\ F = 28.18;\ df = 86$$

Country	Residual	Standard error	Student residual	Cooks'*D*
Bahrain	0.21	0.35	0.59	0.009
Iraq	−0.09	0.37	−0.24	0.000
Kuwait	−0.22	0.37	−0.60	0.001
Oman	0.74	0.37	2.04	0.035
Qatar	n.a.	n.a.	n.a.	n.a.
Saudi Arabia	−0.80	0.35	−2.26	0.094
UAE	−0.21	0.36	−0.58	0.003

Arab countries

$$(2)\ HC = 0.37\,GEY + 1.09\,MEAF - 0.53\,MEGE - 0.41\,GEY74$$
$$(2.37)\quad (2.96)\quad (-4.22)\quad (-3.60)$$
$$-\ 0.90\,YP$$
$$(-2.67)\ R^2 = 0.868;\ F = 15.83;\ df = 17$$

Country	Residual	Standard error	Student residual	Cooks'*D*
Bahrain	0.22	0.23	1.01	0.292
Iraq	−0.22	0.35	−0.62	0.008
Kuwait	−0.53	0.34	−1.52	0.065
Oman	0.31	0.30	1.01	0.083
Qatar	n.a.	n.a.	n.a.	n.a.
Saudi Arabia	−0.76	0.32	−2.42	0.385
UAE	−0.02	0.33	−0.06	0.000

Non-Arab countries

$$(3)\ HC = 0.59\,GEY + 0.32\,MEAF - 0.41\,MEGE - 0.13\,GEY74$$
$$(6.98)\quad (1.57)\quad (-5.01)\quad (-1.71)$$
$$-0.41\,YP + 0.14\,AFP$$
$$(-2.11)\quad (1.66)\ R^2 = 0.648;\ F = 19.09;\ df = 68$$

Note: R^2 = the coefficient of determination; *F* = the *F* statistic; df = the degrees of freedom; ( ) = *t* statistic.

However, as with the total sample, increases in the defense share of the budget (*MEGE*) tended to reduce the growth in human-capital formation.

(c) For the non-Arab countries much the reverse was true. In addition to increased levels of defense expenditures in the central-government budget, these countries as a group experienced negative effects on human-capital formation stemming from increased military expenditures per soldier and the military-participation rate.

Much the same pattern characterizes the two five-year subperiods (Tables 11.3 and 11.4):

Table 11.4 Factors affecting human-capital formation in the World, 1979–84 (standardized regression coefficients)

Third World countries – total sample

$$(1)\ HC = 0.47\,GEY - 0.14\,MEAF - 0.28\,MEGE - 0.18\,GEY74$$
$$\quad (4.58) \quad (-1.37) \quad (-2.79) \quad (-1.92)$$
$$+0.14\,YP + 0.04\,AFP$$
$$(1.49) \quad (0.39)\ R^2 = 0.331;\ F = 7.09;\ df = 92$$

Country	Residual	Standard error	Student residual	Cooks'*D*
Bahrain	−0.20	0.30	−0.68	0.005
Iraq	−1.05	0.20	−5.18	4.834
Kuwait	0.31	0.30	1.04	0.006
Oman	0.09	0.29	0.31	0.001
Qatar	n.a.	n.a.	n.a.	n.a.
Saudi Arabia	0.15	0.30	0.51	0.001
UAE	0.49	0.30	1.66	0.022

Arab countries

$$(2)\ HC = -1.65\,GEY + 3.03\,MEAF - 2.93\,MEGE - 0.11\,GEY74$$
$$\quad (-2.72) \quad (4.35) \quad (-4.87) \quad (-0.76)$$
$$-1.37\,YP + 1.34\,AFP$$
$$(-3.92) \quad (2.55)\ R^2 = 0.839;\ F = 8.71;\ df = 16$$

Country	Residual	Standard error	Student residual	Cooks'*D*
Bahrain	−0.01	0.18	−0.07	0.000
Iraq	−0.02	0.03	−0.74	0.011
Kuwait	0.07	0.19	0.39	0.009
Oman	−0.20	0.17	−1.18	0.148
Qatar	n.a.	n.a.	n.a.	n.a.
Saudi Arabia	−0.13	0.20	−0.66	0.016
UAE	0.27	0.15	1.88	0.681

Non-Arab countries

$$(3)\ HC = 0.74\,GEY - 0.24\,MEAF - 0.28\,MEGE - 0.11\,GEY74$$
$$\quad (7.59) \quad (-2.47) \quad (-3.00) \quad (-1.02)$$
$$+0.07\,YP - 0.06\,AFP$$
$$(0.77) \quad (-0.67)\ R^2 = 0.558;\ F14.49;\ df = 75$$

Note: R^2 = the coefficient of determination; *F* the *F* statistic; df = the degrees of freedom; ( ) = the *t* statistic.

(a) Developing countries as a whole did have a slight stimulus to human-capital formation coinciding with increased military expenditures during the first period, but this turned into a negative (albeit statistically insignificant) effect in the later (1979–84) period.

(b) Developing countries as a group had slower rates of human-capital formation when defense expenditures expanded in the government budget, but this effect was considerably weaker in the second time period as opposed to the first. Apparently, as a group these countries did not experience any retarding effect on human-capital formation resulting from increased military-participation rates.

(c) However, Arab countries were able to expand human capital in line with increased military expenditures per soldier. This effect was fairly strong in both subperiods, and was complemented in the second time period by increased military-participation rates. In both time periods, well over 80 percent of the movements in human capital could be accounted for by the model. As with the 1974–84 time period, an increased share of government expenditures in GNP was not translated into an improvement in the rate of increase in human-capital development.

(d) In contrast, non-Arab countries found their efforts to expand human-capital development little affected by military expenditures, other than increases in the defense share of the budget. In the first time period, increased military expenditures per soldier and increased military-participation rates had a slight positive (but insignificant) effect on human-capital formation, while in the later time period both terms were negative with only military expenditure per soldier statistically significant.

CONCLUSIONS

While it might seem intuitively obvious that shifting public allocations from military toward educational activities would accelerate human-capital development and hence increase a country's long-run growth prospects (while in the case of the Gulf States reducing dependence on foreign workers), the results presented above indicate that this view is too simplistic. Admittedly, this possibility may hold some validity for many developing countries, but it does not appear to be an accurate description of the process by which resources are allocated in the Arab World. For these countries, increases in military expenditure per soldier and in the military-participation rate appear to take place simultaneously with expanded allocations to human capital.

Based on the results presented above, one can only speculate as to the mechanisms linking military expenditures and human-capital formation in the Arab World. Given shortages of skilled labor, particularly in the Gulf, governments in that region might assign a very high priority to attracting available skilled labor to the military services (Cummings *et al* 1980, 42). This could be accomplished through monetary and other incentives. However, since the skilled labor pool is so limited, the private sector might object to sharply increased competition. This is especially so in light of a dwindling number of qualified workers.

A more likely situation is one where the governments are subsidizing education of increased numbers of civilians during periods of stepped-up military expenditures with the understanding that upon completion of training those individuals will serve some time in the military. This strategy would allow the military to absorb the large volume of sophisticated weapons flowing into the region while at the same time not requiring drastic increases in the numbers of foreign military advisers.

This interpretation is consistent with the results obtained above. Given the fairly high correlation between military expenditures and government revenues in the region (Looney 1987), allocations to both defense and education could increase fairly rapidly without either category experiencing significant changes in its share of the budget. Because of the low skill levels of the local populations in these countries, it is unlikely that rapid increases in military expenditures per soldier and in the number of soldiers per capita could be absorbed without accelerated training programs both within and outside the military.

The results presented here suggest that additional analyses should be undertaken. In particular, it would be interesting to see the impact of other types of government expenditures – especially those going to administration and services. It may well turn out that these expenditures have even higher opportunity costs in terms of labor shortages and/or reduced levels of educational attainment.

REFERENCES

Cummings, John, Hossein Askari, and Michael Skinner. 1980. Military expenditures and manpower requirements in the Arabian peninsula. *Scientific American* Winter: 38–49.

Deger, Saadet. 1985. Human resources, government education expenditure, and the military burden in less developed countries. *Journal of Developing Areas* 20: 37–48.

Frederiksen, Peter and Robert Looney. 1983. Defense expenditures and economic growth in developing countries. *Armed Forces and Society*, Summer: 633–45.

Lebovic, James and Ashafaq Ishaq. 1987. Military burden, security needs, and economic growth in the Middle East. *Journal of Conflict Resolution* 31: 106–38.

Looney, Robert. 1987. The impact of defense expenditures on the Saudi Arabian private sector. *Journal of Arab Affairs*, Fall: 198–229.

Looney, Robert. 1988. The role of military expenditures in pre-Revolutionary Iran's economic decline. *Iranian Studies*: 52–71.

Mousad, Mohamed. 1984. Human resources, government education expenditures and the military burden in less developed countries: with special reference to Arab countries. *Bulletin of Arab Research and Studies*: 35–55.

Neuman, Stephanie. 1979. Security, military expenditures and socioeconomic development: reflections on Iran. *ORBIS* 22: 569–94.

Sivard, Ruth. Various years. *World Military and Social Expenditures*. Washington D.C.: World Priorities.

Weede, Erich. 1983. Military participation ratios, human capital formation, and economic growth: a cross-national analysis. *Journal of Political and Military Sociology* 11: 11–19

Whynes, David. 1979. *The Economics of Third World Military Expenditure*. Austin: University of Texas Press.

Wolf, Charles. 1981. Economic success, stability, and the old international order. *International Security* 6: 75–92.

12 Military participation, economic growth, and income inequality: a cross-national study[1]

Erich Weede
University of Cologne

Intuitively, most people feel that the allocation of men and money to the military is a burden. The heavier this burden is, the worse economic performance should be. Men serving with the armed forces are not available for directly productive work. Money spent for armaments is not available for investment. Moreover, it may be argued that defense burdens prevent the establishment or improvement of the welfare state. Under this assumption defense burdens might also contribute to income inequality. In general, the intuitively appealing image of defense is simple: defense *is* a burden. Under specific circumstances it might be unavoidable to carry this burden, but the economic consequences of defense can hardly be positive.

A moment of reflection should suffice to call this image into question. Except for some Communist-ruled societies, there are few nations that have suffered more from threats to their national security and carried heavier military burdens *for decades* than Israel, Taiwan, and South Korea. Taiwan, for example, has a population below 20 million, but maintains armed forces in the same order of magnitude as West Germany, a country with 60 million inhabitants. The purpose of these armed forces is to deter, and to defend against, a Communist invasion from the mainland, that is, less than 2 percent of all Chinese preserve their prosperity and freedom from Communism against the armed forces of a regime commanding more than fifty times as many people. Nevertheless, Taiwan, like South Korea, counts as one of the miracle economies. In foreign-currency reserves, Taiwan is in the same league as Japan and West Germany. Its income distribution is fairly equal, and actually did improve at intermediate levels of economic development where other less developed countries suffered from a deterioration (Fei *et al*. 1980; but, see Chan's Chapter 9 in this volume). Similarly, few countries enjoy a more egalitarian distribution of income than Israel or South Korea.

Of course, specific examples can provide little support for general propositions. The main purpose of my reference to Israel, South Korea, and Taiwan is not to 'prove' the intuitively appealing view wrong and to replace it by its inverse, but to neutralize the impact of another set of cases which seems to dominate more people's minds, that is, the United States and Japan (see Kennedy 1987; Rosecrance 1986). 'Everybody' knows that the United States carries a heavy military burden and suffers from some economic weaknesses, while Japan carries a light burden and outperforms all other developed countries. This comparison fits with the intuitively appealing view, concerns large economies, and is widely invoked.

The following comparisons are rarely made: Whereas Japan carries a light military burden, South Korea and Taiwan carry heavy burdens. Still, the economic performance of the two 'small tigers' is *at least* as good as Japan's. Obviously, one can choose one's examples in order to illustrate just about any putatively *general* relationship between military burdens and economic performance.

It seems preferable to look at quantitative and systematic studies. Here, Benoit (1973, 1978) has argued that defense *expenditures* may actually increase economic growth rates in less developed countries (LDCs). This work has attracted a lot of criticism (reviewed by Chan 1985; Deger 1986; Grobar and Porter 1989). First, Benoit's findings are not robust. Somewhat changing the composition of the sample or the period of observation does generally lead to lower correlations between defense expenditures and growth rates than reported by Benoit (1973). Second, the inclusion of investment and aid in the regression equation turns the beneficial impact of defense burdens at least insignificant, or even negative for Benoit's own data set (Grobar and Porter 1989, 331). By and large, more recent work (such as Deger's 1986) distinguishes between various direct and indirect effects of military spending which may differ in sign, and employs multi-equation models to estimate them by advanced techniques. Unfortunately, I have not yet seen a multi-equation model that takes seriously the idea that defense expenditures might be affected by threats to national security. Therefore, I suspect that at least the defense-burden equations are likely to be misspecified. Full-information methods of estimation spread the effects of misspecification throughout the system of equations. While these caveats may serve to caution one against accepting the claims of some of Benoit's critics, they certainly cannot serve to 'rescue' his findings. Instead Grobar and Porter's (1989, 344) conclusions provide a meaningful summary of the literature: 'overall, military spending has a weak but adverse impact on economic growth in developing countries.'

While a *strong* and *general negative* impact of defense expenditures on economic growth rates remains to be established *if* it should indeed exist, prima facie there seem to be good reasons to expect that equity and national well-being suffer because of defense burdens. 'Guns' could replace 'butter', defense might be financed at the expense of welfare. Again, the plausibility of this argument can be undermined by some reflection. In many societies the welfare state takes much better care of soldiers and veterans than of civilian workers. It may be no coincidence that Bismarckian Germany was characterized by a vulnerable geopolitical location and established a rudimentary welfare state ahead of geopolitically privileged and therefore less 'militaristic' states like Britain and the United States. Conceivably, defense needs can provide something like an opening for the welfare state in hierarchical societies. Turning from specific instances to a systematic study, Russett (1982) did not find a systematic tradeoff between military spending in the United States and its health and education expenditures.

In my view, the dominant branch of research on linkages between defense and economic performance investigated the weaker rather than the stronger effects of defense-related variables on the economy. While the impact of defense *expenditures* on growth rates, welfare, or income distribution *may be* negative, weak, or insignificant, the impact of high military-participation ratios on economic performance is positive, comparatively stronger, and often significant. There even is a relatively large and consistent body of cross-national studies supporting the propositions that countries with high military-participation ratios grow faster than other nations (Marsh 1988; Weede 1983, 1986a; Weede and Jagodzinski 1981; Weede and Tiefenbach 1981a), and also enjoy a more equal distribution of income than others (Chan 1989; Garnier and Hazelrigg 1977; Kriesberg 1979, 379; Weede and Jagodzinski 1981; Weede and Tiefenbach 1981b, 1981c). In addition, Dixon and Moon (1986) demonstrate some positive and significant relationship between military-participation ratios and the physical-quality-of-life index. Assuming that the physical quality of life or basic human-needs fulfillment depends on both economic performance and income distribution, Dixon and Moon's result fits well with the other findings.

The idea that military participation affects production as well as distribution positively has been most vigorously argued by Stanislav Andreski (1968a, 1968b). Concerning growth he wrote:

> The sentiments of national solidarity, the habits of cooperation in a large mass and the concern for efficiency have undoubtedly been stimulated, if not created, by the wars which the European nations have waged during several centuries. And it may not be due to solely material advantages that the nations renowned for efficient military organization, like the Germans or the Japanese, have also been successful in catching up in the industrial race.

More recently, essentially the same view was echoed by Herman Kahn (1979, 334, 457), who related the South Korean and Taiwanese economic miracles to 'very unforgiving external political environments' and the economic stagnation elsewhere in the Third World to the absence of threats to national security: 'One of the real difficulties that many developing nations labor under today is that they have no clear and present danger to face up to.'

Concerning the impact of military participation on inequality, Andreski (1968a, 27, 72) wrote: 'The technical and military circumstances which make the willing cooperation of the masses in the war effort more or less essential, are the most powerful among the factors which determine the extent of social inequalities.' Elsewhere, the proposition is put in these terms: 'The height of stratification tends to covary with the MPR' (that is, the military-participation ratio). Other writers with macrohistorical inclinations, like Lenski (1966) and McNeill (1963, 1982), seem to concur.

How does one make sense of the proposed relationship between relatively large numbers of unproductively employed men, that is of soldiers, on the one hand and of growing economies and comparatively equal income shares on the other hand? First, one may argue that threats to national security have a sobering impact on ruling classes. Where rulers are secure, because they do not threaten to deprive each other of territory, independence, and life, there they can rule arbitrarily, corruptly, inefficiently, kleptocratically, and parasitically. Where rulers feel threatened, they become interested in a thriving economy, a rich tax base, and a powerful heavy industry in order to raise large armies and to supply them with state-of-the-art weaponry. Moreover, rulers become interested in the welfare and loyalty of men from the lower classes, because they need to enlist their loyalty and enthusiasm for purposes of war-making. In a competitive military environment, kleptocrats and whimsical rulers are weeded out. Elites face a powerful incentive to cooperate with the lower classes.

It has even been argued that a fragmented and competitive political setting is one of the background conditions behind both the rise of Europe (compared to the great Asian civilizations of Islam, India, and China) and the limitation of government (Jones 1981; Weede 1989a). For the purposes of this chapter, however, it suffices to claim that threats to national security lead to high military-participation ratios as well as to changes in elite attitudes which promote economic growth and mass welfare.

Second, there is another reason why military participation should positively affect growth rates and income distribution. Where military-participation ratios are low, the military may be an estate or a caste quite separate from civil society. High military-participation ratios, or a *levée en masse*, affect almost all able-bodied young men and require either conscription or some functional equivalent, such as strong social pressure to enlist. In either case, much of the economically active population will be affected in their formative years. The military might become something like 'the school of the nation.'

What is special about the military as a socializing agency? Patriotism, discipline, and taking orders pervade the military curriculum; that is, military training results in mass discipline. Since discipline is important for an industrial workforce, Dahrendorf (1965, 68) hypothesizes: 'Military training on the Prussian pattern might be more useful as a preparation for industrialism than Calvinist creeds might be even under optimal circumstances.' More broadly, one may regard discipline and the readiness to fit into some hierarchical order as a special kind of human capital. Like other human capital, or skills, it should contribute to economic growth. Moreover, widespread possession of human capital is an equalizer of incomes.

In addition to discipline, the military teaches some cognitive skills. This is more important in the Third World than in industrial societies (Pye 1962). In some less developed countries this includes reading, writing, and simple calculations. In most countries it includes some technical skills, like cleaning and maintaining weapons or driving trucks. Some of these skills are quite useful in civilian life, too. So, the army might be a kind of vocational school – and in some countries it is the only one accessible to poor rural youths. Moreover, military demands for literate and numerate conscripts or volunteers even may persuade some governments of the benefits of compulsory, widely available, or better schooling for every child.

Finally, mass armies affect the balance of power between rulers and ruled. It is easy for well-armed rulers to exploit and mistreat unarmed civilians. It is dangerous for rulers to disregard the needs and feelings of well-armed mass armies on whose fighting spirit they might depend tomorrow. By extension, even the parents, sisters, and children of ordinary soldiers benefit from the respect which rulers have to demonstrate towards the lower classes once their sons get armed. The higher the military-participation ratio rises, the less likely elite parasitism becomes, the more likely elites and masses are to share in the available benefits.

For the above-mentioned reasons, high military-participation ratios should promote economic growth as well as the equalization of income distributions. Of course, these relationships are unlikely to be completely general. They might be conditional on other variables. As Andreski (1968a) and McNeill (1963, 1982) have argued, the equalizing impact of the military is likely to depend on military technology. In some historical periods, military technology made mass armies efficient. In other periods, small professional or aristocratic armies have been more efficient. Since I shall focus on the contemporary world in general, and on less-developed countries in particular, I shall assume that military technology still favors large conscript armies. This statement looks less satisfying, however, for NATO or Warsaw Pact armies than for the Third World. In Europe, the availability of nuclear weapons may undermine the military value of mass armies and ordinary soldiers – and the idea that conventional war is either deterred by the shadow of the nuclear bomb or is just an early phase of a catastrophic nuclear war may undermine the seriousness of military training as well as the corresponding benefits.

Moreover, discipline and unquestioning obedience may be a much less important kind of human capital for the frontrunners in the worldwide process of economic development than for those who want to catch up and therefore welcome repetitive and routine jobs, where discipline is more important than innovation or creative thinking. For these reasons, military-participation ratios should be stronger correlates of economic growth or income equality in analyses restricted to the Third World than in global analyses.

A STUDY OF GROWTH RATES

The first set of dependent variables in this investigation is growth rates, as reported by the World Bank (1987, 202–5). One may distinguish between gross-national-product or gross-domestic-product growth rates, and between growth rates of the economy and per capita growth rates. Since I see no theoretical reason why military-participation ratios should be differently related to GNP and GDP, to per capita or other growth rates, I regard all of these measures of growth rates as equivalent for the purposes of this study. Since I can imagine that the choice of some specific period of observation influences results – although it should not, from a theoretical point of view – I want to get at least some feeling for the robustness of my findings against changes in the period of observation. In order not to overwhelm readers and myself with too many regression equations which should turn out to be similar (but might not be so), I shall limit this section to two dependent variables and two slightly different periods of observation: GNP per capita growth rates from 1965 to 1985 and GDP growth rates from 1965 to 1980.

The most important independent variable in this study is the military-participation ratio (per 1000 of working-age population) in 1965, as reported by Taylor and Hudson (1972, 38–41). In order to reduce the weight of outliers and the skewness of the distribution, the raw scores are replaced by the corresponding natural logarithms.[2]

Obviously, the bivariate relationship between the military-participation ratio on the one hand and either GNP per capita or GDP growth rates on the other hand might be spurious and misleading. Ideally, one would wish to control for all other independent variables which affect economic growth rates. Since cross-national researchers rely on a wide variety of lists of control variables and disagree about their relative importance as well as on the proper specification of relationships, almost any conceivable decision about control variables is likely to be controversial. My list is the result of my own previous work (Weede 1983, 1986b; Weede and Tiefenbach 1981a) – in accepting the level of economic development, investment, and human-capital formation as determinants of growth rates as well as in rejecting variables proposed by world-system or dependency theorists.

Looking at average annual growth rates of GNP per capita in our source, one gets the impression that upper-middle-income nations did better than either poorer nations or industrial market economies. This suggests that there might be a nonmonotonic relationship between the level of economic development and growth rates. Upper-middle-income nations seem to enjoy the 'opportunities of backwardness' (Maddison 1969, XXIII). They are advanced enough to borrow modern technologies and to put them to profitable use. By contrast, the most advanced societies have to make their own inventions, which takes more time and might be costly. Very backward societies find it difficult even to borrow foreign technology and therefore do not enjoy the advantages of backwardness.

Borrowing modern technologies by the upper-middle-income countries (or new industrial countries, as some of the most successful members of this category are called) is accompanied by a reallocation of labor from rural and agrarian to urban and industrial or service jobs which improves productivity. By reference to developments over time, Maddison (1969) observes that both Japan and the USSR grew much faster than the earlier industrializers in Western Europe or North America did at comparable levels of economic development; and Kahn (1979) makes a similar observation about the still faster development of the most recent miracle economies in the Far East. Catching up can be faster than pioneering economic development. For purposes of this study this adds up to the desirability of controlling for the level of economic development by polynomial regression. The indicator of economic development levels is GNP per capita in 1965, as reported by Taylor and Hudson (1972, 314–20). According to my own previous experience, the fit between GNP per capita (henceforth: GNPC) and growth rates is maximized by regressing growth rates on the natural logarithms of GNPC and its square.

It has often been claimed that investment is a prerequisite for growth (Kuznets 1976; Maddison 1969; Robinson 1971; World Bank 1981). Therefore, capital formation has to be controlled for. Since capital may be wasted or misallocated, however, the relationship between capital formation and growth rates can turn out to be rather weak. Here, I shall control for gross domestic investment as a percentage of GDP (from Ballmer-Cao and Scheidegger 1979, 43–5), averaged for 1960, 1965, 1970, and 1973.

Finally, primary- and secondary-school enrollment ratios in 1960 (from World Bank 1979, 170–1) are the proxies for human-capital formation. The World Bank (1980, 96–7) is among the most vigorous advocates of human-capital formation and argues that

> there is strong evidence to support the common-sense proposition that human development can make a valuable contribution to growth. Studies at the firm, farm and project level have shown that better education, health and nutrition can raise incomes and average productivity, and the economic rate of return to investment in schooling is high, frequently well above that of physical investment. For primary schooling, the rates of return in a large group of countries average more than 20 percent. At the aggregate level, cross-country comparisons show that developing nations with higher literacy rates grow faster, even when allowances are made for other influences on growth and for reverse causation – the effect of growth on literacy.

My data source for economic growth rates reports GNPC growth rates for 106 and GDP growth rates for 107 countries. Except for China and Hungary, data for centrally planned economies are missing. China will be lost because of missing data on schooling and capital formation. Instead of including a single Communist-ruled country, I decided to exclude Hungary, too.[3] Given the focus of this chapter on the effects of military-participation ratios, dependent territories, like Hong Kong, had to be eliminated, too. Finally, I felt that the inclusion of capital-surplus oil-exporters, like Libya, Saudi Arabia, and Kuwait, might distort relationships and I therefore eliminated them. The three systematic criteria of exclusion (centrally planned economies, dependent territories, capital-surplus oil-exporters) and some missing-value problems made the sample size 93 for the GNPC growth rate (1965–85) and 95 for the GDP growth rate.[4] Taiwan is the most important economy excluded because of missing data rather than for systematic reasons. Since Taiwan is an outlier on both military-participation ratios and growth rates, this exclusion might bias the military participation–growth linkage downwards.

In a straightforward design independent variables refer to some point of time before the measurement of dependent variables. Here, the level of economic development and military-participation ratios refer to 1965, while economic growth rates pertain to the 1965–85 or 1965–80 period. Human-capital formation or schooling refers to an even earlier year, to 1960. Since there is some time lag between schooling and entering the labor force, this lag is quite welcome. As far as these independent variables are concerned, we may rule out reverse causation. It simply does not make sense to argue that later economic performance affected earlier levels of development, earlier schooling, or earlier military-participation ratios.

The situation is somewhat more complicated for gross domestic investment. Since single-year values might be unrepresentative of longer-term levels of capital formation, I felt that it is preferable to consolidate its level by averaging over a number of years. In averaging over the 1960, 1965, 1970, and 1973 scores, I effectively relate investment in the 1960s and early 1970s to growth rates from the late 1960s to 1980 (or 1985). The problem of reverse causation cannot be entirely ruled out, but it should be small. Moreover, my time póints and periods imply some lag between making an investment and reaping the fruits of it.

Table 12.1 presents the regressions of GNPC growth rates 1965–85 and GDP growth rates 1965–80 on the level of economic development, investment, human-capital formation, and the military-participation ratio in its first and third columns. As expected, the military-participation ratio positively affects[5] growth rates. Gross domestic investment and primary schooling also boost both types of growth rates (pertaining to slightly different periods of observation). Secondary-school enrollment is quite strongly related to GNPC growth rates 1965–85, but hardly at all to GDP growth rates 1965–80. While primary-school enrollment seems to affect growth rates more strongly than the military-participation ratio

Table 12.1 Regressions of economic growth rates on the level of economic development, gross domestic investment, human-capital formation, and the military-participation ratio

	Growth rates of			
	GNPC 1965–85		GDP 1965–80	
LN*GNPC*	0.35 0.42	0.61 0.36	3.28 0.04	3.82 0.02
LN*GNPC*²	−0.17 0.12	−0.18 0.10	−0.41 0.01	−0.44 0.00
Beta and significance of b_1 LN*GNPC* + b_2 LN*GNPC*²	1.01 0.00	0.94 0.00	0.91 0.00	0.85 0.00
Gross domestic investment	0.065 0.04 0.21	0.068 0.03 0.22	0.089 0.02 0.27	0.091 0.01 0.28
Primary-school enrollment	0.029 0.00 0.53	0.030 0.00 0.55	0.030 0.00 0.51	0.030 0.00 0.52
Secondary-school enrollment	0.046 0.00 0.51	0.043 0.01 0.48	0.006 0.38 0.06	0.004 0.42 0.04
LN (Military-participation ratio+1)	0.72 0.00 0.39	0.47 0.04 0.26	0.66 0.00 0.33	0.37 0.10 0.19
Defense expenditures/GNP	–	0.12 0.09 0.16	–	0.17 0.06 0.18
Intercept	−0.37	−1.42	−5.73	−7.58
N	91	91	92	92
Adjusted percentage of variance explained	40.9	41.6	31.3	32.5

Note: Except for the third and the last three rows, first cell entries are unstandardized regression coefficients, second cell entries are their significance levels in a one-tailed test, and third cell entries are standardized regression coefficents. The standardized regression coefficients and their significance levels in the third row assess the curvilinear impact of the level of economic development on economic growth. For computation and interpretation of this coefficient, see Jagodzinski and Weede (1981).

(MPR) does, the MPR looks like affecting growth rates more strongly than investment does. Given the importance attributed to investment in the economic literature and the almost universal lack of consideration given to the MPR, this is not a bad performance.

The curvilinear relationship between the level of economic development and growth rates in the upper part of Table 12.1 presents some special problems. Separate *standardized* coefficients for simple and squared terms are meaningless, their absolute sizes are often far beyond unity (Jagodzinski and Weede 1981) and are not reported here. Instead the third row of Table 12.1 provides standardized coefficients summarizing the curvilinear impact of the level of economic development on growth rates. Except for the sign, which is by definition positive, these coefficients permit the usual interpretation. Here, in Table 12.1, they are all close to unity and once even slightly above it. Of course, this indicates a strong degree of multicollinearity between the curvilinear function of the level of economic development on the one hand and the other determinants of growth rates on the other hand. In the regression reported in column 1, it correlates between −0.63 and −0.88 with the other independent variables.

Significance levels for simple and squared terms also may be misleading. In the first column of Table 12.1 they wrongly suggest the absence of a curvilinear relationship between the level of development and growth rates. But omitting the simple as well as the squared term from the equation implies a dramatic fall in the adjusted percentage of variance explained: for column 1 from 40.9 to 25.0 percent. The significance levels of the curvilinear function of development provided in the third row clearly demonstrate that significance is no problem in any one of these equations.

To reiterate the robust findings from columns 1 and 3 of Table 12.1: growth rates are nonmonotonically related to levels of economic development. Investment, human-capital formation in primary schools, and military participation are related to higher growth rates. Despite the literature, some may still argue that military participation does not boost growth rates for the reasons outlined in this chapter, but that military participation serves as a proxy for defense expenditures which actually affect the economic performance for the better. In order to rebut this objection, I have also included defense expenditures as a share of GDP[6] in equations (columns) 2 and 4 of Table 12.1. Given multicollinearity between the MPR and defense burdens, it is to be expected that MPR effects are much more strongly affected by the inclusion of defense burdens in the equations than other effects are. This is indeed the case. Given multicollinearity, a downward adjustment of MPR effects, as observed, is also to be expected. Still, MPR effects look stronger than expenditure effects in the GNPC 1965–85 equation. In the GDP 1965–80 equation, however, the simultaneous inclusion of the MPR and an expenditure term leads to the dilution of both effects.

Above it has been argued that we should expect a stronger positive effect of the MPR on growth rates among LDCs only than in global analyses. Therefore, Table 12.2 provides results where industrial market economies have been eliminated.[7] Focusing on LDCs only clearly establishes that the MPR is the stronger correlate of growth rates than is defense burden. For LDCs, at least, military-participation ratios should *not* be interpreted as proxies for defense expenditures. While MPR effects are significant, however growth is operationalized, defense-burden effects are never significant.

The other substantively interesting finding from Table 12.2 concerns

Table 12.2 Regressions of economic growth rates on the level of economic development, gross domestic investment, human-capital formation, and the military-participation ratio *among LDCs*

	Growth rates of			
	GNPC	1965–85	GDP	1965–80
LN*GNPC*	2.58 0.23	2.42 0.24	5.22 0.09	5.20 0.09
LN*GMPC*²	−0.39 0.12	−0.36 0.14	−0.61 0.05	−0.59 0.06
Beta and significance of b_1 LN*GNPC* + b_2 LN*GNPC*²	0.60 0.00	0.53 0.00	0.43 0.00	0.40 0.01
Gross domestic investment	0.070 0.06 0.18	0.068 0.06 0.17	0.11 0.01 0.27	0.11 0.01 0.27
Primary-school enrollment	0.030 0.00 0.46	0.031 0.00 0.48	0.040 0.00 0.58	0.040 0.00 0.58
Secondary-school enrollment	0.032 0.15 0.17	0.032 0.15 0.17	−0.041 0.12 −0.20	−0.41 0.12 −0.20
LN(Military-participation ratio+1)	0.90 0.00 0.40	0.62 0.04 0.27	0.85 0.00 0.35	0.71 0.03 0.29
Defense expenditures/GNP	–	0.14 0.11 0.16	–	0.085 0.28 0.08
Intercept	−6.06	−6.04	−11.11	−11.25
N	72	72	73	73
Adjusted percentage of variance explained	39.8	40.3	33.9	33.2

Note: Except for the third and the last three rows, first cell entries are unstandardized regression coefficients, second cell entries are their significance levels in a one-tailed test, and third cell entries are standardized regression coefficients. The standardized regression coefficients and their significance levels in the third row assess the curvilinear impact of the level of economic development on economic growth. For computation and interpretation of this coefficient, see Jagodzinski and Weede (1981).

secondary-school enrollments. Among LDCs only, secondary schooling does not seem to affect growth rates for the better. In the GDP equations, even the sign runs contrary to plausible expectations. Although the mitigation of the multicollinearity problem concerning the curvilinear function of economic development and other growth determinants in Table 12.2 and the therefore deflated relationships between level of development and growth rates are reassuring, these facts are of little interest in the context of this study.

Concerning the determinants of growth rates, my findings support the view that human-capital formation by primary schooling or military participation are even more important than investment.

A STUDY OF INCOME INEQUALITY

Inequality data are either scarce or of dubious quality, or both. While the World Bank published Jain's (1975) rather comprehensive compilation some time ago, its more recent publications (such as World Bank 1988, 272–3) provide data for a much more restricted set of nations. Obviously, we would wish as much coverage as possible on the one hand, and decent data quality on the other hand. In practice, however, moving towards one of these goals is likely to move one further from the other one. Worse still, it is not clear which one of these goals is more important – because both of them are vital. Findings based on a small, relatively high-quality data sets might prove unrepresentative for larger data sets, should these some day become available. Similarly, poor data quality might distort findings, too. Given this predicament, I use two radically different strategies.

On the one hand, I shall look to large samples where the compilers tried hard to avoid missing values. Here, my sources are Taylor and Jodice (1983)[8] and Chan (1989, 61–2). My operationalizations of inequality are top 20% and bottom 40% income shares. Two sources and two operationalizations make four dependent variables with broad country coverage. As in the growth analyses, centrally planned economies, dependent territories, and capital-surplus oil-exporters are excluded, even if inequality data were available. *Thereafter*, Taylor and Jodice (1983) provide data for 67 countries and Chan for 56 LDCs.[9]

On the other hand, I shall investigate a much smaller sample provided by the World Bank (1988, 272–3) which covers only 43 countries,[10] 17 of which I regard as industrialized.[11] A comparison of results for the larger and smaller samples of nations will at least give us some feeling for the robustness of findings – or for the lack of robustness.

As in the growth section of this chapter, the logged military-participation ratio is the independent variable of most interest here. As above, we also have to face the issue of including control variables. Since the number of nations in some samples and equations turns out to be quite small, there is an urgent need to limit the list of control variables. Of course, this still should not make one miss the crucial ones. From my own previous research (Weede 1980, 1986b; Weede and Tiefenbach 1981b, 1981c) as well as from Ahluwalia's (1976) or Muller's (1988) lists, I chose the following ones.

First, nations at intermediate levels of economic development seem to suffer most from income inequality. This is Kuznets's (1963) famous inverted U-curve. The rationale behind this relationship is the following. At very low levels of development, subsistence agriculture dominates the economy and there is something like equality in poverty. Economic development implies the creation of some modern and highly rewarded sectors. At intermediate levels of development, the contrast between poor and backward sectors on the one hand and modernized sectors of the economy on the other hand produces much inequality. Thereafter, the poor and backward sectors are slowly eliminated and therefore inequality is slowly reduced. Although one may control for the level of economic development in a variety of ways, here I shall regress income shares on logged GNPC and its square – as has been done in the growth analyses above.

Second, inequality is affected by human-capital formation. If only a small minority of children go to school and become literate and numerate, then they can obtain rewards which are denied to most others. By contrast, compulsory schooling is an equalizer of human-capital endowments – not a perfect one, but still an equalizer. Therefore, one would expect primary- and secondary-school enrollments[12] to decrease top 20% and to increase bottom 40% income shares.

Third, population growth or its corollary, that is, a young population, implies an abundance of labor relative to other factors of production. Since most people do not own capital or land, but have to rely on their labor power only, an abundance of young labor and the corresponding downward pressure on wages contribute to inequality (Lenski 1966; Muller 1988). The indicator for the availability of young labor is the percentage of people below 14 years more than a decade before most inequality data. The source for this variable is the World Bank (1983).[13]

Table 12.3 reports the results of the regressions based on comparatively large numbers of nations. Except for primary-school enrollments, the control variables perform as expected. There is an inverted U-curve relationship between the level of economic development and inequality, as indicated by top 20% income share, or a U-curve relationship between the level of economic development and equality, as indicated by bottom 40% income share. The younger the population is, the higher the income share of the most privileged quintile becomes and the lower the income share of the bottom 40% falls. The higher secondary-school enrollments are, the higher bottom 40% income share becomes and the lower top 20% income share gets. Concerning the military-participation ratio, its effects are weak and not significant at conventional levels. But the sign at least fits with theoretical expectations and earlier findings. Most of the findings in Table 12.3 are consistently significant or insignificant, whether you look at Taylor and Jodice's (1983) data for all nations or at Chan's (1989) data for LDCs only.

Table 12.4 relies on a much smaller set of nations, presumably characterized by better data quality. Unfortunately, this implies that about half of the LDCs still included in Table 12.3 have been lost. Except for the military-participation ratio and the level of economic development, the

Table 12.3 Regressions of income shares on the level of economic development, young population, human-capital formation, and the military-participation ratio

	Taylor–Jodice all countries Top 20	Taylor–Jodice all countries Bottom 40	Chan LDCs only Top 20	Chan LDCs only Bottom 40
LN*GNPC*	18.59 0.03	–8.98 0.03	35.31 0.02	–13.54 0.05
LN*GNPC*²	–1.39 0.05	0.58 0.07	2.92 0.03	0.97 0.10
Beta and significance of b_1 LN*GNPC* + b_2 LN*GNPC*²	0.29 0.01	0.55 0.00	0.42 0.00	0.57 0.00
Young population	0.46 0.01 0.42	–0.25 0.00 –0.50	0.42 0.04 0.26	–0.29 0.01 –0.35
Primary-school enrollment	0.055 0.12 0.18	–0.030 0.09 –0.22	0.057 0.13 0.20	–0.039 0.06 –0.27
Secondary-school enrollment	–0.18 0.02 –0.44	0.095 0.02 0.49	–0.28 0.02 –0.42	0.12 0.04 0.34
LN (Military-participation ratio+1)	–1.33 0.10 –0.15	0.58 0.13 0.14	–0.87 0.22 –0.11	0.79 0.09 0.20
Intercept	–23.26	54.87	–65.10	69.41
N	67	67	56	55
Adjusted percentage of variance explained	45.6	38.1	30.9	38.6

Note: Except for the third and the last three rows, first cell entries are unstandardized regression coefficients, second cell entries are their significance levels in a one-tailed test, and third cell entries are standardized regression coefficients. The standardized regression coefficients and their significance levels in the third row assess the curvilinear impact of the level of economic development on income shares. For computation and interpretation of this coefficient, see Jagodzinski and Weede (1981).

significance and order of magnitude of (standardized) effects hardly depend on the inclusion or exclusion of industrial societies. The (inverted) U-curve relating the level of economic development to inequality is still significantly supported except for the bottom 40% income share among LDCs. The effects of primary-school enrollment remain negligible, as before. Top 20% income share is maximized and bottom 40% income share is minimized by a young population and a lack of access to secondary schools. The effects of the military-participation ratio are clearly significant in reducing top 20% income share and increasing bottom 40% income share, where all available data are analyzed, but no longer where we focus on LDCs only.

Table 12.4 Regressions of income shares on the level of economic development, young population, human-capital formation and the military-participation ratio

	World Development Report (1988) data			
	All countries		LDCs only	
	Top 20	Bottom 40	Top 20	Bottom 40
LN*GNPC*	8.20 0.20	−3.83 0.23	15.36 0.25	−2.57 0.01 −0.47
LN*GNPC*^{2}	−0.48 0.27	0.14 0.37	−1.09 0.29	F-level insufficient
Beta and significance of b_1 LN*GNPC* + b_2 LN*GNPC*^{2}	0.28 0.03	0.54 0.00	0.29 0.04	–
Young population	0.41 0.00 0.44	−0.29 0.00 −0.63	0.47 0.03 0.38	−0.28 0.01 −0.43
Primary-school enrollment	−0.011 0.41 −0.03	F-level in- sufficient	0.04 0.30 0.10	−0.032 0.20 −0.16
Secondary-school enrollment	−0.20 0.00 −0.51	0.10 0.00 0.52	−0.34 0.02 −0.50	0.20 0.01 0.56
LN (Military-participation ratio +1)	−2.08 0.01 −0.27	1.03 0.01 0.26	−1.27 0.16 −0.20	0.61 0.17 0.18
Intercept	13.04	39.03	−13.38	37.13
N	43	43	26	26
Adjusted percentage of variance explained	71.5	66.3	51.4	54.3

Note: Except for the third and the last three rows, first cell entries are unstandardized regression coefficients, second cell entries are their significance levels in a one-tailed test, and third cell entries are standardized regression coefficients. The standardized regression coefficients and their significance levels in the third row assess the culvilinear impact of the level of economic development on income shares. For computation and interpretation of this coefficient, see Jagodzinski and Weede (1981).

Taking regressions from Table 12.3 and 12.4 together, there are consistent findings concerning the effects of young populations, and primary- and secondary-school enrollments. Kuznets's (1963) (inverted) U-curve is generally supported except for the bottom 40% income share in a small sample of LDCs. In the context of this chapter, most worrisome are the inconsistent findings concerning the effects of military-participation ratios. In themselves, results from Tables 12.3 and 12.4 do not permit a clear verdict on whether the MPR is an equalizer of incomes. But both tables together certainly demonstrate that secondary schools and birth control are much more effective equalizers of incomes than the MPR looks like.

CONCLUSIONS

The focus of this investigation has been on the existence and size of a *general or cross-national* relationship between the military-participation ratio on the one hand and economic growth rates and income inequality on the other hand. Concerning growth rates, results from various regression experiments are reasonably consistent with each other. The higher the military-participation ratio is, the higher economic growth rates are. This finding is marginally better supported for LDCs only than for global samples containing both Third and First World nations.

Concerning inequality or income shares, results from various regressions contradict each other. Sometimes, but not consistently, there is a significant and positive relationship between the military-participation ratio and lower-strata income share, or a significant and negative relationship between the MPR and upper-quintile income share. Although the signs of the coefficients consistently fit with theoretical expectations, according to which the MPR should be an equalizer of incomes, the size of the effects is always quite small. Compared to my own previous work on this topic, the results are disappointing. Perhaps, I have previously overrated the beneficial impact of military participation.

All findings from the regression analyses depend on the chosen specifications of the equations. Here, I did control for the curvilinear relationships between the level of economic development on the one hand and growth rates *or* income shares on the other hand, as well as for the linear effects of school-enrollment ratios on either growth rates *or* income shares. Also, gross domestic investment was controlled in the growth equations and age structure in the equations for income shares. Those who cannot accept these lists of control variables need not accept the findings reported above.

From the literature on economic growth and/or income inequality it is obvious that many sociologists and political scientists will find my neglect of dependency indicators disturbing and misleading. I have provided the reasons for this decision elsewhere (Weede 1986b; Weede and Tiefenbach 1981a, 1981b). In addition, I may point to recent work by Marsh (1988) and Chan (1989) who disagree with my evaluation of some dependency propositions and specify their equations accordingly, but who find even stronger and less ambiguous support for some beneficial impact of military participation than I do.

Although I accepted age structure (or young population) as a determinant of income shares from Muller's (1988) recent study, I did not control for the effects of the duration of democracy, as one should according to his findings. In my view (Weede 1989b), Muller's relationship is not robust but is spurious, that is, it disappears once one controls for literacy rates (which, of course, are highly correlated with school-enrollment ratios as used in this paper). Thus, there is no need to control for the duration of democracy.

While military-participation ratios contribute very modestly to the explanation of cross-national differences in growth rates and not even robustly to differences in income shares, one should not entirely disregard the rather weak findings produced here. After all, the beneficial impact of military participation seems stronger than that of investment and more robust over various regressions than the effects of secondary-school enrollments. This is not what most people or most social scientists would have expected. After all, the equalizing impact of high military-participation ratios looks much stronger than corresponding benefits from primary-school enrollments do. Again, this is not what most observers would have expected.

The findings reported here are admittedly weak in a number of respects. First, this holds for their contribution to explaining cross-national variation, and even for their significance, as far as inequality is concerned. Second, a general cross-national and cross-sectional relationship – even if it were stronger than reported here – says almost nothing about what to expect in longitudinal studies for specific nations (see Chan 1985, 1987). Personally, I am not worried about the fact that there are always some nations which do not fit with the general pattern, unless it can be demonstrated that these deviations are systematically related to some measurable characteristics,[14] but I am acutely aware of the desirability of future movements toward pooled designs where cross-national and time-series data are analyzed simultaneously. Unfortunately, meaningful designs of this type need rather long time series. Military-participation ratios tend to be quite stable over time for most nations. Therefore, pooling data from, say, the 1950s, 1960s, 1970s, and 1980s might not go far enough.

Third, the findings reported above are weak in another respect, too. At best, the regressions provide us with 'stylized facts.' At some *superficial* level regression coefficients constitute elements of explanation. At a more demanding level of understanding, there should be reasons *why* military-participation ratios might have some beneficial effects on growth rates or income shares. By pointing to elite discipline and some limitation of kleptocracy because of threats to national security, by reference to the military as a kind of school and an agency for human-capital formation, and by linking less class struggle with better economic performance, I provided an explanatory sketch linking threats to national security, military-participation ratios, and growth rates or inequality. Obviously, the sketch cries out for refinement and does not yet constitute a theory.

Moreover, some of the notions referred to in the sketch could well be investigated at other levels of analysis than at the cross-national level preferred here. To give a simple example: If military participation contributes to human-capital formation, then ex-servicemen should do better in many types of jobs in the civilian economy than other kinds of people. And such a relationship should hold in *many* countries, especially in LDCs. Unfortunately, I simply do not know, nor do I think that the social-science community as such does know, whether this is true or not.

In sum, the size of the beneficial effects of military-participation ratios on growth rates is quite modest. Even the significance of these effects on income shares is still in doubt. Support for any beneficial impact of military participation is strictly limited to cross-sectional and cross-national designs. Therefore, any interpretation of the meaning of the relationship, including my own, must be provisional.

NOTES

1 I appreciate the assistance of Ulrich Albrecht and Juergen Schwuchow in producing this chapter.

2 Since the logarithm of zero is not defined and since Costa Rica scores zero on the military-participation ratio, an increment of one is added to the ratio before logging. Thus, the meaningful zero point of the scale is preserved.

3 If my period of growth observation were to start rather than to end in the mid-1980s, I might have decided to retain the Hungarian case because the country's reforms make it ever more similar to other mixed economies.

4 There is another systematic criterion which should make one exclude certain countries from the analysis. Nobody should expect the economic performance of countries suffering from *protracted* international or civil war to equal the performance of states which succeeded in avoiding these calamities. Since economic growth data for such nations are unavailable, they have been automatically excluded.

5 Of course, the causal terminology is a matter of interpretation. Regressions cannot prove causality. But a properly specified regression may call some causal notions into question.

6 The data source is Taylor and Hudson (1972, 34–6).

7 Here, I adopted the list of industrial societies of the World Bank (1979, 127), but added Israel because of its GNPC in the mid-1960s (Taylor and Hudson 1972, 314). Among the most highly developed countries (in 1965) *in*cluded in the regressions of Table 12.2 are Spain, Greece, and Venezuela.

8 The data tape provides some entries for nations where the book reports missing values. Since these entries look familiar from other widely used sources, and since I want to maximize country coverage, I accepted these additional entries from the tape.

9 Although Chan's (1989) implied definition of LDCs is quite similar to my own in the growth section above, it is *not* identical. For example, Chan regarded Israel as an LDC, while I considered it to be an industrial country. Wherever I use Chan's compilation, I accept *his* definition of LDCs.

10 Actually, the source provides data for 46 nations. Four of them have been eliminated because they were not yet independent in 1965 (Bangladesh, Hong Kong, Mauritius) or was Communist-ruled (Hungary). Since Taiwan has been omitted from recent World Bank publications for political reasons, that is, pressure from mainland China, rather than because of lack of data, I added an older World Bank (1979, 173) estimate for Taiwan.

11 Here, I distinguish between industrialized countries and LDCs in exactly the same way as I did in the growth section above.

12 Data source is as described in the growth section of the chapter.

13 Since most of the inequality data refer to a much later date than the youthfulness of the population (1965), and since children in LDCs start to work early, it makes sense to assume that age structure (in 1965) affects inequality measured

some time in the late 1970s or 1980s (but occasionally earlier in the two broad-coverage data sets).

14 Under such circumstances, it should be possible to modify the regression equations in order to take conditional (nonadditive) effects into account.

REFERENCES

Ahluwalia, Montek S. 1976. Income distribution and development: some stylized facts. *American Economic Review* 66: 128–35.

Andreski, Stanislav. 1968a. *Military Organization and Society* (2nd edn.). Stanford, Calif.: Stanford University Press.

Andreski, Stanislav. 1968b. *The African Predicament*. New York: Atherton Press.

Ballmer-Cao, Thanh-Huyen and Juerg Scheidegger. 1979. *Compendium of Data for World-System Analysis*. Zürich: Soziologisches Institut der Universität.

Benoit, Emile. 1973. *Defense and Economic Growth in Developing Countries*. Lexington, Mass.: D. C. Heath.

Benoit, Emile. 1978. Growth and defense in developing countries. *Economic Development and Cultural Change* 26: 271–80.

Chan, Steve. 1985. The impact of defense spending on economic performance: a survey of evidence and problems. *ORBIS* 29: 403–34.

Chan, Steve. 1987. Military expenditures and economic performance. In *World Military Expenditures and Arms Transfers 1986*, pp. 29–37. Washington, D.C.: U.S. Arms Control and Disarmament Agency.

Chan, Steve. 1988. Defense burden and economic growth. Unravelling the Taiwanese enigma. *American Political Science Review* 82: 913–20.

Chan, Steve. 1989. Income inequality among LDCs: a comparative analysis of alternative perspectives. *International Studies Quarterly* 33: 45–65.

Dahrendorf, Ralf. 1965. *Gesellschaft und Demokratie in Deutschland*. Munich: Piper.

Deger, Saadet. 1986. *Military Expenditure in Third World Countries*. London: Routledge & Kegan Paul.

Dixon, William J. and Bruce E. Moon. 1986. The military burden and basic human needs. *Journal of Conflict Resolution* 30: 660–84.

Fei, John C. H., Gustav Ranis, and Shirley W. Y. Kuo. 1980. *Growth with Equity: The Taiwan Case*. New York: Oxford University Press.

Garnier, Maurice A. and Lawrende E. Hazelrigg. 1977. Military organization and distributional inequality. *Journal of Political and Military Sociology* 5: 17–33.

Grobar, Lisa M. and Richard C. Porter. 1989. Benoit revisited: defense spending and economic growth in LDCs. *Journal of Conflict Resolution* 33: 318–45.

Jagodzinski, Wolfgang and Erich Weede. 1981. Testing curvilinear propositions by polynomial regression with particular reference to the interpretation of standardized solutions. *Quality and Quantity* 15: 447–63.

Jain, Shail. 1975. *Size Distribution of Income: A Compilation of Data*. Washington, D.C.: World Bank.

Jones, Eric. 1981. *The European Miracle*. Cambridge: Cambridge University Press.

Kahn, Herman. 1979. *World Economic Development: 1979 and Beyond*. London: Croom Helm.

Kennedy, Paul. 1987. *The Rise and Fall of the Great Powers: Economic Change and Military Conflict from 1500 to 2000*. New York: Random House.

Kriesberg, Louis. 1979. *Social Inequality*. Englewood Cliffs, N.J.: Prentice-Hall.

Kuznets, Simon. 1963. Quantitative aspects of the economic growth of nations.

VIII. The distribution of income by size. *Economic Development and Cultural Change* 11: 1–80.

Kuznets, Simon. 1976. *Modern Economic Growth*, 7th edn. New Haven, Conn.: Yale University Press.

Lenski, Gerhard. 1966. *Power and Privilege: A Theory of Social Stratification*. New York: McGraw-Hill.

Maddison, Angus. 1969. *Economic Growth in Japan and the USSR*. London: Allen & Unwin.

Marsh, Robert M. 1988. Sociological explanations of economic growth. *Studies in Comparative International Development* XIII: 41–76.

McNeill, William H. 1963. *The Rise of the West. A History of the Human Community*. Chicago: University of Chicago Press.

McNeill, William H. 1982. *The Pursuit of Power: Technology, Armed Force, and Society since A. D. 1000*. Chicago: University of Chicago Press.

Muller, Edward N. 1988. Democracy, economic development, and income inequality. *American Sociological Review* 53: 50–68.

Pye, Lucian W. 1962. Armies in the process of political modernization. In J. J. Johnson (ed.), *The Role of the Military in Underdeveloped Countries*, pp. 69–89. Princeton, N.J.: Princeton University Press.

Robinson, Sherman. 1971. Sources of growth in less developed countries. *Quarterly Journal of Economics* 85: 391–408.

Rosecrance, Richard. 1986. *The Rise of the Trading State: Commerce and Conquest in the Modern World*. New York: Basic Books.

Russett, Bruce. 1982. Defense expenditures and national well-being. *American Political Science Review* 76: 767–77.

Taylor, Charles L. and Michael C. Hudson. 1972. *World Handbook of Political and Social Indicators*, 2nd edn. New Haven, Conn.: Yale University Press.

Taylor, Charles L. and David A. Jodice. 1983. *World Handbook of Political and Social Indicators*, 3rd edn. New Haven, Conn.: Yale University Press.

Weede, Erich. 1980. Beyond misspecification in sociological analyses of income inequality. *American Sociological Review* 45: 497–501.

Weede, Erich. 1983. Military participation ratios, human capital formation, and economic growth. *Journal of Political and Military Sociology* 11: 11–19.

Weede, Erich. 1986a. Rent-seeking, military participation, and economic performance in LDCs. *Journal of Conflict Resolution* 30: 291–314.

Weede, Erich. 1986b. Rent-seeking or dependency as explanations of why poor people stay poor. *International Sociology* 1: 421–41.

Weede, Erich. 1989a. Ideen, Ideologie und Politische Kultur des Westens. *Zeitschrift für Politik* 36: 27–43.

Weede, Erich. 1989b. Democracy and income inequality reconsidered: Comment on Muller. *American Sociological Review* 54: 865–68.

Weede, Erich and Wolfgang Jagodzinski. 1981. National security, income inequality and economic growth. *Social Science and Policy Research* (Seoul, S. Korea) III: 91–107.

Weede, Erich and Horst Tiefenbach. 1981a. Three dependency explanations of economic growth. *European Journal of Political Research* 9: 391–406.

Weede, Erich and Horst Tiefenbach. 1981b. Some recent explanations of income inequality. *International Studies Quarterly* 25: 255–82.

Weede, Erich and Horst Tiefenbach. 1981c. Correlates of the size distribution of income. *Journal of Politics* 43: 1029–41.

World Bank. Various years. *World Development Report*. New York and London: Oxford University Press.

World Bank. 1983. *World Tables*, 3rd edn. Vol. II. Social Data. Baltimore: Johns Hopkins University Press.

13 Do we yet know who pays for defense? Conclusions and synthesis

Richard C. Eichenberg
Tufts University

INTRODUCTION

The contributions to this volume continue a research tradition that began with Russett's (1969) famous article which asked 'Who pays for defense?' Despite over twenty years of research, however, the present book confirms the conclusion that has also been drawn in several recent evaluations of the 'guns–butter' literature: a definitive answer to the question has yet to be found (Chan 1985; Kupchan 1989). Indeed, the research literature is characterized by contradictory and sometimes confusing results: in some times and cases defense spending seems to cause tradeoffs, while in other cases these same tradeoffs disappear. Some research efforts even conclude that defense spending has a beneficial impact.

The purpose of this chapter is to explore the reasons for this confusion. The chapter is divided into four sections. In each section, I outline some of the weaknesses of previous guns–butter research and suggest improvements that are needed to bring cumulation to future research. I also assess the contributions to this volume by asking to what extent they provide a clearer answer to the question of who pays for defense.

Previous research on the guns–butter question has been plagued by four weaknesses. First, research has been *theory-weak*. That is, students of the issue have rarely specified theoretical models or even clear hypotheses that predict both the direction and the strength of the guns–butter relationship. Second, prior research offers *no clear conceptualization* and operationalization of the very nature of a 'tradeoff.' Third, past research is characterized by *major gaps*; that is, there are some theoretically important tradeoff issues that have received almost no treatment in past work. Finally, past research contains almost no work on the external *impact* of the resource-allocation process. As a result, we know very little about the foreign-policy implications of tradeoff decisions, despite the centrality of this relationship in the historical literature (Gaddis 1982; Kennedy 1987; Rasler and Thompson 1989; Tilly 1975).

THEORY

Research on the guns–butter issue has been guided less by *theory* than by the economists' zero-sum *definition* of tradeoffs under conditions of resource scarcity (Pechman 1976, 25): 'From the day he or she opens an elementary economics textbook, the economist learns that economic problems arise from scarcity, and that individuals, businesses, and the nation as a whole must forego some things in order to have other things.' Note that from this perspective, the existence of tradeoffs is not a hypothesis but a logical requirement: there is by definition *always* a tradeoff, since resources devoted to defense can in principle be switched to any number of alternative budget categories or reallocated to the private economy through tax reductions. Note also that the tradeoffs implied by this logical identity are subjective: different observers may find it hard to agree on the comparative utility of resources devoted to defense, social security, education, or private savings. As a result, resource allocations are the result of a political bargaining process rather than a process of utility maximization.

A political theory of tradeoffs must therefore specify both the desires and the power of societal actors who attempt to influence these inevitable choices. A theory of tradeoffs, like any political theory, must specify who gets what, when and how. With very few exceptions, however, past tradeoff research does not contain such a theory. Although scholars have examined the impact of defense spending on social, educational, health, and a myriad of other programs, there is almost no discussion in the literature of the theoretical reasons for expecting that defense tradeoffs will fall on one budgetary category rather than another. As a result, the myriad of empirical findings are most often reinterpreted in a *post hoc* inductive fashion.

There are two exceptions to this generalization. The most important, of course, are Marxist and neo-Marxist theories of political economy, which contain a very specific theoretical structure that relates the preferences of dominant actors (monopoly capitalists) to the outcome of tradeoffs, both between defense spending and civilian public spending and between defense spending and the private economy (Baran and Sweezy 1966). The second set of exceptions is contained in this volume in the contributions of Weede, Rasler and Thompson, and Bobrow. Weede's study (Chapter 12) is both rich and compelling, for it offers a theory with specific predictions relating political structures to levels of defense spending as well as to the size of military forces themselves. Contrary to the economists' zero-sum image, Weede deduces that military spending, military-participation ratios, and several (potential) measures of social policy and equality should be *positively* related:

> Where rulers are secure, because they do not threaten to deprive each other of territory, independence, and life, there they can rule arbitrarily,

corruptly, inefficiently, kleptocratically, and parasitically. Where rulers feel threatened, they become interested in a thriving economy, a rich tax base, and a powerful heavy industry in order to raise large armies and to supply them with state-of-the-art weaponry. Moreover, rulers become interested in the welfare and loyalty of men from the lower classes, because they need to enlist their loyalty and enthusiasm for purposes of war-making. In a competitive military environment . . . elites face a powerful incentive to cooperate with the lower classes. (p. 214)

The appeal of Weede's theory is confirmed not merely by the strength of his statistical results, but also by the resonance of the theory with much of the literature on state-making (Kennedy 1987; Tilly 1975). Although one can agree with Weede that the theory must be tested in time-series models, the clarity of the theory and the crispness of the results emphasize once again the utility of imbedding defense–welfare studies in a larger model of domestic political power.

The same can be said for Rasler and Thompson's analysis (Chapter 3) on the interaction of defense, welfare, and the economy in the process of Britain's economic and military decline. Like Weede, Rasler and Thompson do not stop with the zero-sum logic that necessarily attends a study of resource allocation. Instead, by integrating theories of domestic political change and international hierarchy, they deduce a set of competing hypotheses relating the interaction of the government's military and social allocations to the consumption and investment sectors of the economy. Although temporal sequence and antecedents are open questions in their design, by incorporating a theory of democratic political change in Britain, they produce strong expectations that can be evaluated against the data: 'Given finite resources and rising demands, decision-makers will opt for the choices that are more rewarding politically. Proportional cuts in investment, private consumption, or social services, therefore, are more likely to be avoided than are proportional cuts in defense and foreign policy commitments. (p. 42).' Note that the theories of Weede and of Rasler and Thompson lead them to conclusions that contradict the intuitive notion that 'social' investments lose in the competition with defense. In their theories, leaders must implement tradeoffs to the detriment of defense in order to maintain their political coalitions.

The same can be said of Bobrow's innovative analysis (Chapter 5) on what I will call the Japanese 'security culture.' Bobrow's major contribution is to directly challenge the notion that defense, welfare, and growth are in competition. Indeed, by specifying what he calls 'policy legacies, institutions, and political culture,' Bobrow argues that there are conceptual and political compatabilities between security, welfare, and growth. Like Weede, then, his theory leads him to predict a positive relationship between defense, welfare, and growth – predictions that he finds confirmed by the postwar Japanese experience.

In summary, past research on guns–butter tradeoffs has not been rooted in a political theory of societal values and power. For the most part, it begins with the economist's assumption that spending for defense must by definition come at the expense of other budgetary programs or at the expense of private consumption or investment. The contributions to this volume, in contrast, demonstrate that stronger theory does much to improve our understanding of the empirical defense–welfare relationships that are discovered. By specifying the relationship of national security to the process of domestic coalition-building and to the values that make up political culture, the work of Weede, Rasler and Thompson, and Bobrow provide much sharper hypotheses and thus leave less room for the *post hoc* speculation that has characterized the literature in the past. Of course, these works also point to the necessity for additional research of this kind, for we have as yet very few detailed, let alone comparative, studies of the domestic politics and culture of national security and welfare.

CONCEPTUALIZING TRADEOFFS

Given the influence of the economists' zero-sum definition of tradeoffs, it is not surprising that this conception also dominates the models of other social-science approaches to the tradeoff question. Consider the observations of two leading students of the subject: 'resources assigned to defense are not available for other things' (Greenwood 1972, 7); and 'more for defense has to come at the expense of something else' (Russett 1970, 133).

As noted above, this conception of tradeoff is by definition correct for any discrete allocational decision. However, it may be less applicable to the dynamic, correlational extension of the economists' model that is used in most political-science research. The extension seems plausible: since discrete allocational decisions imply a tradeoff by definition, it is logical to hypothesize that a particular national experience will be characterized by the persistence of a specific tradeoff pattern over time. And this conception can be operationalized using methodologies that are familiar to social scientists: if decision-makers make consistent tradeoff choices, the pattern should be visible in a significant negative correlation between defense spending and other financial categories across time or space.

As I noted earlier, however, it is precisely this operationalization that has produced contradictory and even null results. For example, past research shows that budgetary tradeoffs, which should be the most visible (because they are in principle under the direct control of decision-makers), are in fact very rare. And the impact of defense spending on the macroeconomy remains unclear. At the moment, there is evidence for all three possibilities: positive, negative, and no impact of defense.

Admittedly, the lack of evidence for tradeoffs in past research might very well be attributed to the neglect of theory that has characterized the field. For example, theories of organizational behavior and budgeting have not been applied in defense–welfare research, but it is these bodies of work that could best explain the *absence* of defense–welfare tradeoffs. Because governments are characterized by a division of labor designed to adapt to a complex environment under time pressure, resource-allocation decisions (tradeoffs) are rarely made by comparing the alternative costs and utilities of competing government programs or private-sector endowments. Rather, government resource allocation is a disjointed process, in which individual economic and budgetary decisions are made in isolation (Wildavsky 1975). In addition, under conditions of resource scarcity, governments – like all complex organizations – do not attempt to maximize all goals simultaneously. Rather, they deal with competing goals 'sequentially' (Cyert and March 1967). Following this logic, budgetary tradeoffs can be made against one category in one year and against other categories in succeeding years. Like many individuals and families, governments need not sacrifice the same priority every time they make an allocational decision – they can 'take turns' by favoring different priorities in different years. Under these conditions, we would not expect tradeoffs against particular programs to be systematically visible over time.

The dynamic, correlational conception of tradeoffs may therefore not be appropriate. What little theory we do have suggests that budgetary tradeoffs are not persistent and systematic. Two caveats to this observation are necessary, however. First, despite the disjointed nature of organizational behavior and government budgeting, there may very well be patterns of values and power in society that produce persistent expenditure and economic tradeoffs that could be detected using time-series statistical techniques; we simply have not found them because our theories do not yet provide a sufficiently specific roadmap. This caveat thus returns us to the need for theory in the study of tradeoffs.

The second caveat is that the lack of over-time, correlational evidence of tradeoffs does not obviate the fact that tradeoffs are occurring. The economists, of course, are correct: there is indeed always a tradeoff, but it need not fall the same way in every year. Recognition of this fact should lead us to reconsider our methodologies for studying tradeoffs. One obvious implication is recognized by Chan in his Introduction to this volume: if tradeoffs fall on different programs in different years, then we need disaggregated, program-level data to discover them. Mintz *et al* demonstrate the same point in Chapter 2 on the impact of U.S. defense spending on employment and inflation: by disaggregating the defense budget by detailed categories, they reveal differential impacts on the dependent variables that would otherwise remain hidden in an aggregate model. Similarly, like Keman (1982, 1988) or Eichenberg and Stoll (1989), we might simplify our analyses by focusing only on those years when defense spending increases or on those years when tradeoffs did indeed occur to the detriment of specific programs. Of course, even these improvements might prove futile unless they are guided by theories that specify the competing values and political meaning of particular government programs and their relation to the politics of national security.

Finally, forecasting and simulation methods should be examined for their utility in tradeoff studies. The utility of these methodologies is revealed by the study of Norwegian defense spending in Chapter 4 (for important similar research, see: Cusack and Hughes 1986; and Bremer and Hughes 1990). Significantly, Cappelen and his colleagues are government officials, and they therefore see no need to search for tradeoffs; they are aware that choices – tradeoffs – will have to be made. Accepting this logic, they then pursue the impact of alternative choices by 'forecasting' the economic and budgetary impact of different defense-spending scenarios. Using a sophisticated econometric model of the Norwegian economy, they are able to trace both direct and indirect effects of alternative defense budgets. Their results hold a twofold fascination. First, the sophistication of their model and its complicated feedback loops allows them to reveal the direct and indirect effects of defense cuts on civilian spending, employment, revenues, and government deficits – a picture of resource allocation that is much closer to the complexity of contemporary budgeting than less sophisticated regression models. Second, their 'sensitivity' approach allows them to compare alternative value tradeoffs, as in their exploration of the potential effect of defense cuts on the social-security debate in Norway.

None of these effects could be (easily) studied using the zero-sum, correlational approach to tradeoffs that dominates contemporary research. Tradeoffs do occur, but they occur in a context of disjointed decision-making that may produce different tradeoffs in different years. For all these reasons, scholars should reconsider the correlational conception of tradeoffs that has represented the dominant methodology until now.

GAPS IN TRADEOFF RESEARCH

Some time ago, Frederick Pryor (1968, 123) reminded us that the assumption of a zero-sum resource constraint in government budgeting does not hold for all cases; tradeoffs will occur only under specific circumstances: 'if tax rates remain the same, and if government revenues restrain the growth of government expenditures, then a substitution of defense for civilian expenditures would appear.'

Pryor's analysis points to three paths by which governments can avoid the zero-sum game of budgetary tradeoffs: they can increase taxes, they can engage in deficit spending, or they can do both. Of course, none of these courses of action provide national security for free. Instead, they shift the cost of defense to present and future taxpayers, and as much of the commentary on the American budget debate has shown, deficits may shift costs further by raising interest rates. In the long term, deficits may even make direct tradeoffs more likely, for government budgets will be increasingly burdened by interest payments, and at some point governments may have to 'pay the piper' by implementing the tradeoffs they avoided for so long.

Almost none of this dynamic has been studied in the tradeoff literature, but there are small indications that could guide additional research. Eichenberg (1984), for example, found few tradeoffs between West German defense spending and social spending, but changes in the defense budget *were* positively related to increases in the payroll-tax rate of the social-security system. In effect, increases in the West German defense budget seemed to cause governments to shift the financing burden of social security onto the beneficiaries of these programs. A similar finding emerges in this volume in the study of South Korean defense spending by Moon and Hyun (Chapter 8). Despite a very high defense burden in South Korea, the authors conclude that there are few economic or social-spending tradeoffs in the data. Yet they also point out that, since 1975, the South Korean government avoided expenditure tradeoffs by implementing an earmarked surtax to finance the defense budget; by 1988, this tax raised 43 percent of defense spending! The important point about this chapter, as well as the earlier work of Eichenberg, is that a null finding with respect to *expenditure* tradeoffs obscured an important *revenue* tradeoff that had to be paid by citizens.

Chapter 7 by Ward and his colleagues on the Indian political economy indicates an additional aspect of fiscal structure that may influence tradeoffs. In India, the financial decentralization of many social and educational programs may be one reason for the lack of budgetary tradeoffs in that country's central-government budget. The logic of the authors' argument thus suggests the need for further study of the impact of defense spending on the degree of financial centralization and decentralization: does defense spending 'push' responsibility for social policy onto regional and local governments? Does that responsibility entail increasing taxes or borrowing at those levels? The salience of these questions is highlighted by the recent American experience, where state governments find themselves in increasing financial difficulty, a situation they blame in part on the cuts in federal support for social programs that accompanied the defense increases of the 1980s.

Much more research is needed on these sorts of questions, and they point to the need for better descriptive knowledge of both the revenue and benefit structure of the welfare state. Although our research often focuses on defense–'welfare' tradeoffs, the fact is that welfare states vary greatly in their revenue structure (the mix of progressive, general revenue financing, and self-financing payroll taxes) as well as their benefit structure (universalist benefits such as family allowances or public assistance versus individualist benefits such as 'earned' pensions or health insurance).

The variation in fiscal structure is evident in Table 13.1, which shows the

Table 13.1 Revenue sources as a percentage of total revenues, 1985

	Personal income	Employee social-security tax	Employers' social-security tax
Austria	23	13	16
United Kingdom	26	8	9
Denmark	50	2	2
France	13	12	28
Germany	29	16	19
Italy	27	7	25
Japan	25	11	15
Netherlands	20	19	18
Norway	23	6	14
Sweden	39	0	24
United States	36	11	17

Source Organization for Economic Cooperation and Development (1987, 85ff).

relative dependence of selected Western advanced economies on various sources of revenue. As the table suggests, states face very different levels of flexibility when they seek to avoid tradeoffs, and thus the frequency of budgetary tradeoffs necessitated by defense spending will be mediated by these and other fiscal variables. For example, the prospensity to raise defense spending should be conditioned by the ability of states to shift the costs of defense by raising payroll taxes on social programs or by shifting the tax burden to employers or to lower levels of government. Note the similarity with state-building theories, all of which emphasize the interrelationship of political coalitions, economic policy, revenue mobilization, and the enhancement of the state's national-security capabilities.

These consideration also reinforce the need for better theories of tradeoffs in the overall context of resource allocation. The financial structure of the welfare state as well as the degree of fiscal centralization are a function of the values and power of societal actors. A theory of tradeoffs must therefore specify both the values of these actors as well as their political needs and power. The contributions to this volume demonstrate that additional intellectual investment in the study of the revenue side of tradeoffs will be well worth the effort. In fact, defense–welfare research would benefit greatly from additional attention to the entire literature on the fiscal, political, and economic bases of the welfare state (see especially Flora 1987).

THE EXTERNAL IMPLICATIONS OF TRADEOFFS

One of the exciting features of this volume is the extension of tradeoffs studies to include explanations of foreign-policy behavior and grand strategy. Of course, there is already a rich historical literature that describes the interrelation of state-building, domestic politics, economic policy, and external behavior, but that literature is almost totally theoretical or descriptive (Gaddis 1982; Kennedy 1987; Tilly 1975).

In this volume, there are two chapters that begin to specify and test the linkage between the politics of resource allocation and external behavior. The first work focuses on the long term. Continuing their earlier work on state-building, Rasler and Thompson in Chapter 3 now focus on the effect of domestic allocation decisions on the long-term decline of British power. In their earlier work, Rasler and Thompson had modeled the relationship between domestic coalitions, the economic base, government revenue and spending, and the grand strategy of major powers. They now ask whether the long-term decline of British power is a cause or a consequence of the allocational tradeoffs that occur through the process of domestic political change. As noted earlier, their theory leads them to expect that social policy and private economic endowments will be increasingly favored in allocational decisions. More importantly here, they also begin to clarify the timing of these connections between domestic tradeoffs and decline. By and large, the findings confirm their theory of the primacy of domestic political priorities, but it is especially clear *after* the onset of decline. In any case, their results link nicely with Weede's because the data (especially for the later years) show that defense spending is relegated to a secondary process as the tradeoffs forced by decline are implemented.

The interesting Chapter 10 by Mintz and Russett is similar in inspiration to the Rasler–Thompson work, but it focuses on the short-term conflict system of the Middle East rather than on long-term change. They show that domestic economic factors (corporate profits) as well as political factors (the electoral cycle) are strongly related to Arab and Israeli conflict behavior. They thus build on the work of Mintz and Ward (1989), who showed that the Israeli defense budget is itself related to economic conditions. Like Rasler and Thompson, therefore, Mintz and Russett conclude that the allocational dimensions of domestic politics and economics are inextricably tied to the external policies of states.

In summary, the work in this volume brings us closer to more refined empirical research on the foreign policies and grand strategies of states. Influential historical works had suggested that external policy is a function of economic policy and growth (Gaddis 1982) as well as the nature of domestic coalition politics (Kennedy 1987). While compelling, most of these ideas had not been subjected to empirical test. The chapters in this book thus point the way to closing an important gap in the literatures on foreign policy and grand strategy.

CONCLUSION

This book will not be the final word on the political and economic relationship between guns, butter, and growth. Indeed, what is exciting about the chapters in this book is that, by pointing to improvements and extensions to a research tradition that is already well established, they will stimulate additional research and thus contribute to better cumulation of results.

As concerns *theory*, this book suggests that our future work must be more firmly grounded in theories of political structure and change than has been the case in the past – a challenge that will require scholars to move beyond the inductive approaches of the past. In addition, stronger theories will require us to acquire a fuller understanding of the political and fiscal structures of modern welfare economies.

Second, several contributions to this book indicate that the *correlational conception* of tradeoffs has its limits. Since tradeoffs patterns may vary over time and across budgetary and economic categories, we must seek alternative – perhaps simpler – methods to identify the impact of tradeoffs. Forecasting and simulation are attractive methodologies for tracing these impacts. Nonetheless, even these methods will yield paltry results if the theoretical task is ignored, for the identification of tradeoffs at the level of detailed budgetary and economic policy requires a roadmap that is equally detailed.

Third, several findings in this volume highlight important gaps in the defense–welfare research. Most pertinent here is the study of the impact of national-security policy on revenue burdens and structure. There are indications, for example, that defense burdens influence several dimensions of tax structure, including the division of responsibility for financing social programs and the degree of centralization in fiscal systems. Indeed, a study of the relative impact of fiscal centralization on allocational tradeoffs is clearly needed.

Finally, several chapters in this book point to an exciting research agenda on the impact of allocational politics on foreign policy and grand strategy. Although there has been much speculation and historical inquiry on this connection, there has been little empirical work. As is true of each of the suggestions made in this concluding chapter, the intellectual pursuit of these relationships will bring us much closer to a definitive answer to the question of who pays for defense.

REFERENCES

Baran, Paul and Paul M. Sweezy. 1966. *Monopoly Capital*. New York: Monthly Review Press.

Bremer, Stuart A. and Barry B. Hughes. 1990. *Disarmament and Development: A Design for the future*. New York: Prentice-Hall.

Chan, Steve. 1985. The impact of defense spending on economic performance: A survey of evidence and problems. *ORBIS* 29: 403–34.

Cusack, Thomas and Barry Hughes. 1986. Using GLOBUS to explore alternative taxation and security policies in the West. In Margaret P. Karns (ed.), *Persistent Patterns and Emerging Structures in a Waning Century*, pp. 237–72. New York: Praeger.

Cyert, Richard and James March. 1967. *A Behavioral Theory of the Firm*. Englewood Cliffs, N.J.: Prentice-Hall.

Eichenberg. Richard C. 1984. The expenditure and revenue effects of defense spending in the Federal Republic of Germany. *Policy Sciences* 16: 391–411.

Eichenberg. Richard C. and Richard Stoll. 1989. Straightjacket: public support for defense spending in four democracies. Paper presented at the annual meeting of the American Political Science Association, Atlanta.

Flora, Peter. 1987. *Growth to Limits: the West European Welfare States Since World War II*. Volumes I–III. New York: de Gruyter.

Gaddis, John Lewis. 1982. *Strategies of Containment*. New York: Oxford University Press.

Greenwood, David. 1972. *Defense Budgeting*. London: Royal United Services Institute.

Keman, Hans. 1982. Securing the safety of the nation-state. In Francis G. Castles (ed.), *The Impact of Parties*, pp. 177–221. London: Sage.

Keman, Hans. 1988. Welfare and warfare: critical options and conscious choices in public policy. In Rudolf Wildermann (ed.), *The Future of Party Government*. New York: de Gruyter.

Kennedy, Paul. 1987. *The Rise and Decline of the Great Powers*. New York: Random House.

Kupchan, Charles. 1989. Defense spending and economic performance. *Survival* 31: 447–61.

Mintz, Alex and Michael D. Ward. 1989. The political economy of military spending in Israel. *American Political Science Review* 83: 521–33.

Organisation for Economic Cooperation and Development. 1987. *Revenue Statistics of OECD Member Countries*. Paris: Author.

Pechman, Joseph. 1976. Economic policy making. In Nelson Polsby and Fred Greenstein (eds.), *The Handbook of Political Science*. Reading, Mass.: Addison-Wesley.

Pryor, Frederick. 1968. *Public Expenditure in Communist and Capitalist Countries*. Homewood, Illi.: Irwin.

Rasler, Karen and William Thompson. 1989. *War and State-Making*. Boston: Unwin Hyman.

Russett, Bruce. 1969. Who pays for defense? *American Political Science Review* 63: 412–26.

Russett, Bruce. 1970. *What Price Vigilance*? New Haven, Conn.: Yale University Press.

Tilly, Charles (ed.). 1975. *The Formation of Nation-States in Western Europe*. Princeton, N.J.: Princeton University Press.

Wildavsky, Aaron. 1975. *Budgeting*. Boston: Little, Brown.

Index